Astrological Healing

The History and Practice of Astromedicine

Reinhold Ebertin

SAMUEL WEISER, INC.
York Beach, Maine

First published in 1989 by
Samuel Weiser, Inc.
Box 612
York Beach, Maine 03910

The original German language edition was first published by Ebertin-
Verlag, Freiburg/BRD under the title of *Sterne Helfen Heilen* von
Reinhold Ebertin. Copyright ©1982 Ebertin-Verlag, Freiburg.

Translated from the German by *Transcript*,
Wales, Great Britain

Library of Congress Cataloging in Publication Data

Ebertin, Reinhold.
    Astrological healing.

    Translation of: Sterne helfen heilen.
    Includes index.
    1. Astrology and health.   2. Healing--Miscellanea.
I. Title
BF1729.H9E2413 1989   133.5'8613   89-9129
ISBN 0-87728-643-4 hardbound
ISBN 0-87728-711-2 paperback

Typeset in 11 point Garamond
by Sans Serif, Inc.
Printed in the United States of America
by Edwards Brothers, Inc.

CONTENTS

PART ONE

THE FOUNDATIONS OF ASTROMEDICINE

CHAPTER ONE

THE SOURCES OF ASTROLOGY

THE ORIGINS OF ASTROLOGY ARE LOST IN THE mists surrounding the early cultures of the human race. Old Indian sources assign to it an age of several hundred thousand years. Rock paintings discovered in northern lands and in the Sahara lead us to suppose that people were taking an interest in the starry heavens overhead, and in the movements of the Sun, Moon and planets, some ten to twenty thousand years before our own era.

Boll has established that as long ago as the period between 2000 and 1000 B.C. an astrologically oriented system of medicine arose under the name of *iatromathematics*.[1] Abraham of the Old Testament has been numbered among the fathers of astrology. Moses (ca. 1250 B.C.) is also alleged to have been one of the astrologers of antiquity. Because of his wisdom, he was treated with religious respect by the Egyptian priests.[2] The cosmo-religious significance of Moses is deducible from the fact that he has been depicted as a lunar deity with two horns and that the Law was given on Mount Sinai, the Moon mountain.

The Chaldean priests (named for the land of Chaldea watered by the lower course of the rivers Euphrates and Tigris) were also physicians who incorporated the astrological knowledge of their time in their medical work. These doctor-priests and astrologers took care that women brought their children into the world under the best possible cosmic conditions. In accordance with the time of birth, water was taken from certain transparent vessels of different colors, and medicinal plants were sought which bore resemblance to certain planets.

In the Orphic mysteries of Greece (seventh–sixth centuries B.C.), a large part was played by tonal vibrations, music and consecrated oil. Even in those days, it was realized how important beautiful and harmonious surroundings were for the healing process.

Kurt Pollak writes in his book *Wissen und Weisheit der alten Ärzte — die Heilkraft der frühen Hochkulturen:*

> The astrological signatures found in chance or natural omens were doubtless the most important for, according to the old oriental mode of thought, the stars are the handwriting of heaven. Since accurate astrology required highly-trained interpreters . . . its use was confined to affairs of state and for consulting the welfare of kings, etc. Observations were made of the Moon, the Sun, the planets and the stars and also of atmospheric phenomena. According to Jastrow, astrology was also employed to determine the course and prognosis of a disease, especially in respect of the day of the month on which it began or in respect of special phenomena observed in the Moon and planets while it lasted. Thus in one text, for example, we read: "When a child is born, if the Moon is rising the life will be brilliant, good, and long." Astrological medicine in the strict sense of the word first developed in Egypt during the Hellenistic period and reached its apogee in the Middle Ages and the Renaissance.[3]

Even the physicians of ancient Greece were able to draw on rich Egyptian sources. The Egyptian masterpiece, the works of Hermes Trismegistus, which received their final form around 300 B.C., were known to the Greek medical practitioners.

The Greek philosopher and doctor Empedocles (490–430 B.C.), who practiced on the southern coast of Sicily, had a reputation as a wonder-worker and was regarded by his followers as a god. He taught that all life was derived from the "root of things," the four elements (fire, earth, air and water), and that out of the various mixtures of these arose love and hate and, above all, diseases.*

The physician Hippocrates (460–377 B.C.) of the island of Cos in the Aegean Sea, is still honored today as the "Father of medicine." His first school on Cos was highly respected. This was also the site of the famed shrine of Aesculapius, the god of healing.

A piece of writing has been ascribed to Hippocrates, in which relationships were worked out between the entire heavens of the fixed stars and the human body. He is said to have assigned the middle of the thorax, or solar plexus, to the Sun; but to have assigned the body as a whole to the Moon. He also left us an interesting example of astrological dream interpretation. When, for instance, the dreamer sees the stars dimmed or completely obscured by atmospheric influences, one can determine from this the severity of the disease, its cause and the appropriate remedy. Hippocrates is also said to have written a treatise entitled *On the Astrology of Physicians*.

The Greek philosopher Aristotle (384–322 B.C.) was Plato's most gifted pupil. Aristotle laid the foundation of the astrological picture of the world accepted in his day and age. According to him, the universe is eternal. Immovable in its center rests the earth, surrounded by variously revolving spheres to which the heavenly bodies are attached. The spheres and the heavenly bodies are formed from the ether; mundane things are formed from the four elements (fire, earth, air and water). Aristotle paved the way for the rational-scientific approach of Hellenistic astrology. The correspondences in table 1 may be traced to him and his contemporaries.

Professor Wilhelm Gundel has authored a compendious work entitled *Neue astrologische Texte des Hermes Trismegistos — Funde und Forschungen auf dem Gebiet der antiken Astronomie und Astrologie.*[4] Hermes Trismegistus (as we spell his name in English) has had attributed to him forty-two hermetic writings with an astronomical-astrological, medical and philosophical-magical content. In the late Hellenistic period, these works were translated from Egyptian into Greek and to some extent formed the basis of the

---

*Rather love and hate were supposed by Empedocles to be active forces continually uniting and separating the elements. *Tr.*

Table 1. Hellenistic Correspondences

Humors	Element	Astrological Signs		
Hot–Dry	Fire	Aries	Leo	Sagittarius
Hot–Wet	Air	Gemini	Libra	Aquarius
Cold–Wet	Water	Cancer	Scorpio	Pisces
Cold–Dry	Earth	Taurus	Virgo	Capricorn

development of astrology in the East. Especially in the medical texts, there are early references to correspondences between the signs and degrees of the zodiac and bodily parts and organs.

With the observation of the cosmic correspondences of diseases began the change-over from universal astrology, with its emphasis on the fate of mankind, to individual astrology, which is concerned with the fates of single individuals.

An unknown astrologer in 379 B.C. cited from the writings of Hermes Trismegistus the statement that, according to their placements in certain decans (10° sections of the zodiac), the malefic planets send diseases and infirmities to those parts of the body that are ruled by the decans concerned. This is particularly likely when Saturn in a night birth or Mars in a day birth rules the place which could cause the trouble.

In the *Buch des Hermes Trismegistos an Asklepios über die Pflanzen der sieben Sterne* (The Book of Hermes Trismegistus to Asclepius on the Plants of the Seven Stars), medicinal plants corresponding to the signs and decanates are discussed. "Zodiacal plants" are said to develop their full potency when they are gathered, prepared and used at the time when the Sun is posited in the appropriate sign. At the same time, the Moon should be trine the Sun (aspecting it by 120°).

With Alexander the Great (356–323 B.C.) there was a new epoch in the development of astrology. His conquests had a unifying effect on Oriental and Grecian views on the subject. We are indebted to the astronomer and mathematician Hipparchus of Nicaea (161–127 B.C.) for the division of the zodiac into 360°. He extended the scheme by which bodily parts and organs are assigned to the zodiac and the planets.

Astrology in Rome

When Greece was drawn into the orbit of Rome ca. 196 B.C., there was in increase in cultural exchange between Greece and the Roman Republic; and so astrology became known in Rome too. However, it was there that the art began to deteriorate, so that steps were taken against its practitioners and it was even prohibited from time to time. In 33 B.C. Augustus had all "astrologers and wizards" expelled from Rome. Even then there was a big difference between serious astrological study and mere superstition.

We are informed that the Roman emperor Tiberius employed a court astrologer whom he also treated as a friend. This was Thrassilos of Alexandria (died 36 A.D.). Around the middle of the first century A.D. the physician and astrologer Thessalos was active, to whom we owe an iatromathematical, or astromedical, herbal.

Claudius Ptolemaeus, or Ptolemy (ca. 100–178 A.D.), was, as mathematician, astronomer, astrologer and physicist, the last of the great scientists of antiquity. In his writings, he took into consideration the findings of earlier astrologers. His fundamental work on astrology, *Tetrabiblos*, is still extant and has been translated from Greek to Latin by Melanchthon.[5] The exposition of Ptolemy, the "king of astrologers," anticipates many of the principles of present-day cosmobiology. For instance, he made allowance for heredity, taught free will, and rejected fatalism.

Among other things, he wrote on the action of Saturn from a medical point of view: "induces general disorders and deterioration through cold and, in particular, chronic diseases of the human body—pulmonary tuberculosis originating from catarrhs, secretory disorders, fluxes, quartan fever." He thought that Mars had an affinity with tertian fever, hematemesis (vomiting blood), painful diseases and excessive infant mortality. Right up to modern times, the work of Ptolemy has formed the basis of many astrological textbooks.

Galen of Pergamum (129–200 A.D.) was the most celebrated medical man of imperial Rome. He first practiced as a gladiatorial surgeon and then became personal physician to the emperor Marcus Aurelius. Galen wrote numerous medical treatises and remained for centuries an authority on the healing art. He held the view that the true physician must also be a philosopher. He wrote about Hippocrates and Plato and is supposed to have developed the doctrine of temperaments based on Hippocrates' humoral theory.

In his book on the prognosis of diseases in which the patient is confined to bed, he argues that the Moon and the five visible planets provide important clues for both astrologer and doctor. Thus he recommends that blood-letting and purging should be performed only when the Moon is waxing and the aspects are favorable. When the Moon is in Cancer or Virgo no laxatives should be given, because at these times patients will not tolerate them but will suffer from nausea. On the other hand, this form of treatment may be dispensed when the Moon is in Aries, Taurus or Leo. Also when the Moon is in Scorpio purges should be prescribed, because every source of trouble can then be traced by the Moon and the body can be purified from within. With the Moon in Capricorn purges must be avoided, however, since they would produce bowel cramps.

Ca. 335 A.D. Firmicus Maternus (dates of birth and death unknown) wrote what was then the most comprehensive text book of astrology, the eight-volume *Matheseos libri*. In the works of Firmicus Maternus we find still current the correspondences of the signs of the zodiac to the human body. For instance, Aries corresponds to the head, Taurus to the neck region, Pisces to the feet, etc. For him, astrology was a divine science.

The Influence of Christianity

In the fifth and sixth centuries, astrological empiricism and Christian theology became increasingly mixed with one another. As far as Christianity was concerned, the stars do not rule our fates but act solely as pointers to the future.

Incidentally, it is interesting to note that the numbers three, four, seven and twelve, which from the earliest times have been regarded as sacred, have entered both into astrology and into Christianity. There immediately spring to mind the four elements, the four cardinal signs, the four evangelists, the twelve zodiac signs and the twelve disciples of Jesus.

The Middle Ages through the Renaissance

One of the most influential personalities of the Middle Ages was Count von Bollstädt, known to history as Albertus Magnus. He is thought to have been born in 1193 in Lauingen/Donau, and he died on the 15th November 1280, in Cologne. As theologian, philosopher, natural scientist and astrologer, he was a famous *doctor universalis*. He taught chiefly at Cologne and Paris. One of his scholars later became the great Catholic theologian Thomas Aquinas.

In his *Speculum astronomiae*, he divided star lore into theoretical astronomy and practical astrology. The latter he subdivided into a theoretical and a practical part, and this practical part he split up into nativities, revolutions, questions and elections.

As far as astromedicine is concerned, his attitude to the triplicities (elements) is rather intriguing. Thus he claimed that images of the fiery triplicity (Aries, Leo, Sagittarius) would abort fevers, dropsy, paralysis, etc.; images of the airy triplicity (Gemini, Libra, Aquarius), on the other hand, would moderate a fever accompanied by sweating and make a person inclined to peace, friendship and a punctilious observance of the law; the images of the watery triplicity (Cancer, Scorpio, Pisces) were supposed to alleviate hot, parching fevers, but also to give a disposition to lying, inconstancy, injustice and self-indulgence; the images of the earthy triplicity (Taurus, Virgo, Capricorn) were supposed to be cold and dry in their effects and were thought to be good for acute diseases and to make a person religious and inclined to rural life.

The attitude of Albertus Magnus to astrology is well expressed in the following lines from his work *De mineralibus*:

> Everything produced by nature and by art is affected by the celestial powers. The constellations and the heavenly bodies were there before all created things, and so they exercise an influence on everything that is subsequent to them. It necessarily follows that, when a correctly observed celestial pattern depicts any work of nature or of art, some of the powers of the former will influence the latter.

Who would deny, in the light of this, that Albertus Magnus occupied himself with astrology? He also wielded a sharp sword against conservative teachers and scholars who clung to the old and did not want to learn anything new. For example, he exclaimed:

This is what I have to say about sundry idle windbags who are looking for excuses for their idleness and poke their noses into books only in order to find something to revile: such people killed Socrates, drove Plato from Athens, and expelled Aristotle. In the kingdom of knowledge they are what the liver is to the body. In each body there is bile; this spreads through the body and makes it bitter. Equally, in the realm of scholarship, there are some bitter and ill-natured people who make everyone else bitter and do not allow the truth to be sought in sweet fellowship.

The abbess Hildegard von Bingen (1098–1179 A.D.) occupied a special place in the 12th century, which also produced such distinguished figures as Albertus Magnus, Bernard of Clairvaux, Bernard of Chartres and others. From her birth, Hildegard was trapped in a net of pain and disease. Her physique is said to have been ethereal or airy. Every change in the weather and every cosmic constellation exerted the most profound influence on her; but this very sensitivity enabled her to grasp things that remained hidden from others. She saw visions, and speaking of them said:

In these visions, my souls soars by the will of God to the heights of the firmament and to the shiftings of the winds, and straddles lands and expanses of space. I enter, as it were, into the wavering and wandering of clouds and into other mutable things. Everything is clear to my spirit. My eyes are open. No ecstasy enfolds me. I gaze on my visions day and night, awake and not adream; but often deathly sick and deadly tired.

On the whole, as a contemporary biographer noted, her teaching was sound. For as the Codex Latinum shows she set "man" in her Cosmos Table with outstretched arms in the center of the universe, which rotates around him as he stands on the earth surrounded by the

cosmic spheres. The latter radiate on him, meet in him and cause the
human being, as their point of intersection and crystallization center,
to reflect into the universe.

> As the partner of the world, man is the mirror of the uni-
> verse. In predestined union, body and soul belong together
> as man and wife, as heavenly and earthly, earth and water,
> sun and moon, winds and birds in the air, bread in the
> oven, and the comb with its honey—the delight of the soul
> is to be busily creative in the body.

In Hildegard's view,

> We could call the sun the cap of the firmament; it illumi-
> nates the whole firmament and also the earth and the
> waters, and sheds its warmth on them in varying measure.
> In the middle regions of the earth its rays are strongest.
> Owing to the sun's action, the earth is extremely vigorous
> there; everything, both fruits and living creatures, is more
> powerfully developed than in other places on earth.

> The moon too, in her phases, has an influence on the fluid
> balance in human beings. Fluid assimilation can not be
> regarded in the same way as when it is tempered by the sun;
> this gives a much more stable equilibrium, so that it neither
> increases nor decreases. Now, the phases of the moon do
> not rule human nature as if she were a goddess, nor can
> human beings apply anything to or withdraw anything
> from the moon. Rather the moon affects people's life activi-
> ties by means of the taste of the air; therefore blood and
> other humors can be moved according to the lunar phases.
> Patterning himself on the moon, man understands himself
> to be a "*homo mutatus*" whose humoral complex is subject
> to atmospheric influences in many respects.[6]

When God created the world, He reinforced it with the four
elements: fire, earth, air and water. The doctrine of the elements,
which Hildegard apparently adopted from the Greek philosophers,
played a big part in her thinking as it did in that of others. Humans
live by virtue of the four humors just as the universe is composed of

four elements. Fire with its forces resides in the brain and marrow. In humans, these fire forces manifest themselves as a glow in the visual faculty, as cold in the sense of smell, as wetness in the sense of taste, as air in the sense of hearing and as movement in the sense of touch. Air and its forces are expressed in respiration and in the reason. Water with its fifteen forces is found in the fluids and in the blood. Earth is encountered with its seven forces in the tissues and bony system. As long as the elements preserve their correct order in the organism, the individual is healthy; but as soon as they deviate from their functional order the individual falls ill.

In her *Heilkunde*[7] Hildegard speaks of the formation of mankind in accordance with cosmic laws, of sexual behavior, of the human being between sleeping and waking, of diseases from the head to the feet, of nourishment and digestion, of metabolic disorders, of remedies, of a healthy regime, of the quality of the physician and of the chart of life.

At the period in which she lived, Hildegard was instrumental in formulating a body of knowledge which, over the centuries, had become lost to view and only then was brought to light again. Here we have room for just a few quotations to give readers an insight into the work of the "prophetess of Rupertsberg."

> When the blood increases in the organism with the waxing of the moon, the human being, man or woman, is ready for procreation, that is to say for the production of progeny. For when the moon is waxing there is an increased supply of blood and the seed is strong and vigorous; but when the moon is waning there is a diminished supply of blood and the seed is weak and infertile.

> Also in trees, which become green from the root, the sap increases in the waxing moon and decreases in the waning moon.

> If noble and healthful herbs are picked (either by cutting them or by pulling them out by the root with their juices intact) under a waxing moon, they will prove better for the preparation of electuaries (medicinal pastes), ointments

and similar remedies than if they are gathered under a waning moon.

As the moon waxes and wanes, so the blood and humors in the female organism are purified at the time of the monthly flow. Otherwise the woman could not survive, since she is much richer in humors than the man and could become very unwell.

A strong man should be bled every three months, because after two changes of the moon the blood has its maximum strength and its optimum fullness. The operation should be performed on the first day of the waning moon, but in any case within six days of the change of the moon. Blood-letting is inadvisable when the moon is waxing, because the blood and the morbid matter in the blood system are then very difficult to separate. Since morbid matter naturally preponderates in the elderly, bleeding is advisable sooner in their case. In special instances, bleeding may be performed as early as the twelfth year in males. However, no more blood should be drawn than will fill both shells of a nut. Up to the fifteenth year and after the fiftieth, bleeding should be performed once. In old age, bleeding is rather harmful; in special cases it is preferable to use blisters, say with earline (*Vardi nigra*), corrosive types of *carlina* or similar herbs. When the blister bursts, the harmful fluid between the skin and the flesh can be discharged.

Besides *Heilkunde*, her book *Gott ist am Werk*[8] is also worth mentioning. According to the latter, the creation of the world in God's likeness is a system of correspondences between the macrocosm and the microcosm for "in the circle of the macrocosm the human being appears as homo quadratus spreadeagled on the world cross in a quadruplicity of elements, winds, qualities and temperaments."

Man is like the sun and moon. . . . And so these heavenly luminaries are meant to serve a person as inner signs of how he should sigh, pray, cry to God and call on the Holy Spirit to help him. But they may also teach him the correct use of the signs and how to employ them for his own and his neighbour's use.

In the picture of the twelve months, Hildegard shows her knowledge of natural history and of the story of the life and sufferings of Christ. Everything in the pattern of the universe, in human anatomy, and in history, is worked into a grand design which presents us with a mature Christian anthropology.

The abbess Hildegard was one of the commanding personalities of her age, and was the prophetess of the century; emperor and pope kept in touch with her and her influence pervaded the whole of Western Europe. Hildegard's main works have been republished since 1954 but are mostly out of print again. As the leading expert on them, Professor Schipperges has performed a great service in his translation and commentary.[9]

A famous contemporary of Albertus Magnus and Hildegard was the Archduke Leopold of Austria, bishop of Freising, who published his *Tractatus decem de astrorum* ca. 1200. And in the thirteenth century, astrology was strongly supported by princes. The Emperor Frederick II employed the famous astrologer Michael Scot as his personal physician. The latter was born in Balwirie, Scotland, in 1214, was educated in France, and then attached himself to the emperor, to whom he prophesied the place and nature of his death. Scot was killed in 1291 when a stone fell on him inside a church. At the emperor's command, he had written several volumes on the secrets of nature and on chiromancy, physiognomy and astrology. His book *Compendium magiae nigrae* was translated into German by the historical Johann Faust under the title, *Fausti Hoellenzwang oder Mirakel-Kunst und Wunderbuch* (Faust's Ruler of the Infernal Powers or Miracle Art and Wonder Book).

Gilbert Anglicus (William of England) wrote ca. 1219 a treatise on *The Diagnosis of Disease by Astrological Rules Without the Inspection of Urine*. In this manuscript, a copy of which is in the Austrian National Library, the relationship of the seven planets to the twelve zodiac signs as well as to the then known organs and diseases is depicted in eighty-four sections.

The fame of Alphonso X of Castile rests on the Alfonsine tables named for him. The latter were completed in 1252 and enabled astrological calculations to be performed with greater accuracy and reliability than had previously been possible. For this reason he was nicknamed "Astrologus."

Guido Bonati, one of the most celebrated astrologers of the thirteenth century, was born in 1230 at Cascia near Florence. At first he read law, but soon added astronomy and astrology to his studies, and his skill in these earned him the title "Siderabilissimus." He was appointed court astrologer to the Emperor Frederick II. Later he lectured at Paris and Bologna and then entered the service of Count Guido of Montefeldro and advised the latter on the art of gunnery. In his old age, Bonati joined the Franciscan order and died at the monastery in Ancona in 1300. He wrote a comprehensive treatise, which in 1572 was published in Basel under the title *Auslegung der menschlichen Geburtsstunde* (An Exposition of the Hour of Human Birth).[10] His view was that the Ascendant must always lie centrally between two planets, and so he founded the doctrine of half-sums or midpoints.

Peter of Albano (1250–1316) was a physician, astrologer and magician. Initially he studied medicine and philosophy, gaining doctorates in both; then, after a short stay in Constantinople, he settled in Padua where he became the first professor of medicine. He charged very high fees for his treatments and would not make house calls for less than thirty crowns. When he was treating Pope Honorious IV, he came under suspicion of being in league with the devil and was thrown into prison, where he took poison in 1316.

In front of Padua city hall, a statue has been erected in his honor describing him as a physician and astrologer. In his book, *Astrolabium planum*, he showed how to find the places of the planets with fair accuracy by graphical means without recourse to calculation. To some extent, therefore, he was the father of today's graphic ephemerides.

Cichus Asculus (1250–1327), whose given name was Francesco della Stabili, was a well-known physician and astrologer who named himself for his home town of Cecco d'Ascoli. He studied philosophy, theology, medicine, mathematics, astrology and poetry. He was a friend of Dante and, for a short time, was personal physician to Pope John XXII. During the years 1322 through 1325 he taught at the University of Bologna. An attempt to interpret the life of Christ astrologically landed him a charge of heresy; upon which he renounced his theory and did penance. In 1326 he was appointed personal physician and astrologer to Duke Charles (the landless) of Calabria. But when he foretold from the charts of the Duchess, Marie of Valois, and of her two-year-old daughter, that they would both lead immoral lives, he fell into disfavor. His enemies renewed the charges of heresy and on 15th September 1327 he was burned alive at Florence.

On the threshold of modern times, Nicolaus Cusanus (1401–1464), whose real name was Nikolaus Chypffs or Krebs, appeared at Kues (Cusa) on the Moselle. He was born a year after Johann Gutenberg, the inventor of book printing. In his youth there occurred the Council of Pisa, the birth of Joan of Arc, and the start of the Hussite war. In 1425, Cusanus became episcopal adviser to the Court of Mainz, and was ordained in 1439. In 1436 he published a treatise on calendar reform, was raised to the cardinalate in 1448, became bishop of Brixen in 1450 and, in 1459, was created curial cardinal.

As far as Cusanus was concerned, the hierarchical cosmos of the ancient world no longer had any reality. For him, the earth was the cosmic position of the human race; it was not the center of the universe, for humans had now begun to see themselves as creatures to whom it was impossible to assign a fixed station in the All, because their existence signified a single stage in the endless unfolding of being.

Cusanus stood between ancient and modern times. He still relied on the perceptions of Hermes Trismegistus and yet was an early precursor of Copernicus. He rent the medieval fabric of the heavens in order to look beyond to new worlds. His attitude to astrology was formulated chiefly in his work *Conjecturis*. In this book, *The Art of Conjecture*, he incorporated the earth in a network of cosmic activities. Theology, cosmology and anthropology were made mutually dependent and were welded into a unity.

The individual was proved by Cusanus to have a measure of autonomy with regard to the whole: "Each being in the universe rejoices in its uniqueness, which it shares with none other." At this point, personal astrology began to come increasingly to the fore while universal astrology receded into the background.

Agrippa von Nettesheim, who was born on the 14th September 1486 in Cologne and died on the 18th February 1535, was a scion of an old, wealthy and aristocratic family which bore the name Nettelhym. He studied law, but took a particular interest in books on the occult sciences. He understood eight languages, six of which he knew so well that he "spoke them elegantly, and was able to dictate and translate them." In about 1507 he went to Paris, where he founded an "occult society." There he changed his residence several times, becoming a soldier and then a man of learning again in quick succession. He made use of astrology and the secret arts in earning his living. In 1505 he was installed in Burgundy as a lecturer in theology, but soon came into conflict with the clergy. Because he was so persecuted by the monks, he went to England in 1510 but speedily returned to Cologne, where students crowded to his lectures.

On a trip to Würzburg he got to know the abbot Trithemius, stayed at his monastery and learned much from him. He wrote three books of occult philosophy, was appointed an imperial councilman and undertook the inspection and improvement of the mines. In 1522 he was a captain in the imperial army waging war against the Venetians and was dubbed knight for his bravery. In the meantime he had graduated as a doctor of law and a doctor of medicine.

On the 12th July 1513, he received a letter from Pope Leo X praising his zeal for the Apostolic See. In the following years he delivered lectures at Pavia on Hermes Trismegistus. In 1518, on the recommendation of his friend Syndikus, he was appointed orator and advocate to Metz. When he espoused the cause of innocent people who were accused of witchcraft, saving many of them from torture and prosecution, he was attacked by the monks and was forced to leave Metz in 1519. He then returned to his native city, Cologne.

After the death of his wife in 1521, he went as a physician to Geneva and Freyburg in Switzerland, where he married again. In 1524 he decided to reside in Lyons. There the reputation of his practical skill was so great that Francis I granted him a pension and the Queen Mother chose him as her personal physician. In 1527, however, he was dismissed for refusing to chart the progress of French affairs with the help of astrology. In July 1528 he arrived in Antwerp, where he gained public recognition as a great healer. Here the plague killed his second wife, who had borne him seven children. In 1529 he received an invitation from Henry VIII of England. Then he accepted the position of imperial archivist and historiographer to the Regent Margaretha. But persecution was soon renewed against him and on the death of Margaretha he was left to starve. His enemies slandered him to the emperors Ferdinand and Charles and his salary was not paid. In 1531 he was even thrown into prison in Brussels for a short time. In 1532 he paid a visit to the Archbishop of Cologne, to whom he had dedicated his *Occult Philosophy*. Defying the inquisitors, he saw an improved version of his *Occult Philosophy* through the press and the book was published in 1533. In the same year he went to Bonn, and died in the house of a nobleman on the 18th February 1535.

Because he travelled so widely and became acquainted with the great thinkers of his era, Agrippa acquired extraordinary knowledge and perception, which unfortunately led the ignorant to suppose that he possessed supernatural powers and even that he was in league with the devil. In his second book, he commented: "As soon as the common people see something out of the ordinary, they fondly imagine in their ignorance that demons are the authors of it, or treat as a marvel what is simply a work of scientific or mathematical art."

In his astrological researches he developed the subject beyond the state in which he found it. It is true that he looked for its foundations in the elements, but he also set out an extensive range of correspondences for the individual planets. Here are one or two examples:

> To Jupiter correspond, of the elements air, of the humors blood, together with the vital spirit and everything to do with nourishment and growth, of the tastes favorite foods, of plants and trees the silk-cotton tree, basil, ox-tongue, mace, lavender, mint, violet, horse-chestnut, beech, poppy, hazel-bush and others.

> To Mars correspond, of the elements fire, together with all pungent and hot things, of the humors bile, of the tastes bitter and pungent — burning the tongue and making the eyes water, of plants and trees hellebore, garlic, horse-

radish, large radish, spurge laurel, aconite and all plants armed with thorns.

To Venus correspond, of the elements air and water, of the humors phlegm, plus blood and semen, of tastes what is sweet, fatty and pleasant, of plants and trees vervain, violet, maidenhair, valerian, sandalwood, coriander and all spicy plants together with delicious and favorite types of fruit such as pears, figs, and pomegranates.

To Mercury correspond, of the elements water, of the body fluids the mixed humors in particular, of trees and plants the hazelbush, cinquefoil, fumitory, salad-burnet, marjoram and parsley.*

On the subject of disease, we read in his fourth book:†

To know whether a patient will recover or die, look to see if Saturn or Mars or the Dragon's Tail is associated with evil planets in the first house. If evil planets occupy the angles, this is a bad sign for the patient. If you wish to know whether you can cure the patient, note whether Jupiter, Venus or the Dragon's Head are in the Ascendant or Descendant, for this is a good sign. If the Moon is with a benefic planet, go and give the patient remedies; if she is with a malefic planet, or if malefics occupy angles, do not go for you will be unable to help the patient. If the signs are good, try to discover where or in what member his trouble lies; for Aries rules the head, Taurus the neck, Cancer the chest and lungs, Leo the heart, Virgo the abdo-

---

*The violet and hazelbush each appear twice in these lists. The violet is assigned to Jupiter and Venus, and the hazelbush is assigned to Jupiter and Mercury. Culpepper, in his Herbal, is simpler and says of violets, "They are a fine pleasing plant of Venus," and of hazel nuts, "They are under the dominion of Mercury." *Tr.*

†The so-called Fourth Book of Agrippa's *Occult Philosophy* is spurious in the sense of being wrongly attributed to him, although based on genuine old texts by other writers. *Tr.*

men and intestines, Libra the navel and the kidneys, Scorpio the anus and the genitals, Sagittarius the hips and buttocks, Capricorn the knees, Aquarius the calves and Pisces the feet.

These anatomical correspondences have held good right down to the present day, but are certainly not always applicable, because the zodiac signs taken on their own are not decisive.

Large chunks of the works of Agrippa von Nettesheim, which were reprinted in 1921, were occupied with contemporary magic, but he always upheld the principle, "In everything turn to the Lord, and think, say and do nothing outside the will of God."*

Whereas the past votaries of astrology relied heavily on the teachings of Hermes Trismegistus and Claudius Ptolemy, the moderns have in some areas broken entirely new ground as science has won fresh knowledge.

Johann Müller of Königsberg, who was named Regiomontanus† for his birth place, introduced a new system of house division based on the rotation of the earth. This work was the result of his education. He was born in Königsberg on the 6th June 1436, and from his twelfth year studied in Leipzig logic, spherical astronomy, arithmetic, and geometry. He completed his training in Vienna and, together with his teacher, Purbach, improved planetary theory. In 1464 he was summoned by Matthias Corvinus, the king of Hungary and Bohemia, and cured the latter of a depression into which he had fallen through fear of a solar eclipse. He became celebrated for his numerous scientific works and was installed by Pope Sixtus IV as bishop of Regensburg, being called to Rome in 1475 for a planned calendar reform. Here he died on the 6th June 1476, of poison administered by the sons of George of Trebizond. Regiomontanus is accounted the greatest astronomer in the period between Ptolemy and Copernicus, and is known as the "father of German astronomy."

---

*Agrippa did use pious expressions from time to time, but his detailed exposition of magic as a "philosophy," rather than as something of antiquarian interest, leads one to suspect that he was really a pagan at heart. Tr.
†Latin form of the German, meaning "King's Mountain." Tr.

Hieronimus de Manfredi of Capua was professor of medicine at Bologna at the end of the 15th century. He endeavored to combine astrology and medicine, being the first to publish calendars with medical elections, i.e., giving information about which days of the year are good or bad for taking medicine, bleeding, and cupping. His work *Centiloquium de medicis et infirmis* was printed in Bonn in 1489.

It is interesting to note that in 1496, a broadsheet was issued on the subject of syphilis by the physician Dietrich Uelzen (Ulsenius), and in it was a woodcut by Dürer.[11] It has been reproduced as figure 1 on page 22. In the upper part of the picture we see the zodiac circling a sphere. Scorpio, which generally is characteristic of diseases of the sexual organs, contains the Sun, Moon and two planets. These planets are taken to represent the grand conjunction of Jupiter and Saturn which occurred in 1484, the year inscribed within the zodiac belt. In the main part of the print, a man is represented who is marked with syphilis. His face and upper leg are covered with eruptions. The title, "Lichnica genesis," refers to the origin of the disease.

Theophrastus Bombastus von Hohenheim (1493–1541) of Einsiedeln deliberately named himself Paracelsus, i.e., "above (or greater than) Celsus," Celsus being a renowned ancient physician. Paracelsus was a medical man who had gained his doctor's hood at Ferrara in 1517. He interested himself in philosophy, pharmacy and astrology.

Paracelsus turned against the astrological tradition of his times, and especially against Galen's doctrine of humors. He regarded man as a microcosm and spoke, among other things, of the *"Astrum in corpore,"* or the star in us. He believed that to be proficient, a doctor must also practice astronomy and astrology — without the art of astrological interpretation, a doctor was a "pseudomedicus." For him, the pattern of the heavens was a pointer to both diagnosis and therapy. He categorically rejected the fatalistic doctrine that "the star makes the man," and did not speak of Mars and Saturn as ruling over us but as being in us. On the power of medicinal plants we find him saying, "The power of herb comes not only from the earth but also from the planets; the *Corpus* (body) is from the earth however."

One of the fundamental discoveries of Paracelsus was the doctrine of signatures, according to which, from the appearance and

Figure 1. A Dürer woodcut showing the astrological indications of syphilis.

structure of plants, we can draw conclusions about their medicinal action on the organs and other parts of the body. For instance, he saw in the walnut a resemblance to, and thus a relationship with, the human brain. His doctrine of signatures was adopted by the anthroposophical medical practitioners and by the alchemists.

The Paracelsian researcher, Dr. Bernhard Aschner, M.D., said of him, "Paracelsus was not a wonder-doctor but a wonder of a doctor." C.G. Jung saw in him a pioneer not only in medicine but in empirical, psychologically oriented healing.

Martin Pegius lived in the 16th century as a royal councilman in Salzburg and concerned himself with the astrology of his times with great success, being the first to publish a comprehensive textbook on the subject in German (in 1570).[12] On the relationship between therapeutics and astrology, he says, among other things:

> I think that physicians are to blame chiefly for not seeing that skill in reading the stars is requisite to their medical art; since Paracelsus gave them all such a bad time, they practice medicine without reference to stellar science. . . .
> Diseases will occur in those parts of the body that are indicated by some sign of the Zodiac. Thus Aries signifies the head, Taurus the neck, Gemini the arms, etc.; Saturn signifies the right eye, the spleen and the bladder, Jupiter the right hand, the lungs and the ribs, Mars the left eye, the left ear and the penis, the Sun both eyes (especially the right), the face and the entire right side of the body, Venus the buttocks and the liver, Mercury the tongue and the interior of the nose, the Moon the right side of the throat, the uvula, the stomach, the womb, the vulva and the left side.

These anatomical correspondences do not quite coincide with modern opinions, but can nevertheless be regarded as a useful attempt to combine medicine with astrology.

Tycho Brahe (1546–1601) was a Danish astronomer who built the Uranienborg and Stjerneborg observatories. He was confirmed in his astrological beliefs when in 1563 the plague broke out in Europe at the same time as there was a conjunction of the outer planets in the nebula Praesepe in the sign of Cancer.

Johann Antonius Maginus (13th June, 1555–11th February, 1617) was born in Padua. He became professor of mathematics of Bolgona and was invited by Pope Gregory XIII to take part in reforming the calendar. Maginus cast the horoscopes of almost all the princes of Europe, compiled ephemerides, and wrote a book on the use of astrology in medicine.

One of the most famous astrologers of the 17th century was Jean Baptist Morin (23rd February, 1587–6th November, 1656). He was born in Villefranche in the south of France, learned medicine and mathematics, became a doctor of medicine and finally went to Germany to study mining. Here he became acquainted with astrology. In 1621 Morin was appointed personal physician to the Duke of Luxembourg, and there followed a similar appointment to Louis XIII of France. The French statesman, Richelieu, and Cardinal Mazarin sought his advice. When he died in 1656, he left behind him his huge opus, the *Astrologia Gallica*. One of Morin's special developments was the doctrine of determination, which was an attempt to elaborate a comprehensive theory of combinations. The multi-volume *Bausteine der Astrologie*, published between 1926 and 1928 by Sinbad-Weiss in Munich, was to some extent based on the teaching of Morin.[13] In this are to be found notes on astromedicine and medicinal plants.

From the hand of Abdias Trews (12th July 1597–Easter 1669), who was born in Ansbach and studied theology, philosophy and mathematics at Wittenberg, appeared a treatise entitled, *Astrologia Medica*. His "groundwork of improved astrology" was reprinted in 1927. In the astromedical section of the book he remarks:

When I and my family have something the matter with us [he was twice married and had twenty-two children], I consult the doctor, tell him what the trouble is . . . as far as I understand it, and accept what he prescribes. But I myself choose the time when the remedy is used and, God be praised, find myself well again by doing so. In fact, because of all the illnesses and accidents in my own family, I have had more opportunities to put my ideas to the test than I

would have wished. What I am revealing here is based
partly on personal experience and partly on the use of
reason.[14]

Placidus de Titis was born in Perugia in 1603. He worked out a
new house system which is still popular. His table of houses appeared
in 1657. He criticized the house systems of Regiomontanus and Cam-
panus. Later he wrote a commentary on the works of Ptolemy and
also published an astronomical treatise entitled, *De diebus decretoriis
et agrorum decubio*.

Modern Astrology

In the 18th and 19th centuries, we find a whole series of astrologers
who advised clients and even wrote books but made hardly any contributions to medical astrology. We know that Wolfgang von Goethe,
Friedrich von Schiller, Friedrich Wilhelm Schelling, August Wilhelm
Schegel, Joseph Karl Benedikt von Eichendorff, Ludwig Tieck, Friedrich Hölderlin and Novalis (Friedrich Leopold von Hardenberg)
were very interested in astrology. Johann Wilhelm Pfaff (born on the
5th December, 1774), the last professor of astrology at the University
of Erlangen, was a keen advocate of his subject.

But we do come to an important figure for astromedicine in the
person of R.C. Smith, who styled himself "Raphael." Raphael's ephemerides, which were first published in 1800 and have appeared
annually ever since, owe their inception to R.C. Smith. In his book
on medical astrology, Raphael confirmed the findings of Paracelsus
when he wrote: "Among our native plants, there are medicinal herbs
suitable for diseases of all types and, provided they are used in
accordance with astrological principles, they offer unlimited help in
every complaint and illness."

At the end of the last century, the Hamburg astrologer Albert
Kniepf became well known and, in 1898/99 he published pamphlets
on *Die psychischen Wirkungen der Gestirne* (The Influences of the
Planets on the Psyche) and *Die Physik der Astrologie* (The Physics of
Astrology). In his opinion, the effects of the planets are due to
electromagnetic stimulation, and he maintained that the human aura
is much more sensitive than a selenium cell to planetary radiations.

In July 1909, Alexander Bethor launched the periodical *Zodiacus*, and in Leipzig a year later the *Astrologische Rundschau* (The Astrological Review) came out under the editorship of Brandler-Pracht, who from 1914 onwards also edited the *Astrologischen Blätter* (Astrological Papers). In these magazines one could always count on finding articles on "Diseases Caused by Stellar Influences."

In 1850, the death of Professor Wilhelm Pfaff occurred in Erlangen. He had taught astrology at the university there. From that time forward there were no more academic lectures and seminars on astrological themes. Although astrological books were still published in the second half of the 19th century, the subject led a more or less shadowy existence. But, with the arrival of the 20th century, people in scientific professions, especially physicians, began to take an interest in it once more.

Dr. Friedrich Feerhow's *Die medizinische Astrologie*[15] came out in 1914. In it, he mentions, among other things, that he was the first to try and find a scientific causal explanation of the cosmobiological relationship.[16] Dr. Feerhow provides a wealth of astromedical material, including details from the charts of patients, and refers to other authors who had studied astromedicine in depth. Thus he calls the Parisian physician Dr. R. Allendy a "clinical pioneer in the field astrological diagnosis."[17] And he continues:

> Dr. Allendy states that it is foolish to disregard the assistance offered by astrology, seeing that it gives the doctor a practical guide, and its role in pathology is very important. . . . From a series of instructive natal charts, he exemplifies this (planetary) influence, even demonstrating from several of them how difficult diagnoses were made with their help when the usual clinical tests had been unsatisfactory or actually misleading.[18]

This quotation refers to the discussion of a report made to the Second International Congress for Experimental Psychology held in Paris March 25–30, 1913.

We could consider 1926 a turning-point in the history of astrology; for that was when the compendious work of the qualified physician Baron Herbert von Klöckler was published.[19] On the subject of astromedicine, von Klöckler has this to say:

> In view of the putative and, to my mind, completely established relationship between the horoscope on one hand and heredity and body-shape on the other, we do seem entitled to look for some connection between the stellar pattern at birth and specific physical functions and their disorders. If it is possible to find clear-cut relationships between chart factors and the shape of the body, then this is the first step to a medical understanding of the chart; for without doubt there is a link between types of human physique and certain predispositions to disease, since even academic medicine has led to the recognition of constitutional types (sthenic, asthenic, apoplectic, etc.).

> Perhaps it would be easier to accept astrological data if astrology could be restricted, in addition to the specification of astrological constitutional types, to the discovery of the timing of biological periods for which analogous processes have been discovered by modern science—seen, say, in the coincidence between the frequency of epileptic fits and certain phases of the Moon.[20]

Dr. von Klöckler was also one of the first to use statistics to put astrology on a scientific basis. A year after Klöckler's breakthrough, Dr. Karl Th. Bayer produced his dissertation, *Die Grundprobleme der Astrologie* (The Fundamental Problems of Astrology), in which he said that "astrology can fulfill all the requirements for making it a science," and that "it occupies a well defined position vis-à-vis natural philosophy and psychology."[21] In fact, Bayer saw a particularly close link between astrology and psychology.

One of those who drew support from the findings of Dr. Bayer was Professor Georg Anschütz in his book *Psychologie* (Psychology),[22] published in 1953. He said:

> The attempts made by astrology to find a connection between human types and the sun, moon, planets and signs of the Zodiac, has so far not been taken very seriously

by science. Part of the reason lies in the fact that outsiders notice complicated and imprecise concepts which give them the impression that the whole thing is nothing more than the popular typology of a byegone age.[23]

And:

The method of erecting a so-called natal chart (radix) may be regarded as scientific to the extent that the calculation is performed on the basis of spherical trigonometry to make an astronomical picture of the heavens for a given moment of time and for a given geographical point in space. The Ascendant and the Meridian are determined in a generally accepted way, but how best to calculate the inner houses is a matter of dispute. Recently, attempts have been made to dispense with house calculations altogether. . . . The various modes of calculation and interpretation reveal extraordinary subjectivity. But this does not negate their intrinsic reasonableness.[24]

Cosmobiological phenomena in the widest sense were dealt with by Professor Wilhelm Hellpach in *Geopsyche – Die Menschenseele unter dem Einfluss von Wetter und Klima, Boden und Landschaft* (Geopsyche – the Human Psyche Under the Influence of Weather and Climate, Soil and Landscape).[25] Although the author expresses considerable reservations with regard to astrology in this book, he is well worth reading because he shows so clearly that, in addition to the cosmic factor studied by cosmobiology, a host of other factors affect mankind and these too must be taken into account in cosmobiology and astromedicine.

In 1929, Dr. Hans Hermann Kritzinger brought out a book with the strange title *Todesstrahlen und Wünschelrute* (Death Rays and Divining Rod). In his chapter "Man in the Cosmic Forcefield," he studies the influence of the higher atmospheric layers on variations in the earth's magnetism and the relationship between these and air pressure and weather. He quotes the results of the psychiatric physician Dr. Heinrich Lahmann, who found that a fall in atmospheric pressure regularly produced disorders in the digestion, the circulation of the blood, the nervous system and the mental condition.[26]

The physician Dr. Fritz Schwab, whose book *Sternmächte und Mensch* (The Stellar Powers and Humanity) was published in 1923,[27] repeatedly found cases of the same type occurring together in his clinical work. Thus, on the same day, two girls with appendicitis were admitted to hospital; "by chance" they occupied adjacent beds, they simultaneously suffered from peritonitis and their operations took place at the same time. In both, an abscess had to be opened from below. No similar cases were treated for the next three months. On many occasions, it "rained" hernia patients; other days were conspicuous for the number of patients suffering from heart failure, and so on. At first, he was completely baffled.

Schwab goes on to mention the seven-year period of Swoboda, the theory of periodicity advanced by Dr. Fliess, and the number symbolism of antiquity, and quotes the statements made by Professor Ruth in *Neue Relationen im Sonnensystem* (New Relationships in the Solar System):

> A survey of the many connections and numerical proportions in the solar system and in the universe may well give the impression that what we are looking at is not so much a system as an organism. . . . We are facing the greatest challenge to science—the question of the psychic character of the universe.[28]

Schwab put his findings into the form of statistics which, although not extensive, were a preliminary attempt to obtain significant data from the birth picture.

The physician and psychotherapist Dr. Olga Freifrau, of Ungern-Sternberg, came across astrology in the 1920's and studied it in connection with medicine and psychotherapy. In her book published in 1928, *Die innerseelische Erfahrungswelt am Bilde der Astrologie* (The World of Inner Experience as Represented by Astrology), a second edition of which appeared in 1975, she sought to tie astrological terminology in with psychological terminology. She comments:

> Therefore, when expressed in psychological terms, Saturn represents the ability to give shape to things, Mars represents tonicity and libido, Venus represents contrast and sensibility, Mercury represents nervous sensitivity and mental

ability, Jupiter represents the desire to synthesize and the power of realization.[29]

A great deal has been written on the Sun and Moon as cosmic powers, but only a brief mention of the subject can be given here. According to Dr. Guthmann,[30] there is almost a one hundred per cent increase in menstruation around the times of full moon and new moon. Also the number of births runs parallel to the phases of the Moon. Dr. Hilmar Heckert writes, "The outwardly visible phases of the Moon indicate a rhythmic play of forces hidden from our eyes, which acts in such a way on the human organism that it finds its final external expression in an increase in male births and a decrease in female births when the Moon is increasing in light, and in a decrease in male births and an increase female births when the Moon is decreasing in light."[31]

The American physician Dr. Andrews[32] ascertained from the statistics of one thousand tonsillectomies that eighty-two per cent of severe hemorrhages after tonsil operations occurred one to three days before full moon.

Regular contributions on medical and psychological themes have been a feature of the Conferences on Cosmobiological Research held since 1949 in Aalen and then since 1980 in Stuttgart. The *Kosmobiologischen Jahrbucher* (Cosmobiological Yearbooks), published in Aalen since 1950 and partly still obtainable from the Ebertin Verlag, Freiburg im Breisgau, are replete with working and research material.[33]

CHAPTER TWO

PIONEERING RESEARCH BY HEALERS

S INCE ANCIENT TIMES, PHYSICIANS WITH A COS-mic outlook have searched for healing agents with some rela-tionship to the stars. The oldest texts on the subject cannot be evaluated today, because we have no botanical descriptions of the medicinal plants to which they refer. However, recent centuries have bequeathed to us an expanded knowledge of herbs and other remedies. In fact, we still have among us physicians and pharmacists who work in accordance with cosmic laws, although their remedies are often offered under names that make it hard to recognize that they have been cosmically prepared. In one or two instances the cosmic factors are acknowledged. But a further problem is that the experts differ because their experiences and their interpretations of the doctrine of signatures do not agree. G.W. Surya gives the follow-ing ascriptions in *Pflanzenheilkunde* (Herbal Medicine):

> If we inspect the vegetable kingdom to see whether any plants have characteristics of a planetary nature, we find that a Martian plant will exhibit sharp leaf edges, and thorns and stinging hairs on the leaf and stem. Nettles and plants with blistering, pungent secretions and juices belong

Table 2. Relationships between Plants and Planets (after G.W. Surya)

Planet	Growth	Form	Color	Smell	Taste
Saturn	slow	long, sad-looking	dark, little color	stinking, narcotic	astringent, often toxic
Jupiter	luxuriant	stately, compact	blue, violet, gorgeous	pleasant, soothing	sweet, good
Mars	varied	thorny, bristly	red, reddish blue	pungent, penetrating	tingling, bitter
Sun	rapid	noble, colorful	yellow, orange	aromatic, balmy	sweetish sour, strong
Venus	lively	colorful, smiling, pretty	cheerful, light, green, blue, pink	sweet, soporific	palatable, perfumed
Mercury	rapid	unusual, bent, small	variegated	faint, aromatic	sourish but weak
Moon	varied, often rapid	mysterious, unusual	whitish yellow, pale violet	scentless	tasteless, mawkish

to the Mars type. Examples are the great and small stinging nettle (*Urtica dioica* and *Urtica urens*), horseradish (*Cochlearia amoracia*), field buttercup (*Ranunculus acris*), etc. We can say of such plants that they possess the planetary signature.

This doctrine of signatures can therefore be put on an astrological footing, even though it is not always easy to discover the signature or ruling planet for a given plant.

Paracelsus and other investigators have endeavored to present the relationships between plants and planets in the form of short catchwords. But, and the "but" is important, we must not treat this sort of information as the absolute truth when we find it is astrological books. Corrections and improvements are often necessary.[34]

Table 2 indicates relationships between planets and plants as conjectured by Surya. See page 32. It must be emphasized that they should not be regarded as authentic until they have been confirmed in practice by a number of doctors.

Research Done by Dr. M. Duz

Anyone who examines the more recent astromedical texts will find that most of the spadework was done by the French physician Dr. M. Duz, whose opus was printed in Geneva in 1910 in only 510 copies and was soon sold out. It was thanks to the Kosmobiophysische Gesellschaft e.V., Hamburg, that a translation of this book by Curt Knupfer was issued in German—to be sure, only in duplicated form—and even so it is still almost unobtainable. Dr. Duz wrote, among other things:

Astral science builds from the ground up, because it returns to origins. Thus it permits us to understand the role of body humors in physiology and in pathology—it opens fresh horizons in regard to the constitution, and summarizes the pathological picture; in hygiene it shows us the proper course to take, in climatology it reveals favorable and unfavorable times in yearly, daily and other periods, in therapeutics it provides us with a simple law that is in harmony with nature, the law of similars, and finally in sociology it shows us, from the dispositions of our children as revealed in their natal charts, the training needed to fit them for social life.

One apparently highly important feature is that the cosmic correspondences are quite different in different regions of the globe. On this point, Dr. Duz says:

It is a fact that in hot climates in particular there is a prevalence of acute diseases, especially those affecting the liver; by expanding the vessels, the heat causes an impairment of the blood and so the liver becomes congested. Indeed, hepatic disorders and acute diseases are very frequent in the countries concerned for this reason. Now, whereas people living in warmer climates are subject to liver trouble, those in cold and damp climates suffer from chronic (earth-type) or lingering disorders.[35]

In his section on "Physiological Synthesis," Dr. Duz expressed the opinion that "physiology is the science dealing with the nature and constitution of the body, i.e., of the endowments of life. But, since life itself eludes our investigations, astrophysiology is restricted to the consideration of the effects of the heavenly bodies, especially the Moon, on living cells. As we shall see, the Moon is very closely involved with things animate and inanimate, and its journey through the twelve signs of the zodiac affects the body." It must be remembered that the following tables were originally written in French; so when we read of this or that organ being "affected" we must not start thinking in terms of cause and effect: all that is meant is a correspondence between cosmic factors and human organs. (See tables 3 and 4 on pages 35–37.)

Table 3. Correspondences between the Zodiac Signs and the Human Body (after Dr. Duz)

Sign	Physical Correspondence
Aries	affects the cerebral nervous system, the head and what is dependent on it. It gives a predisposition to liver disease. Elementary quality: dry heat.
Taurus	has to do with the thyroid gland and thyroid cartilage, the thymus, which disappears in adulthood, the pituitary, the neck, and the throat and its ancillaries. There is a predisposition to kidney disease. Elementary quality: dry cold.
Gemini	affects the respiratory system (superior lobes of right and left lung), the innervation of the lungs, the arms and the first, second, third and fourth vertebrae. It gives a predisposition to diseases of the cranium. Elementary quality: wet heat. (While on the subject of lung disease, we might consider the statistics of Dr. Schwab, which suggest that Libra plays the main role in these disorders. Also, we must remember that the positions of the planets in the zodiac are made better or worse by aspects and midpoint aspects.)
Cancer	affects the digestive organs (stomach, pit of stomach, epigastrium) and their adjuncts, as well as the diaphragm, the inferior lobes of the lungs (two right, one left) and the pleura. It predisposes to diseases of the head and abdomen. Elementary quality: wet cold.
Leo	corresponds to the cardiac and circulatory system (heart, large blood vessels), the upper third of the stomach, the orifice of the stomach (cardiac, and the fifth, sixth, seventh, eighth and ninth vertebrae. It predisposes to heart disease. Elementary quality: dry heat.

Table 3. Continued

Sign	Physical Correspondence
Virgo	has to do with two-thirds of the right lower stomach, the solar plexus, the pyloric valve, the left lobe of the liver, the caudate lobe of the liver, the pancreas, and their adjuncts, the abdominal-epigastric stomach system and everything dependent on it. It predisposes to diseases of the cranium. Elementary quality: dry cold.
Libra	relates to the kidneys, the left and right region of the navel and the hypogastrium (lower abdomen), i.e., the left and right regions of the groin, part of the small intestine, the urinary bladder in children and the uterus during pregnancy. It gives a predisposition to kidney disease. Elementary quality: wet heat.
Scorpio	relates to the urogenital system, bladder, uterus, and pituitary (also to the corresponding nose-and-throat system) and to the endocrine glands (e.g., to the suprarenals, ovaries, testicles, etc.). It predisposes to liver disease. Elementary quality: wet cold.
Sagittarius	relates to the musculature, also to the cardiac system, the blood vessels, the peritoneum, the bladder muscle, the lumbar region and the thighs. It gives a predisposition to chest diseases. Elementary quality: dry heat.
Capricorn	concerns the skin and mucous membranes, the cell tissues, and the knees. It gives a tendency to diseases of the spleen. Elementary quality: dry cold.
Aquarius	affects the circulatory system (and the blood itself), the shins and the ankles. It predisposes to diseases of the spleen. Elementary quality: wet heat.
Pisces	has to to with the fibers and tendons, and more especially with the respiratory organs and the synovia* (joint oil), also with the calcaneum and the feet. It gives a predisposition to diseases of the chest. Elementary quality: wet cold.

*A term coined by Paracelsus from the Greek *syn* = "with" and the Latin *ovum* = "egg."

Table 4. Correspondences between the Planets and the Human Body (after Dr. Duz)

Sign	Physical Correspondence
Sun	rules cell vitality. Disease: inflammation.
Moon	governs cell modularity. Diseases: hyperemia and degeneration of the blood.
Mercury	maintains the nerves. Diseases: neurosis, metastases (harmful subsidiary growths).
Venus	controls the intercellular fluid. Diseases: dystrophy (defective nourishment), infections.
Mars	stimulates the cells. Diseases: inflammations, fevers, organ lesions.
Jupiter	rules cell regeneration. Diseases: toxic conditions, mercury poisoning, lead poisoning, iodine poisoning, bromine poisoning, food poisoning, allantiasis (botulism, sausage poisoning), syphilis, gonorrhea, etc., dyscarsia (faulty condition of the blood—defective humoral mixture).
Saturn	contracts the cells and rules the protoplasm. Diseases: asthenia (weakness), stenosis (stricture), chronic disorders.

*Uranus, Neptune and Pluto are not included, since at the time Dr. Duz was writing they had not been sufficiently studied. *Tr.*

Research Done by G.W. Surya

G.W. Surya called himself a student of the occult. However, in this connection it must be pointed out that he was active in the first quarter of the 20th century, when all knowledge that was not academically approved was branded as "occult." Today, many things once thought of as occult knowledge have been incorporated in science or in parapsychology. The book *Astrologie und Medizin* (Astrology and Medicine),[36] which Surya produced with his friend Sindbad

(Schwickert), is one of the volumes of *Okkulte Medizin* (Occult Medicine). The first printing was in 1921, to be followed by several improved and enlarged editions.

After a brief historical survey and an introduction to astrological techniques, Surya stresses that the insight of the practicing physician and the wisdom of an accomplished astrologer, are both required in order to make good use of astrodiagnosis. Let no one think that "with such intellectual equipment as an old emphemeris and a freshly sharpened pencil, he can cure a chronic patient in a quarter of an hour." The task is impossible, in any case, since Surya, like other authors, regarded it as essential to calculate the directions, especially the secondary directions or progressions. I know from personal experience, especially since preparing many life diagrams, that this is the only way to detect chronic disease, especially cancer, many years before the symptoms appear.

> Therefore even Paracelsus emphasized that astrology is only *one* of the pillars of medicine; even in diagnosis and prognosis, there is need for philosophy and virtue—both of which are to be understood in their Paracelsian sense.
>
> In uniformity with most other authors, and for the sake of brevity, we will speak of the astrological factors in a nativity as if they "affected" or "influenced" things. This is in keeping with the law of correspondences, which states that when two phenomena occur simultaneously they are related as cause and effect or are both effects of one and the same cause. Anyway, that is how we hope to be understood. See Cicero's dictum, "It is sufficient to experience *what* happens, even if we do not know *how* it happens."[37]

In contrast to traditional astrologers, who had been limited to seven planets, Surya mentions the pathological influences of Uranus and Neptune proposed by the English astrologer Raphael.

Schwab—Hickethier—Schussler

Dr. Schwab, to whom reference has already been made, wrote that we shall be able "to use astrology to introduce a measure of calculation or, as Maack says, of 'genuine mathematics,' into medicine. And wasn't this what alchemy was always after — namely to pinpoint the right remedy?" A year after it was published, he came across an interesting confirmation of the astro-biochemical system announced in 1928. At Easter 1929, he was on holiday in Wiesbaden and went to pay respects to a colleague. During a stroll, they were chatting on this subject, when the friend suddenly exclaimed," Doctor, you really should study Hickethier's book, in which the choice of biochemic remedy is set out according to type and complexion."

Having secured a copy of the *Lehrbuch der Antlitzdiagnostik* (A Manual of Facial Diagnosis), Schwab found that the author had reached the same conclusions as he had, although approaching the subject from a completely different angle. Hickethier proposed eleven clearly defined types, e.g., the cheesy face (Calc. phos.), the puffy face (Silicea), the red, hollow-eyed face (Ferr. phos.). Since his types are more or less identical with the astrological ones, we can naturally replace his notation with appropriate astrological symbols: e.g., Cancer for Calc. phos., Pisces for Silicea, Aries for Ferr. phos., etc.

On that basis, Schwab drew up Table 5 on pages 40–44, which has now been brought up to date. The table combines signs with physical symptoms and how they relate to homeopathic remedies.

The obviously striking correspondences in Table 4 corroborate one another. "For example, when Aries is the rising sign, the native, if a true Arian, will also belong to the Ferr. phos. type. Therefore Ferr. phos. comes under Aries."*

Indeed, Schüssler says of Ferr. phos. and of Kali sulph. that they transport oxygen and promote oxidation. They exactly corres-

---

*It is interesting to compare the zodiac attributions of the biochemic cell salts given in this book with those given by Dr. George Washington Carey (see *The Zodiac and the Salts of Salvation*, by Inez Eudora Perry, published by Samuel Weiser, York Beach, ME in 1971). Dr. Carey's scheme has often been quoted more or less accurately by others (for example, by James Vogh in *Astrology and Your Health*, Granada Publishing, 1980), apparently without questioning its truth. However, the attributions mentioned in this present book differ in almost every instance from those of Carey; the one exception being Na. sulph. for Taurus.

The discrepency is so striking that it raises the suspicion that both schemes are wrong. At any rate, it shows how easily a strong subjective element can enter into the

Table 5. Remedy Selection according to Appearance,
Sign and Disease

Remedy	Appearance	Sign	Disease
Ferrum phos.	Feverish look, hollow-eyed, shadows under eyes as if greatly fatigued, red forehead, hectic flush.	Aries. Hard look, eagle-eyed, often prone to fever-ishness, head always hot, red face, especially in the forehead.	Inflammatory hyperemia, inflammations, hemorrhages, pneumonia, encephalo-meningitis.
Natrum sulph.	Greenish yellow face and skin, impression of slow metabo-lism, abnormal redness.	Taurus. Usually yellowish color of skin and face, metabolic disorders due to faulty diet (food usually too rich), gallblad-der and skin troubles.	Metabolic dis-turbances due to defective regulation of the water econ-omy, bilious-ness, diabetes, skin complaints.
Magnesium phos.	Pale pink face, crimson over the cheek bones, numer-ous patches like red blushes, inner restless-ness, hectic red in neuralgias.	Gemini. Fresh colors, nervy, always on the go, tendency to feverish-nervous disorders, e.g., tuberculosis, otherwise cramps and neuralgias.	Cramps, stom-ach cramps, bladder spasms, colic, neural-gias, chorea (St. Vitus' dance), tuberculosis, scrofulism.

Table 5. Continued

Remedy	Appearance	Sign	Disease
Calcium phos.	Waxy face, like white-wash.	Cancer. Pallid, soft, flabby skin, anemia, relaxed tissues and the consequences of these, disorders of the glands and serous membranes; rickets in children.	Exudates, rickets. (This remedy regenerates the cells.)
Kali sulph.	Brown color.	Leo. Animated, light sun-tan color, tendency to heart disorders, pleurisy, distension of the aorta, vertigo.	Vertigo, palpitation of the heart, catarrhs.
Natrum mur.	Well-known cooking-salt face, rather spongy and puffy, often sweaty, occasionally watery eyes.	Virgo. Seems tired and lacking in energy, wears a look of suffering as in intestinal disorders, rather puffy skin, tendency to diseases of the stomach and intestines.	Drowsiness and coldness, watery diarrhea, stomach trouble, water brash.

Table 5. Continued

Remedy	Appearance	Sign	Disease
Kali mur.*	Delicate brownish, milky skin, like alabaster, swollen glands, leukorrhea.	Libra. Fine delicate complexion, metabolic disorders, unbalanced state of the detoxifying organs—glands, skin, serous membranes, kidneys.	Exudates, diphtherial deposits in body cavities, catarrh with plastic exudations.
Kali phos.	Ash-grey, as if the face was unwashed.	Scorpio. Generally dusky, grey face color, (red cheeks are rare in Scorpio), nervous conditions, diseases of the brainworker, venereal diseases, sexual neurosis, serious infections, typhus, dysentery.	Disturbed neurotrophy, weak memory, neurasthenia, vasomotor disturbances of the sympathic nervous system, severe dynamic conditions, typhus, sepsis, syphilis.

*Not Kali chlorat. as the German. Kali mur. is a *chloride* of potassium not a *chlorate. Tr.*

Table 5. Continued

Remedy	Appearance	Sign	Disease
Natrum phos.	Oily exudations in the folds around the eyes and nose, greasy appearance, disorders of the sebacious glands, blackheads, general overoxidation, rheumatism and gout.	Sagittarius. The skin often displays impurities, moles, blackheads, liver disorders, overoxidation, articular diseases, especially in the hip.	Excess of lactic acid and its consequences, uric acid diathesis and its consequences, polyarthritis, hyperacidity of the stomach, diarrhea, children's diseases.
Calcium fluor.	Longitudinal and transverse creases on a dark reddish-blackish substratum, in the angle made by the eye the nose.	Capricorn. Poor blood supply to the skin, a furrow in the crease between the nose and eye, the complexion is often red with dark shading, degenerative conditions, deformities, bad posture, enteroptosis (prolapse of the bowels), spots, indurations.	Bone diseases, displacement of the abdominal organs, skin complaints such as fissures, cracks, hardened exudates, nodules in the breast.

Table 5. Continued

Remedy	Appearance	Sign	Disease
Aluminum* Probably a complex of biological ash	†	Aquarius. Delicate complexion, light color, cramps and other nervous conditions, intestinal gases, flatulence, diseases of the limbs and joints, the typical demineralized individual.	Nervous impulses, disorders of the smooth musculature of the intestines, bladder, and larynx, nasal catarrh and pharyngitis, muscle weakness and spasms, failing sight in old age.
Silicea	Facial skin translucent or as if covered in varnish, crow's-feet, often baldness.	Pisces. Thick skin, fresh complexion, sometimes with a glassy look, tendency for crow's-feet at corners of eyes, septic foci, lumps, proud flesh, cancer.	Diseases of the connective tissue, pus spots, effusions are resorbed, gout, gravel in the kidneys, cataract.

*Calc. sulph. is the English equivalent here. *Tr.*

†This space is blank in the German text. Hickethier described only eleven types; one less than the astrological and biochemical twelve. *Tr.*

pond to the signs Aries and Leo, for they fit the typology. In astrological nomenclature, these two signs are known as fire signs, and this tells us among other things that they have something to do with biological combustion. (The typical members of the signs have a good color and produce plenty of blood and body heat). On the other hand, Schüssler says of Nat. sulph. and Nat. mur. that they attract tissue water and help to regulate the water economy of the body. Their signs, in our scheme, are earth signs; that is to say, they are dry and readily absorb water. Their natives are very sensitive with regard to water balance.

Richard Herlbauer-Virusgo

In 1935, the Ebertin Verlag, Erfurt, published *Praktische Astro-Medizin* (Practical Astromedicine) as a manual for the "Dulcanoster" therapeutic system developed by the author on the basis of cosmo-biological principles. With the assistance of IosWerk in Regensburg, he prepared a homeopathic complex of remedies corresponding to the zodiac signs, to the elements and to the planets. In the foreword to his book, Herlbauer-Virusgo writes:

> Several astromedical (cosmobiological) systems of therapy have been worked out to meet the requirements of the New Age, but their novelty and their more or less complicated modes of operation have prevented them from reaching a very wide circle.

---

question, and, as a matter of fact, anyone who takes the trouble to read Carey's reasons for matching certain cell salts with certain zodiac signs will find that whenever he could not match them on medical or biological grounds, he made do with some mineralogical analogy. And yet, presumably, people are still taking regular doses of "their" birth salts in the belief that they have a sound scientific reason for doing so.

Quite possibly, it is a mistake to try and make a one-to-one pairing of the biochemic salts and signs. Although there are twelve of each, the areas they cover are not the same. The signs represent body sections and organs, whereas the salts affect the functioning of body tissues shared by many different body parts and organs. *Tr.*

The "Dulcanoster" therapeutic system explained in this book has made a big change in the situation and represents a practical healing system which is easy to use and has a sound cosmobiological basis. It is not simply a symbolic relationship with the signs and planets, but guarantees a treatment tailored to the needs of the individual. In this system, pure herbal remedies are combined with homeopathic compounds.[38]

In preparing his remedies, Herlbauer-Virusgo relied chiefly on the findings of Dr. Allendy and Dr. Feerhow, whose research has already been described. Numerous physicians and health practitioners have been using his system for many years. It was characteristic of the period of its inception that, in order to recruit as many physicians as possible, the manufacturers used labels of two types. For those who believed in astrology, the remedies were labeled with the names of the signs and planets but, for sceptics, only the names of the active constituents were mentioned and the fact that the composition had a cosmic basis was suppressed. This usage was retained by the Göppingen firm which later manufactured the "Dynoplex" remedy according to Herlbauer's instructions. For example, Silicea with the addition of Belladonna, Cochlearia off., Opecuanha, Natrium chlor., Nux vomica, Pulsatilla, etc., corresponded to the sign Cancer. Herlbauer's system offered compound remedies for each sign of the zodiac, for the individual planets, and for the elements, as well as a selection of tisanes for the various signs. Physician and cosmobiologist Dr. H.G. Müller-Freywardt of Munich has formulated a new range of zodiac teas.[39] In choosing the right tea, however, it is not always the Sun sign or the Ascendant which is the decisive factor; any sign that exercises a particularly strong influence must also be taken into account. Table 6 is another listing of homeopathic remedies that can be used by sign or planet.

In using the individual remedies and in deciding the correct dosage, a qualified homeopath should always be consulted, since it is important that the correct attenuation is prescribed.

Table 6. Homeopathic Sign and Plant Remedies formulated by
Albert Lang

Sign	Remedy	Planet	Remedy
Aries	Cimifuga D	Sun 1	Cactus D
Taurus	Guaiacum D	Sun 2	Lycopus D
Gemini	Bryonia D	Moon 1	Agaricus D
Cancer	Silicea D	Moon 2	Senecio D
Leo	Kalmia D	Mercury 1	Baptisia D
Virgo	Colocynthis D	Mercury 2	Valeriana D
Libra	Cantharis D	Venus 1	Primula D
Scorpio 1	Scilla D	Venus 2	Fucus D
Scorpio 2	Gelsemium D	Mars 1	Hypericum D
Sagittarius	Chamomilla D	Mars 2	Apis D
Capricorn	Viola D	Jupiter 1	Asclepias D
Aquarius	Dulcamara D	Jupiter 2	Salvia D
Pisces	Urtica D	Saturn 1	Taxus D
		Saturn 2	Pimpinella D
		Uranus 1	Veratrum D
		Uranus 2	Stramonium D
		Neptune 1	Passiflora D
		Neptune 2	Helleborus D

Dr. H.G. Müller-Freywardt

Dr. Müller-Freywardt was a regular speaker from as early as the Second Conference for Cosmobiological Research in 1950. He was absolutely convinced of the relationship between the cosmos and humanity and constantly used astromedicine to help him in his practice, and even made himself so proficient in astrology that he listed astrologer as his profession on his passport. "Kosmisches Denken: Eine praktische Realitat arztlichen tuns und lassens" (Cosmic Thinking: A Practical Guide to What Is Done and Not Done in Medicine) was one of his subjects at the meetings. Here are a few sentences from this fundamental lecture:

When we come to look at the course of human life — the life-portrait if you like — within the framework of time and space, it is particularly important for those of us who are physicians to try and do so in the context of disease. Disease is part of the life-portrait of an individual even when it does not stand in the foreground. The old adage about "dying in good health," which is something we would all still like to do at the end of a healthy life, proposes a goal that is harder to achieve than it used to be.[40]

Dr. Reich, co-founder of the Cosmobiological Academy at Aalen e.V., agreed with leading researchers and experts in the field that a natural and holistic therapy is essentially cosmic. For him, cosmic thinking was a practical guide to medical do's and don'ts. He saw one of the secrets of the zodiac as its very arrangement, which is both a progress and a rhythm. During his travels in Japan, Korea and Bali, Dr. Reich learned of the reliance placed by the Asiatics on symbols. Out of his own experiences, he confirmed the dictum of C.G. Jung that "the astrological symbols are the archetypes of mankind, and are deeply rooted in our psyches."

Here, perhaps, we should mention a few of the more important basic cosmobiological laws:

1) Especially important in a nativity are those planets that are as nearly as possible in exact hard or easy aspect with one another according to classical theory.

2) In every case, the dominant planetary influences are those uniting several personal points in themselves.

3) In the hierarchy of personal points the MC is the chief; then come the Sun, ASC, Moon, lunar nodes, IC and DC.

The fundamentals of astromedical practice were laid down by Dr. Müller-Freywardt in his lecture, "Sinn und Unsinn astromedizinischer Diagnosen" (Sense and Nonsense in Astromedical Diagnosis) at the 21st Conference in 1969. He said:

The psychologist and the expert on psychosomatic diseases tell us in technical jargon nothing else than what astrologers have been maintaining for centuries, that the mode of life favored by the astrological type Leo frequently leads to disorders of the heart and circulation, while behavior characteristic of Pisces often results in impaired mobility due to diseases of the shanks, ankles and feet. This certainly does not mean that any and every emphasis on Leo in the chart will signify cardiac problems. The natural law by which each event has its astrological counterpart does not work both ways; therefore we must refrain from making medical diagnoses from the radix alone without corroboration.

Many patients have been filled with fear and despair by astromedical diagnosis and by some even less reliable prognosis from the stars. One would have to be very brash to say a patient, "Forget that new job for the moment—you will be having a heart attack some time in the next few months."[41]

A case is known to the author in which an astrologer advised a pregnant woman to have an abortion, since her child would be handicapped. The woman was reassured by professional advice and bore a perfectly healthy child. In another instance, a man was given the prognosis that he would die at the age of forty-five. One can imagine the fear into which he was thrown at that age. He was counselled by another practitioner and survived; the progressed aspects did come into operation, but released their influence as a loss of employment. Facts such as these are one reason why astrologers should produce evidence of their skill and would do well to belong to a professional association.

Dr. Müller-Freywardt continued that in the main he made use of the circle of the elements of Dr. Folkert and the homeopathic compounds of Herlbauer-Virusgo, because the progress of a cure was often more satisfactory with biological medicaments chosen on the *similia* principle rather than on the *contraria* principle of allopathy.

Dr. Wilhelm Folkert

The Dr. Folkert to whom reference was made by Dr. Müller-Freywardt first spoke at the 11th Conference for Cosmobiological

Research at Aalen in 1959, just after the publication of his basic textbook on his life's work, *Sphäron*.[42] I had already made the acquaintance of Dr. Folkert in 1950 at a discussion held in Radio Frankfurt's big studio. (The main speakers were myself on behalf of astrology and cosmobiology and Max Gerstenberger on behalf of astronomy.) During the discussion, Dr. Folkert first drew attention to his working methods and also remarked on the absolute necessity of including heliocentric constellations as well (we shall return to this point later). In his lecture, Dr. Folkert said, among other things:

> Until now, since nothing of the kind yet exists in our professional literature, none of you has read a book clearly showing in a scientific way the effect of cosmic influences on the individual — even though Mr. Ebertin has written an article pleading that such a work is badly needed.
>
> My own practice is a synthesis of East and West. Acupuncture has been adopted from Eastern medicine and is already being taught at university level by our French neighbors. [In 1959 acupuncture was still relatively unknown in Germany, but many books on the subject appeared in the next decade]. The foundations of Chinese philosophy are the principles of Yang and Yin on which the celebrated Chinese book of wisdom, the *I Ching*, is based. Nothing that happens, none of the tension in living nature, would be conceivable without the opposition they produce between positive and negative, light and dark, dry and wet, etc. In medical work extending over thousands of years, the Chinese have discovered hundreds of sensitive points on the human body and have realized that they mark the course of a continuous stream of energy flowing through the body. In disease, this energy flow is disturbed.
>
> With the help of X-rays, scientists have counted the elements and know today that ninety-two elements occur naturally. . . . Now if each atom is like a tiny planetary system, ought not the elements as a whole to have the same appearance? . . . I have succeeded without difficulty in establishing an unforced connection between our solar system and the periodic system of the elements. As far as I know,

nobody has done this before. What you are learning now is something new; the fruit of my studies over the past ten years or more.

I have arranged the elements in a circle with special reference to Yang and Yin. The odd elements are Yang and the even elements are Yin. The circle runs continuously from the lightest elements through the heaviest and back to the lightest again.

In this circle we can also arrange the Chinese [acupuncture] points. These are distributed all over the body. They are each the size of a pin's head, and when they are manipulated correctly they are very sensitive — especially in disease. The points are all interconnected and we have to assume that a continuous flow is taking place through our bodies through definite channels, similar to the flow of an electric current through a wire. The flow takes twenty-four hours to return to its starting point. This explains the variation in the reactions of the organs according to the time of day — on account of which I give my remedies at exactly determined hours.[43]

Speaking on the significance of the Sun's place in the radix, Dr. Folkert made the interesting statement that patients born on the same day exhibit similar symptoms. He discovered this by running through more than twenty-five thousand medical cards, and Dr. Muller-Freywardt confirmed the observation from his own records.

In the book *Sphäron*, the following cases are adduced. A female birth took place on 10th July, 1925 at 5 P.M. At the age of five months the child suffered from convulsions which lasted several hours. One week after vaccination on 17th June, 1937, she had a fit of convulsions, and this was repeated several times. Body cramps also supervened. A male patient born on the same day at 3 A.M. suffered from a spasm of the esophagus at the age of six months. And a female patient born on the same day at 2 A.M. had an attack of vaginismus (vaginal spasm) at the age of twenty-four.

Various individuals who shared 21st November, 1901 as their birthday suffered from sexual disorders. A male patient born on this day at around 3 P.M. fell into a state of mental confusion in 1940, and kept writing love letters which were heavily underlined and full of eccentricities. Another male patient born on the same day, who suffered from chronic psoriasis, was covered in 1940 by a fiery red, burning, itching eczema from his abdomen to his anus. A third patient, born at 12:30 P.M., came for treatment in 1950 suffering from giddiness, strabismus, depression and an evil-smelling discharge from the testicles and the region of the inguinal glands. A female patient came for giddiness, buzzing in the ear and listlessness in 1953; in 1928 an operation had been performed on one of her ovaries. Another female patient, weighing one hundred and ninety-three pounds, complained of giddiness and headaches. She suffered from a persecution complex and had a growth the size of two fists in her abdomen.

The Sun is 28° Scorpio here and, according to the *Anatomische Entsprechungen der Tierkreisgrade* (The Anatomical Correspondences of the Zodiac Degrees)[44] 25°–28° have to do with the fallopian tubes, perineum, anus and mucous membranes; as can also be seen in the similar scheme developed by Fritz Brandau in his *Organuhr* (Organ Clock).[45]

The Daily Rhythm of the Human Organism

We have mentioned several times already how important it is, in diagnosis and therapy, to recognize the diurnal rhythm in the human organism. This is linked with meteorological and physical processes occurring during the day. Günther Wachsmuth explored the subject in great detail in his book *Erde und Mensch* (Earth and Man).[46] As may be seen from tables 7 and 8, definite phases occur at 3 A.M., 9 A.M., 3 P.M. and 9 P.M. (See pages 53–54.)

At 3 A.M. barometric pressure is at minimum; there is maximum conductivity of the vertical electrical current and a variational change in the earth-current. At 9 A.M. barometric pressure is at a maximum, there is a turning-point in the movement of the air, the valley wind starts to blow, and there is a matutinal increase in the potential gradient and variations in the earth-current. At 3 P.M. barometric pressure is at a minimum and there is a change in the movement of the air. At 9 P.M. barometric pressure is at a maximum; there is a

Table 7. Daily Meteorological and Physical Processes (after Dr. Wachsmuth)

3 P.M. Phase	9 A.M. Phase
Minimum of barometric pressure, of oscillations in the earth's magnetism, of the potential gradient (in the lower layers), and of radioactivity near ground. Hour of change for air movement and wind vectors, for variations in terrestrial magnetism, and for variations in the earth-current.	Maximum of barometric pressure, and of oscillations in the earth's magnetism. Hour of change for air movement and wind vectors, and for variations in terrestrial magnetism. Onset of the valley wind. Morning increase in the potential gradient. Variations in the earth-current.

9 P.M. Phase	3 A.M. Phase
Maximum of barometric pressure, and of oscillations in terrestrial magnetism. Hour of change for air movement. Onset of the mountain wind. Hour of change for variations in terrestrial magnetism and for variations in the earth-current. Evening increase in the potential gradient.	Minimum of barometric pressure (in the double daily wave), of air movement near the ground, of oscillations in terrestrial magnetism, and of the potential gradient. Maximum of conductivity of the vertical electric current, and of radioactivity in the layers near the ground. Hour of change for variations in the earth-current.

Table 8. The Daily Rhythms and Phases of the Internal Processes
(after Dr. Wachsmuth)

3 P.M. Phase	9 A.M. Phase
Maximum of: secretory activity of the liver and kidneys, glycogen mobilization (emptying of the liver), bile production and secretion, diuresis (at local time when travelling).	Maximum of: body temperature (at local time when travelling).
Increase in: blood pressure, circulation, vital lung capacity, oxygen consumption and release of carbon dioxide.	Increase in: the activity of the liver and kidneys, diuresis (morning urination), the discharge of dissimilation products, circulating erythrocytes, leukocytes (red and white blood corpuscles) and thrombocytes, bile secretion, blood sugar.
Minimum: glycogen storage in the liver, fat resorption in the wall of the intestine.	
Afternoon temperature peak.	

9 P.M. Phase	3 A.M. Phase
Decrease in: kidney activity	Maximum of: glycogen storage in the liver, fat resorption in the intestinal wall, blood enrichment in the lungs and legs, water retention in the blood, increase of melanophoric hormone, contraction of the capillaries.
Accumulation of glycogen in the liver.	
Greater frequency of labor pains.	
Evening maximum of blood pressure.	
Sharp fall in body temperature around 10 P.M.	Minimum of: bile secretion, diuresis, water excretion, pulse rate, heart frequency, blood pressure, circulation, venous reflux, heart minute volume, vital capacity of lungs, oxygen consumption and release of carbon dioxide, metabolism, body temperature.
Maximum venous return between 9 P.M. and midnight, then sudden change in the circulation of the blood.	

change in the movement of the air and variations in the earth's magnetism. These are the most significant phases, which belong to rhythms controlled partly by the cosmos and partly by the earth.

If we now take a look at the rhythm of the liver, we find a maximum concentration at 3 A.M., with storage of glycogen in the liver; at the same time bile production commences. The glycogen content starts to decrease slowly; blood sugar and bile secretion increase. At 9 A.M. the liver reaches an intermediate stage of secretion until, at 3 P.M., a maximum of bile production and bile secretion is reached. After this the secretion and storage of glycogen in the liver commences, with a half-way stage at 9 P.M. and maximum concentration at 3 A.M.

And just as the rhythmic functioning of the liver plays an important part in metabolism, so the rhythmic functioning of the kidneys plays an important part in water elimination. Incidentally, it has been found that these processes are independent of meal-times. We can distinguish a morning flow starting at about 3 A.M., a maximum secretion at around 3 P.M. and a minimum secretion around midnight. These phases persist even during world travel and correspond to the current local time of the traveller. The circulation of the blood has a daily rhythm, in that the heart minute volume shows a marked increase between 10 P.M. and midnight and a marked decrease between 2 A.M. and 4 A.M.; the difference being six to ten per cent.

In the respiratory process it has been established that the vital capacity, the respired-air content of the lungs, peaks in the morning and afternoon. The evening decrease represents eight to twenty per cent of the morning capacity. The actual figures for pulmonary blood engorgement are ca. 300–800 c.c. of blood, which accumulate in the lungs between 2 A.M. and 6 P.M. and between 10 P.M. and 2 A.M.

According to Schenk (Wachsmuth, p. 391) blood formation in the bone marrow is most intense around 4 A.M., and the number of circulating leukocytes is greatest around 4 P.M.

In the endocrine system, the adrenal glands are most active during the day, whereas the pituitary gland is more active at night. And, in the nervous system, the sympathetic nerve predominates by day and the vagus by night. The evening drop in body temperature is also characteristic.

Here we have only given some of the basic points from Wachsmuth's copious volume, which is particularly useful for judging the proper time to take medicaments.

In this connection, mention must also be made of the investigations of Dr. E.W. Stiefvater and his book *Die Organuhr* (The Organ Clock).[47] The author published a large diagram, the bare outline of which is reproduced here as figure 2. This diagram is very similar to Wachsmuth's tables, but actually improves on them as a survey of the body's daily activities. Yin and Yang relationships and many other details have been omitted from the annexed drawing.

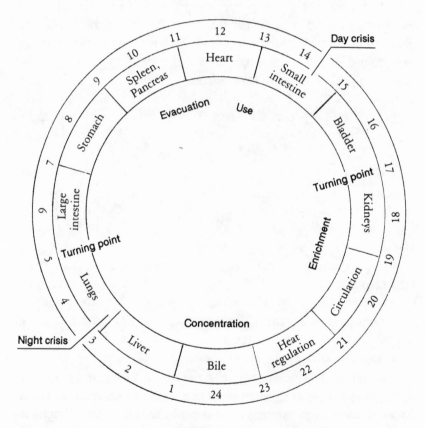

Figure 2. The 24-hour clock and physical activity in the body (after E.W. Stiefvater).

Alexander von Bernus

Alexander von Bernus came of an old aristocratic Frankfurt family, but shortly after his birth he was adopted by his uncle, Friedrich Alexander von Bernus. In the main, he is known as a poet and as the publisher of a magazine which received contributions from well-known contemporary writers. Following the death of his uncle, he became lord of the manor at Stift Neuburg, a place steeped in the traditions of a mighty past. Even as a chid, von Bernus had a taste for supernatural and metaphysical things, and he went on to immerse himself in the writings of Paracelsus and in rare alchemical texts, which he acquired from Gustav Meyrink in 1914. He devoted himself more and more to alchemy, came to know Rudolf Steiner, and finally founded the Laboratorium Soluna at Schloss Neuburg, later removing it to Schloss Donaumünster.

Alexander von Bernus died in 1965. A great exhibition from his estate was mounted in Karlsruhe State Library in 1971. In his list of medicaments there are no more than one or two references to "Astro-sophie" but, on the other hand, it emerges from his book *Alchemy und Heilkunst* (Alchemy and the Healing Art), published in 1948, just how interested he was in cosmic correspondences, on which he had in fact relied when preparing his remedies. He called astrology as exact empirical science.

How seriously he took his research appears from a quotation he made from Rudolf Steiner: "The laboratory bench must become an altar restored." He also expressed the opinion that the hour in which medicinal plants are gathered is a vital factor since, it they are not picked at the right time of day, the medicine will, as Paracelsus said, pass through the body without doing any good at all. (The literal words of Paracelsus are that, if the herbs are not picked at the right time, the medicine prepared from them "goes uselessly through the arse.")

The aim that Alexander von Bernus set himself was, as we read in the preface of his book, "to place the cosmogenetic and philosophical system known as alchemy in its true light as a scientific discipline quite distinct from modern physics and chemistry, and to produce evidence of its genuineness." For: "Through astrology we finally introduce an element of calculation — Maack even goes so far as to say of mathematics—into medicine. And wasn't this the very thing that alchemy was always trying to do, namely to pinpoint the right remedy?"[48]

Alexander Müller

Between 1924 and 1927, the pharmacist Alexander Müller lectured on "Cosmic and Telluric Rays as the Causes of Disease." The lectures were collected under the title *Kosmos und Mensch* (Cosmos and Man).[49] On the basis of his experiments, which he was scrupulous to perform only on living beings, he came to the conclusion that, with the help of electrically active salts, one could imitate every climatic influence without exception and, to some extent, could artificially produce the atmospheres of meadow, upland and mountain. Understandably, to begin with, he met with strong resistance on all sides, being branded by some as a visionary and by others as a swindler. He said:

> Generally speaking, electrolytes are thought of as salts which have the property of breaking up in aqueous solution into their molecules, atoms, electrons and ions, and there-fore of generating an electric current due to the friction between colliding particles as the material flies apart. Their solutions also have an increased capacity for carrying electric currents from outside sources.
>
> My recognition that all the causes of disease are invari-ably to be sought in the disruption of the minutest vessels of the organism paves the way for a cure.
>
> Then it occurred to me to use two stimuli of different kinds, corresponding to cosmic vibrations, and to impart special properties and a special direction in our bodies to the stimuli applied to our nerves. In addition, the means used had to bring uric acid, calcium, oxalate and insoluble phosphates into solution. I had been successful thus far, after countless attempts, especially in influencing the activ-ities of the glandular organs, when the thought struck me that I could derive all stimulation from my electrolysis of the solar plexus, the true function of which is totally unknown to science.

Müller also recognized that cosmic rays have completely different effects at different times of day. Around noon, and in the evening, the radioactive radiations bring about an involuntary contraction of the finest capillaries in the organism and the large vessels
expand under pressure. At night, on the other hand, the radioactive
influences of the Moon (according to phase) appear to regulate the
spinal nerves; especially as, when the body is recumbent, the earth
currents are driven to increasing activity by them. Müller realized that
related ideas were to be found in the work of the Dornach anthroposophist, Dr. Günther Wachsmuth, after he had been presented with
the latter's book *Die ätherischen Bildekräfte in Kosmos, Erde und
Mensch*.[50] Alexander Müller also exchanged ideas with Mrs. Elsbeth
Ebertin; who regularly took and recommended his preparations,
since the twenty-four different salts contained in the remedy Sepdelen are compounded on cosmic principles.

Like a number of other research workers, Alexander Müller took
the view that all epidemics are the consequence of strong solar flares.
He named his field of research sepdelenopathy. However, those who
take the well-tried Sepdelen today seldom know that it has a cosmic
basis.

Carl Friedrich Zimpel

Carl Friedrich Zimpel was born in Sprottau/Schlesien in 1800. In
addition to being a professional engineer, he was an officer in the
Prussian guards and an aide to the King of Prussia. When his suit for
the hand in marriage of the daughter of a high-ranking officer was
rejected, he tried to elope with his sweetheart. However, his plan was
discovered and he was sentenced to confinement in a fortress. By
favor of the king he was permitted to travel to America. There he
purchased needles, ribbons and similar items and began peddling his
wares in Canada. In this way he familiarized himself with the country
and its inhabitants and learned to speak the language. But it was not
long before he resumed his old profession, working for the mines and
railways, and eventually built houses in New York where he became

the owner of more than one hundred properties. However, he lost everything in a great slump and returned to his homeland as an American citizen. By this time he had lost his enthusiasm for building railroads and turned to the study of medicine, graduating as a Ph.D. and being awarded the diploma of a homeopathic physician by Dr. Lutze. He was later decorated with the Prussian Gold Medal for Art and Science and was made an honorary member of the University of Jena.

In 1849 he went to London in order to practice as a homeopath and became interested in theosophy* and mysticism. It is not know when he started to study spagyrics and the writings of Paracelsus. He spent his professional fees on travelling to France, Spain, Italy, Liguria, San Remo, Morocco, Tunisia, Egypt, the Holy Land, Lebanon and whenever he could win acceptance for homeopathy and could spread the knowledge of its benefits.

In Italy he made the acquaintance of, among others, Count Cesare Mattei, the founder of electro-homeopathy (a system similar to electro-homeopathy was produced by Professor Krauss in conjunction with Iso-Werk, Regensburg). Dr. Zimpel visited Italy a number of times, where he achieved striking success with his remedies during a terrible outbreak of cholera. In 1873 he moved house to Naples, and collaborated with the resident pharmacist, Hartenstein. And the same year he met Dr. Mauch of Göppingen, who acquired all Zimpel's manuscripts and original prescriptions. The Zimpel remedies, all of which bear the head of Paracelsus on the label, are still available and are prescribed by registered physicians and lay medical practitioners alike.

In Dr. Zimpel's description of the spagyric system of healing, nothing is said about the remedies being prepared under specific cosmic laws; in fact the word astrology is avoided in order not to ruffle any academic feathers. However, mention is made of the hermetic sciences and of occultism in the Paracelsian sense.[51]

---

*Clearly not the Hindu-type "Theosophy" of the Theosophical Society, founded in 1875, as the latter was not yet in existence; more likely the older German theosophy of Meister Eckhart and Jakob Boehme.

Rudolf Steiner and Anthroposophy

Rudolf Steiner was born on the 27th February 1861, in Kraljevec (Königsdorf) on the Hungarian-Croatian border. In 1879 he passed his school-leaving examination and entered the College of Science and Technology in Vienna, but also attended lectures in philosophy and medicine at the university there. In 1884, on the recommendation of his tutor, he was invited by Josef Kürschner to edit Goethe's scientific writings with an introduction and notes. The fact that Steiner came to Goethe by way of natural philosophy was particularly significant to him. The immediate consequence of Steiner's work was that he was called to the Goethe-Schiller Archiv in Weimar. Thus an opportunity was presented to him to make contact with representatives of the intellectual world.

A big step in Steiner's life was his transfer to Berlin in 1897. Here he edited the *Magazin für die Literatur des In- und Auslandes* ('The Magazine for German and Foreign Literature') and was able to come to grips with the equivocal cultural trends of the turn of the century. In his numerous articles he was already displaying those constructive abilities which were to prove so fruitful. He founded Anthroposophy as a science and, by the time of his death on March 30, 1926, had formulated his spiritual researches in more than six thousand lectures. In 1913 he erected the Goetheanum in Dornach as a center for the anthroposophical movement and, when this was destroyed by fire on New Year's Eve 1922/23, designed a second building in a new architectural style.

Steiner made a special study of medical and anthropological problems, one of his most pregnant sayings being: "In order to join forces with health, it is necessary to see the entire cosmos in man." He said this in his treatise *Krankheitsfälle und andere medizinische Fragen* (Cases of Disease and Other Medical Questions).[52] At Easter 1920, he delivered a course of lectures to thirty-five doctors and medical students in which he laid the foundation for an expansion of medical science by the addition of knowledge drawn from spiritual science. This and other courses led to the demand for a place where remedies could be developed and manufactured in accordance with the findings of spiritual science, and the foundation of a manufacturing company was laid at Arlesheim. In 1924, the German firm Weleda was set up in Stuttgart and Swabian Gmünd.

The firm endeavors to cultivate medicinal plants in their natural habitats and to use appropriate fertilizers. Due consideration is also given to the correct ecological conditions, so that the herbs encourage one another's growth. Plants are harvested at the right time of day and in the proper season. It is known, for example, that the healing properties of the dandelion vary according to whether the herb is gathered in spring or in autumn. The toxicity of many species of Ranunculus is greater in June than in October. Thorn-apple leaves picked in the morning have a higher alkaloid content than those picked in the evening. And foxglove leaves are most potent when picked and prepared on a sunny afternoon.

Dr. Rudolf Hauschka

Dr. Rudolf Hauschka is an anthroposophist. From 1928 through 1940 he collaborated extensively with Dr. Ita Wegmann at the Clinical Therapeutic Institute founded by her in Arlesheim, Switzerland. Dr. Wegmann was a close associate of Dr. Rudolf Steiner in the twenties. Dr. Hauschka has published the results of his investigations in the books, *Substanzlehre*, *Ernährungslehre*, and *Heilmittellehre* (The Doctrine of Substances, The Doctrine of Nutrition, and The Doctrine of Remedies)[53] and put them into practice at his Wala Remedy Laboratory in Eckwalden bei Bad Boll. I had the privilege of knowing him personally, and was amazed at the care taken over the manufacture of his medicaments. It is a tribute to the happy atmosphere of the enterprise and to the confidence of the staff in the methods used for preparing the remedies that willing workers were always on hand to harvest the medicinal plants in the early morning and at sundown. Within the compass of a few pages, it would be impossible to give anything like an adequate idea of Hauschka's wealth of learning and practical experience. A few extracts from the section of stellar influences in earthly substances will have to suffice.

Many old writings allude to the powers of the zodiac pictures and to the significance of their names, but we have lost our insight into this way of representing reality. Science, in particular, has severed every link with traditions recorded for our benefit in the tomes of the ancients. However, the spiritual science founded by Rudolf Steiner has resurrected, in a form suited to modern minds, the knowledge of the connections between constellations, earth and man. Many ways have been advertised as leading to a knowledge of the universal creative principles, and yet all the while we have been gazing with unseeing eyes at their images in the stars.

We are gradually realizing that everything has arisen from the essence of this stellar pattern, which builds the earth and the human body. Now, if we want to cooperate intelligently with these formative forces of the fixed stars and planets which affect us here below, we would do well to ask ourselves what are the ultimate physical results of their action? In the twelve signs, the names of which were bestowed by the old seers, four images hold a leading position: the Lion, the Eagle (Scorpion), the Water Bearer and the Bull. These four, known to us in mythology and in the Book of Revelation, have always been seen as depicting the makeup of the human being:

— the Eagle represents the power of thought, which is associated with the head;

— the Lion, with its powerful chest development, represents the energy of the heart;

— the Bull (or cow), which is a treasury of metabolic products [milk, meat, leather and horn], represents the metabolism;

— the Water Bearer, finally, represents the harmonizer of the other principles in the earthly organization of the human being — which is why the ancients called it the Man or Angel.

Thus, in Atlantean times, four human types could be distinguished: the Eagle or cerebral, the Lion or pectoral, the Bull or metabolic, and those who for the most part kept these in balance—the Water-Bearer people.[54]

As an aid to understanding what he was going to say next, Dr. Hauschka supplied the diagram reproduced here as figure 3.

The four leaders of the zodiac, the lion, water bearer, bull and eagle, represent the four essential substances hydrogen, oxygen, nitrogen and carbon, which build the entire organic world. According to Dr. Hauschka, the harmonization of these four chemicals forms protein, the basis of all life. Protein is so versatile when we

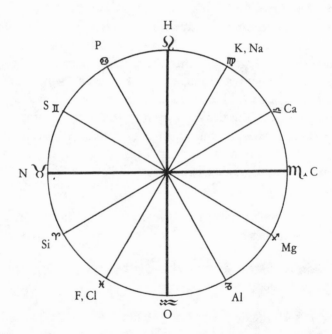

Figure 3. The four essential substances and the chemicals of the zodiac. Nitrogen (N) is Taurus, Oxygen (O) is Aquarius, Carbon (C) is Scorpio, and Hydrogen (H) is Leo. The other substances in order from Aries: Silicon (Si) is Aries; Sulfur (S) is Gemini; Phosphorus (P) is Cancer; Sodium (Na) is Virgo; Calcium (Ca) is Libra; Magnesium (Mg) is Sagittarius; Aluminum (Al) is Capricorn.

observe that it is constructed of these four elements, each with its distinct and extensive sphere of action yet together producing the matrix for the development of living, ensouled and spiritually activated substance!

Consider the difference between human and vegetable protein. In making vegetable protein, the formative forces of these four elements flow together from the four corners of the universe, which we have now learned to identify by the four images of the signs. The pure cosmic forces are forever renewing vegetable forms. Thus the plant is plugged straight into macrocosmic energies; the human being, on the other hand, is a microcosm, i.e., a small copy of the macrocosm, and bears within the celestial forces of the planets and of the zodiac. These express themselves organically and synthesize human protein as a microcosmic imitation of the macrocosm.

Cyrill von Korvin-Krasinski

The four elements as exemplified by the cardinal signs of the zodiac are widely known among all peoples, and so are their interrelationships. It is only their names that differ. Father Cyrill von Korvin-Krasinski made a special study of Tibetan medicine and produced a comprehensive work on the subject. The easily grasped fundamentals are set out in his book, *Mikrokosmos-Makrokosmos* (Microcosm-Macrocosm). Tibetan medicine is based, in fact, on three principles: chi, schara and badgan. To which are added further elements, corresponding to our four Western elements — fire, earth, air and water. The following excerpts may serve to give some idea of the researches and ideas of the father from Maria Laach abbey.

> Mental and physical well-being ultimately consists of harmony between the three basic principles (regarded as perfectly objective), and of their uniform control over all areas of human life. Any one-sidedness is a form of disease; and the wise physician's task is to counteract the one-sided excess of deficiency of one of the three above-mentioned ultimate basic aspects of the human being, by using the two other basic aspects to counteract or to supplement it.

It goes without saying that the lama-physician must also be a philosopher in order to understand and correctly apply this doctrine of the three principles; just as he needs to have a great deal of ordinary medical knowledge in order to work out the proper regimen for his patients. Especially interesting is his appreciation of the many microcosmic and macrocosmic correspondences linking man with his environment and, above all, with the vegetable kingdom. The physician displays his skill by exploiting the highly-developed science of the Tastes; which enables him to discover some plant or plant-part having a mysterious, though by no means magical, affinity with the diseased organ.* A few of the more important and more readily understood correspondences are given here.

The woody framework in trees corresponds to the human skeleton. And so we have "anthropoid" plants such as the cedar, oak and lime, standing erect like human beings; whereas others such as the weird-looking cacti and scrubland bushes, lianas and so on, are quite unlike us and seem to spread out in all directions. The human liver corresponds to the flat leaf of the deciduous trees, the bile to the green chlorophyll (and in the cosmos the sun). The outspread hand corresponds to the finger-like leaf structure of trees such as the chestnut, the palm and the rhododendron. The intestines correspond to the roots, which draw liquid nutrients from the soil; the nails to the colored petals of the flower; the finger-tips to the sensitive tendrils of climbers such as the pea, the vine, the ivy, etc. The mother's breast, full of nourishing milk, has it counterpart in fruits such as the grape, orange or cherry, in which the juice collects around a tough, usually unpalatable, pip or stone; on the other hand, hard fruit with husks or shells enclosing the

---

*The herbalism of ancient Europe also relied on a knowledge of the tastes and "temperatures" of plants; but this seems to have been increasingly ignored as herbs were classified according to their physiological and medicinal action. *Tr.*

nutritious part, fruit that is to say such as almonds and rice and other nuts and grain, correspond to the brain. Plump seed cotyledons, which for a time look like two small wings, correspond to the two halves of the brain. They are particularly noticeable in peas and beans and, on account of the similarity, these were recommended as foods for brain-workers, even though the Tibetans had no inkling that they contain phosphorus. Analysis by formal analogy of shape and appearance seems to have done service for chemical analysis. The similarity between the head on one hand and nuts and corn on the other is also the reason for Tibetan offerings of peas and grain in human skulls—obviously as a substitute for earlier blood sacrifices in which the brain was offered, as evidenced by the skull cemeteries still found near Chinese temples.[55]

In another section of his book, the author deals with the link between mankind and the zodiac.

• • •

To summarize now the relationship between healer and remedy, Friedrich Husemann always said that a doctor has to treat human beings, but cannot confine himself to them if he wants to help them. He needs to take note of the curative properties of the animal, vegetable, and mineral kingdoms as well. In other words, a doctor must strive to comprehend nature. There will be no end to his striving as long as he has not gotten to the bottom of what nature is all about. The physician needs two pictures: one of the human being and one of the universe. These pictures should match in the sense that when the picture presented by human beings changes—through illness—the undisturbed universe will show where the possibilities of healing lie.

CHAPTER THREE

COSMIC STRUCTURES OF REMEDIES

VARIOUS ACCOUNTS HAVE BEEN WRITTEN PURporting to show the cosmic correspondences to herbs and other medicaments, but their writers are frequently at odds with one another. For example, Dr. Duz associated Abrotanum with Mercury, whereas Asboga associates it with the Sun, and Busse listed its cosmic correspondent as Jupiter.

Interested students can research the various correspondences further in the original literature, and the contradictions could be greatly extended. For now it is only important to note that the contradictions are explained by the fact that on different occasions different organs or diseases are activated through the correspondences. For this reason I conceived the idea, as long ago as 1952, of expressing the multifaceted correspondences in terms of remedy structure. My investigations were published in part in current issues of the magazine *Kosmobiologie*, and they brought to light some interesting relationships, especially those between the signs. Some structures displayed square correspondences, others sextile, others quintile, etc. An example of this is shown in Table 10, which shows the cosmic structure of remedies.

This chapter will focus on correspondences of homeopathic remedies. Each remedy will be followed by an illustration of how the energy would manifest based on my research. Other homeopathic remedies follow, giving the reader an idea of how the homeopathic remedies relate to the signs.

Table 10. Cosmic Remedy Structure

♃ Nutrition, weight increase, liver (bile), lungs	☉ Heart, circulation, blood, eyes, cerebrum, vitality	M Ego problems, psychological disorders, complexes, repressions	☽ Fluid balance serum, lymph, mucous membranes, stomach, cerebellum, psyche	♄ Skeleton, joints, stone formation, deformities, indurations, leukocytes
☿ Motoric nervous system, organs of speech and hearing, hands and fingers				♀ Overdevelopment, drastic measures, collective events, accidents, operations, amputation
A Reactions to environmental influences				☊ Reactions to social life, hospitalization, confinement in an institution
♂ Muscles, tendons, red blood corpuscles, bile				♀ Glandular system, neck, tonsils, kidneys, veins, cheeks, skin, bladder
☋ Life rhythm, spinal cord, meninges, pituitary				♇ Solar plexus, pineal gland, paralysis, cellular exhaustion, disorders caused by the subconscious
SA Choleric, bilious constitution, digestive organs	SI Melancholic, lymphatic-nervous constitution, blood, anemia, growths	Horse chestnut Aesculus hippocastanum	LA Sanguine, bilious-sanguine constitution, congestion of blood, lesions	LI Phlegmatic, lymphatic-nervous constitution, metabolism, elimination

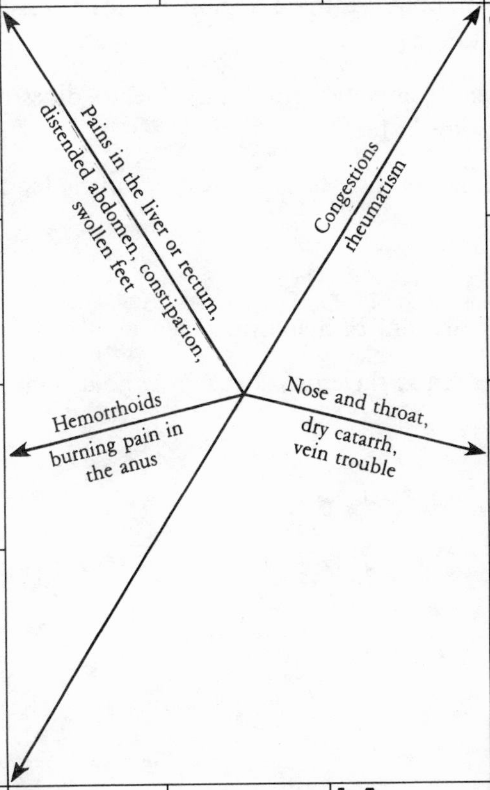

Diagonal labels within the table:
- Pains in the liver or rectum, distended abdomen, constipation, swollen feet
- Congestions rheumatism
- Hemorrhoids burning pain in the anus
- Nose and throat, dry catarrh, vein trouble

Abrotanum

Abrotanum, or Southernwood (lad's love), has its main correspondences with four signs:

Cancer: Stomachache, constriction in the chest, pleurisy.

Leo: Anemia, stabbing pain in region of heart, cardiac neurosis, backache and lumbago.

Virgo: Depression, anxiety, irritability due to digestive disorders, emaciation in spite of feeding well.

Aquarius: Circulatory disorders, emaciation of the legs.

Planetary disorders:

Sun: Heart, circulation, cardiac insufficiency.

Saturn: Skin, eczema, skeleton, stiff joints, gout, emaciation.

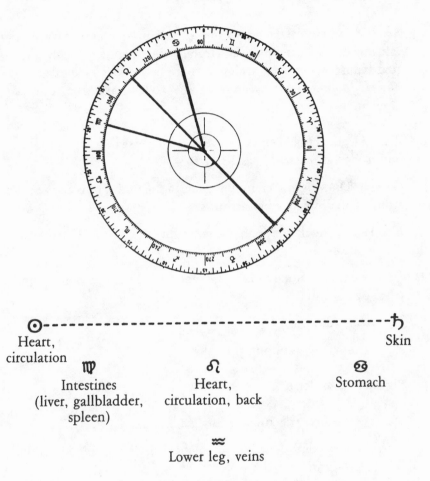

Figure 4. Cosmic remedy structure for Abrotanum (Southernwood).

Aconite

Aconite, or Monk's-Hood, is one of the most poisonous yet most valuable of medicinal plants. Naturally the tincture is highly attenuated before being used, unless it is applied under medical supervision. The structure of aconite in the zodiac takes the form of a hexagon.

Aries: Head, cranial nerves, frontal headache, swimming head, buzzing in the ear, earache, nasal catarrh.

Gemini: Drawing and cramping pains in the limbs, pins and needles, atony of the muscles, polyarthritis.

Leo: Heart, circulation, palpitation of the heart, cardiac anxiety, cardiac neurosis.

Libra: Kidneys, urinary bladder, scanty urine with pain and urging, relief by sweating.

Sagittarius: Sciatica.

Aquarius: Veins, cramp in the calf.

Planetary disorders:

Mercury: Nerves, trigeminal neuralgia.

Mars: Nerves controlling size of blood vessels and blood pressure, fever, chills, inflammations.

Uranus: Cerebral nerves, nervous twitches, attacks of cramp, restlessness, general uneasiness.

Aconite is a remedy of the first rank for all the inflammatory conditions (Mars) and is given until the patient perspires.

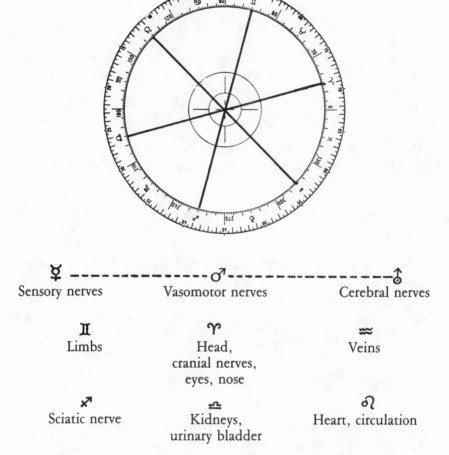

☿	♂	⚷
Sensory nerves	Vasomotor nerves	Cerebral nerves
♊	♈	♒
Limbs	Head, cranial nerves, eyes, nose	Veins
♐	♎	♌
Sciatic nerve	Kidneys, urinary bladder	Heart, circulation

Figure 5. Cosmic remedy structure for Aconite (Monks-Hood).

Aesculus Hippocastanum

Aesculus hippocastanum, or Horse Chestnut, has its main correspondences with Taurus, Leo, Scorpio and Aquarius:

Taurus: Dryness of nose and throat, scanty secretions, feeling of swelling at back of nose, dry cough, catarrh of the nose and throat.

Leo: Lumbar weakness, dull ache in small of back and around the hips, rheumatism.

Scorpio: Sense of fullness in abdomen, griping pains, diarrhea or constipation, hard stools, pains in anus, mucous diarrhea, intestinal disorders, hemorrhoids.

Aquarius: Swelling of lower leg when standing, phlebitis, thrombosis.

Aesculus is a remedy mainly for phlebitis and hemorrhoids, although, in addition to helping the veins, it benefits the other organs mentioned in the cosmic correspondences. Many sufferers from rheumatism keep a homeopathic attenuation of horse chestnut on hand to ward off their disease. Often the correspondences with the planets are more important than those with the signs. In the diagram for Aesculus the arrows point to the following planets and their correspondences:

Jupiter: Pains in the liver or rectum, distended abdomen, constipation, swollen feet.

Mars: Hemorrhoids, burning pain in anus, inflammations.

Venus: Diseases of the nose and throat, dry catarrh, vein problems.

Saturn: Congestions, rheumatism.

Finally, Aesculus is a special remedy for the SA type (externally tense).

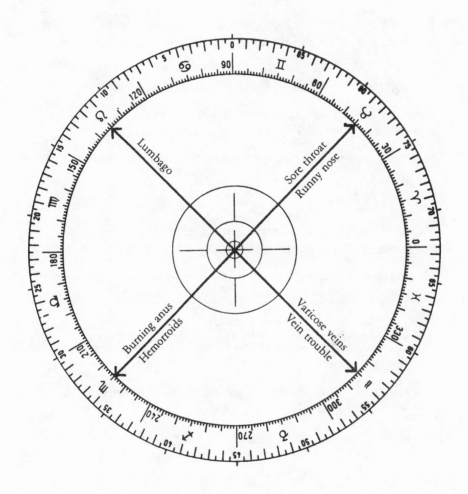

Figure 6. Cosmic remedy structure diagram for Aesculus (Horse Chestnut).

Agaricus

Agaricus muscarius, or Fly Agaric, has the structure of the rune 'Man' = man, with its axis between Aries and Libra and its side-arms running to Virgo and to Scorpio.

Aries: Central nervous system, meninges, pituitary, giddiness when walking, headaches, better on going to stool or on passing wind, cillosis (twitching of the eyelids).

Virgo: Nervous stomach and intestinal disorders, colic.

Libra: Cystoparalysis (paralysis of bladder), vesical spasms (bladder spasms), heavy perspiration with suppressed urination.

Scorpio: Diseases of the rectum, sexual debility, pruritis.

Planetary disorders:

Uranus: Central nervous system, meninges, pituitary, fibrillation of the muscles, uncertain gait, spasms.

Mercury/Uranus: Fits of excitement, irritability, restlessness, over-stimulation of the nerves, effects of mental overwork.

Mercury/Mars: Disorders of the motor impulse, cramps.

Mars/Uranus: Disturbances of the functional rhythm, tremors, writer's cramp, squint.

Saturn: Obstructions, feeling of (icy) coldness under the skin, sudden plunge from cheerfulness into melancholy.

Venus: Relief of functional disorders by secretion from the lachrymal (tear), salivary and intestinal glands, perspiration with suppression of urine, temporary interruption of the flow of urine.

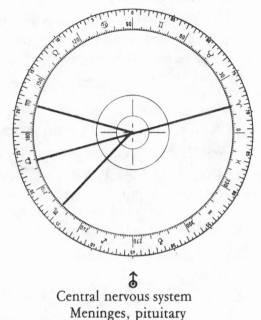

☊

Central nervous system
Meninges, pituitary

☿☊   ☿♂   ♂☊

Sudden onset   Motor nervous   Disturbances of
of nervous disorders   system   the functional
                   Nerve irritants,   rhythm,
                   reflexes   tremors

♄   ♀

Obstructions in the   Relief of functional disorders
organism showing themselves   by secretions from the
in the skin: formication,   lachrymal, salivary and
pins and needles, chilly   intestinal
feeling of nervous origin   glands, perspiration

♈

Central nervous system

♍   ♎   ♏

Intestinal nerves   Urinary bladder   Rectum
                Transpiration
              through the skin

Figure 7. Cosmic remedy structure for Agaricus muscarius (Fly Agaric).

Aloe

Aloe socotrina is often grown in flower pots as a domestic remedy, since the freshly cut leaves make an excellent application for burns and inflammations. The cosmic structural pattern of the aloe is the same as that of Fly Agaric but has another meaning.

Aries: Rush of blood to the brain (cerebral congestion), pain in the forehead and vertex (top of head), headache better in fresh air, worse from bending and movement.

Virgo/Scorpio: Heaviness and fullness in the intestines, often involuntary bowel motions, weakness of the anal sphincter, burning and itching of the anus, colitis with involvement of the liver, intestinal ulcer, hemorrhoids. Aloe is a drastic purgative.

Libra: Frequent urging to urinate, dark-colored urine, often involuntary stools during urination.

Planetary disorders:

Mars: Burns, elimination of morbid matter and metabolic products by inflammation, suppuration and fever, bitter and sour taste in the mouth.

Saturn: The feces forms balls; biliary stasis in gout and hypochondria, general congestion, exhaustion, unsociableness.

N.B. Aloe is suitable only for occasional short-term use.

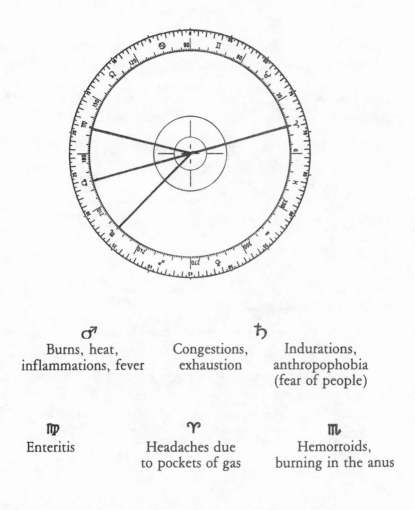

♂	♄
Burns, heat, inflammations, fever	Congestions, exhaustion	Indurations, anthropophobia (fear of people)

♍	♈	♏
Enteritis	Headaches due to pockets of gas	Hemorroids, burning in the anus

Figure 8. Cosmic remedy structure for Aloe socotrina (Aloe).

Alumina

Alumina, or Aluminum Oxide, is an important constituent of clay and loamy soil. Its structural pattern is that of half a six-pointed star.

Taurus: Nasal catarrh and sore throats of various kinds, including "clergyman's sore throat" due to weak vocal cords, nose bleed.

Cancer: Dyspepsia, cold in the stomach, gastritis, anxiety and fear of becoming a permanent invalid, psychoses.

Virgo: Colic, flatulence, constipation.

Scorpio: Chronic enteritis, intestinal lesions, blood in the stools.

Planetary disorders:

Moon: Stomach disorders due to the state of mind, small ulcers in the stomach and small intestines.

Saturn: Chronic diseases, constant fatigue, thinness, lack of body heat, tendency to take cold, pruritis, hair loss.

Neptune: Aggravation of diseases of over-indulgence in alcohol.

Alumina acts slowly but deeply and needs to be taken for a fairly long time.

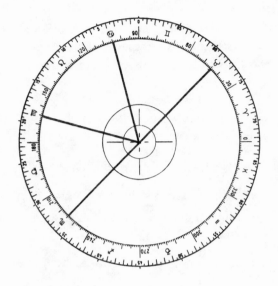

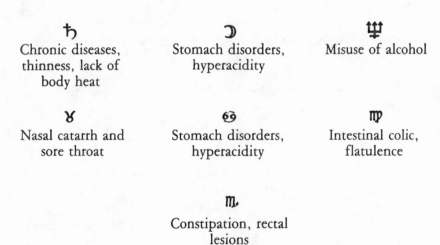

♄	☽	♆
Chronic diseases, thinness, lack of body heat	Stomach disorders, hyperacidity	Misuse of alcohol
♉	♋	♍
Nasal catarrh and sore throat	Stomach disorders, hyperacidity	Intestinal colic, flatulence

♏

Constipation, rectal lesions

Figure 9. Cosmic remedy structure for Alumina (Aluminum Oxide).

Arnica

Arnica montana contains an antiseptic essential oil. It should be used well diluted. The structural pattern is a cross embracing the signs Taurus, Leo, Scorpio and Aquarius, with an additional side-arm to Aries.

Aries: Cerebral congestion with coldness of the extremities due to venous stasis, headache worse through coughing and bending.

Taurus: Inflammation of the throat, buzzing in the ear.

Leo: Stabbing pain in the heart, angina pectoris, backache.

Scorpio: Foul-smelling flatulence, involuntary stools, diarrhea containing pus and blood.

Aquarius: Phlebitis, varicose veins, cramps in the calves.

Planetary disorders:

Mars: Injuries, inflammations, sore joints, sprains, hematomas, nerviness, quarrelsomeness.

Saturn: Weakness, exhaustion, worn-out feeling, rheumatism.

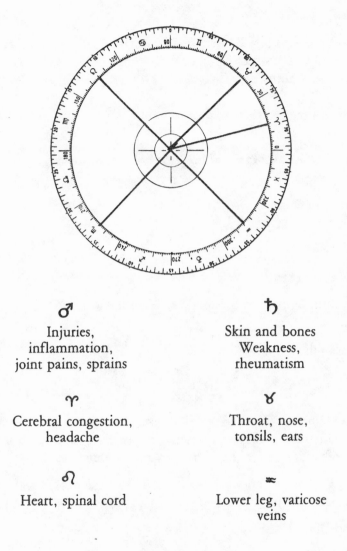

♂

Injuries,
inflammation,
joint pains, sprains

♄

Skin and bones
Weakness,
rheumatism

♈

Cerebral congestion,
headache

♉

Throat, nose,
tonsils, ears

♌

Heart, spinal cord

♒

Lower leg, varicose
veins

Figure 10. Cosmic remedy structure for Arnica montana (Arnica).

Arsenicum

Arsenicum album, or White Arsenic, acts on a great many organs in accordance with a structural pattern that includes all the signs of the zodiac from Taurus through Scorpio.

Taurus: Laryngitis, head cold, sore mouth, difficulty in swallowing, goiter.

Gemini: Cough, shortness of breath, restlessness, sticking pain in the lungs.

Cancer: Indigestion, gastritis, nausea, unquenchable thirst.

Leo: Disorders of the heart and circulation, angina pectoris.

Virgo: Pedantry, irritation over trifles, digestive disorders, and predisposition to cancer.

Libra: Burning pain in the urethra, incontinence, lumbago.

Scorpio: Diarrhea with foul-smelling stools, burning in the anus, hemorrhoids.

Planetary disorders:

Saturn/Neptune: Diseased condition of the whole organism, general sepsis, faded features, deep rings around the eyes; the tip of the nose and the hands and feet feel cold; toxins not eliminated.

Mars/Neptune: Tendency to weeping eczemas, ulceration, infections.

Moon/Neptune: Sensitive stomach, dyspepsia, sense of anxiety, hallucinations.

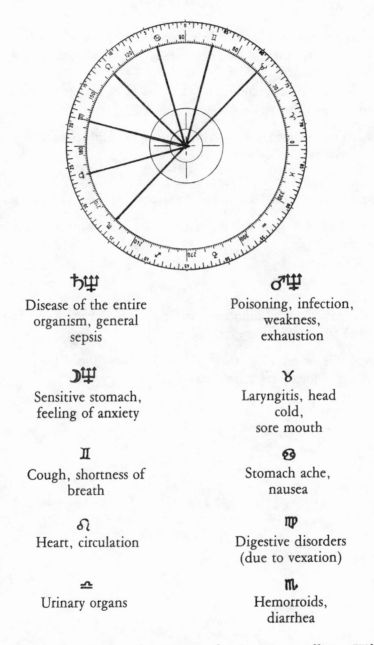

ħ♆
Disease of the entire
organism, general
sepsis

♂♆
Poisoning, infection,
weakness,
exhaustion

☽♆
Sensitive stomach,
feeling of anxiety

♉
Laryngitis, head
cold,
sore mouth

♊
Cough, shortness of
breath

♋
Stomach ache,
nausea

♌
Heart, circulation

♍
Digestive disorders
(due to vexation)

♎
Urinary organs

♏
Hemorroids,
diarrhea

Figure 11. Cosmic remedy structure for Arsenicum album (White Arsenic).

Aurum

Aurum metallicum, or Gold Leaf, is a splendid remedy for the central nervous system and the solar plexus.

Aries: Cerebral congestion, red, bloated face, boring pains in the head, pain in the cranial bones.

Taurus: Bitter taste in the mouth, halitosis (bad breath) due to digestive disorders.

Leo: Palpitation of the heart accompanied by fear and a sense of constriction, irregular heartbeat, coronary sclerosis, angina pectoris.

Scorpio: Redness and swelling of the nose, nasal obstruction, pains in the sexual organs.

Planetary disorders:

Sun/Moon: Diseases connected with the psychological state, chronic diseases, diseases of the eyes.

Saturn: Dejection, lack of self-confidence, lack of initiative, depression, skin complaints, sensitivity to cold.

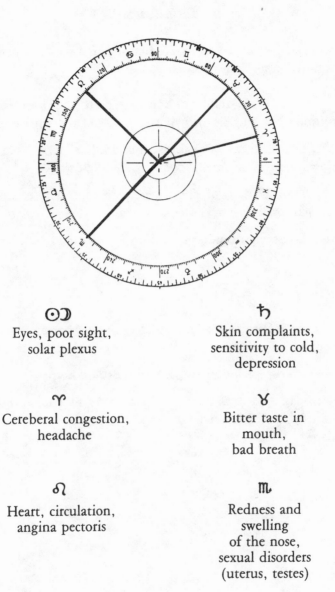

☉☽
Eyes, poor sight,
solar plexus

♄
Skin complaints,
sensitivity to cold,
depression

♈
Cereberal congestion,
headache

♉
Bitter taste in
mouth,
bad breath

♌
Heart, circulation,
angina pectoris

♏
Redness and
swelling
of the nose,
sexual disorders
(uterus, testes)

Figure 12. Cosmic remedy structure for Aurum metallicum (Gold Leaf).

Belladonna

Atropa belladonna, or Deadly Nightshade, is structured mainly on the negative signs (apart from Aries).

Aries: Cerebral congestion, throbbing headache, hot head and face, teeth-grinding during sleep, hypersensitivity of the sense organs.

Taurus: Dry throat, inflamed throat and tonsils, start of a sore throat, functional disorder of thyroid, pain in middle ear.

Cancer/Virgo: Disease of the digestive organs, nausea, stomach cramps, gastric ulcer, appendicitis.

Scorpio: Intestinal disorders, burning in the urethra, abdominal cramps.

Planetary disorders:

Mars: Fever, inflammation, muscular cramps, shooting pains in all the limbs.

Saturn: Skin complaints, pimples and pustules, herpes.

Uranus: Spasmodic conditions, sudden severe functional disorders, symptoms that quickly come and go, restlessness, hypersensitivity, epilepsy.

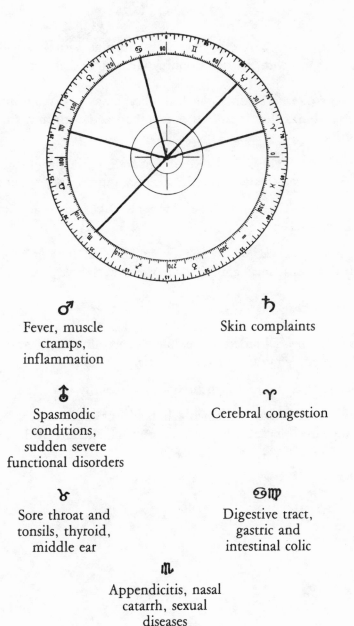

♂
Fever, muscle
cramps,
inflammation

♄
Skin complaints

♇
Spasmodic
conditions,
sudden severe
functional disorders

♈
Cerebral congestion

♉
Sore throat and
tonsils, thyroid,
middle ear

♋♍
Digestive tract,
gastric and
intestinal colic

♏
Appendicitis, nasal
catarrh, sexual
diseases

Figure 13. Cosmic remedy structure for Atropa belladonna (Deadly Nightshade).

Bryonia Alba

Bryonia alba, or White Bryony, has a structural pattern that forms a Maltese cross with the tips spanning Gemini/Cancer, etc.

Gemini/Cancer: Pleura, bronchial tubes, lungs, dry cough with feeling of thirst, chest pain when coughing and with any vibration, gastritis.

Virgo/Libra: Lack of bile secretion, jaundice brought on by anger, dry stools, constipation, burning pain in anus, kidney weakness.

Aries/Pisces: Great thirst for cold water to slake body heat, often also chills and shivers.

Sagittarius/Capricorn: Feeling of weakness in the limbs, muscle pains, rheumatism, pain on any movement.

Planetary disorders:

Moon/Saturn: Disorders of the fluid balance, dryness, great thirst for cold water, agitation, irritability, anxiety.

Jupiter: Liver disorders, pneumonia and pleurisy.

Mars: Excited states, inflamed gallbladder or appendix (cholecystitis or appendictitis), muscle pains, redness and swelling of the skin.

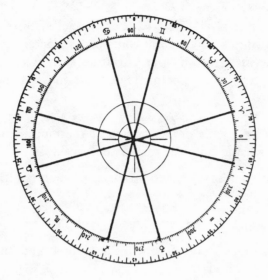

☽♄

Great thirst due to
internal heat and
dryness

♃

Diseases of the
lungs
and liver

♂

Inflamed
gallbladder
or appendix, muscle
pains, diseases due
to anger

♊♋

Bronchitis,
pneumonia, pleurisy

♍♎

Intestines,
appendix,
kidneys

♈♓

Alleviation of heat
by cold

♐♑

Limbs, joints

Figure 14. Cosmic remedy structure for Bryonia alba (White Bryony).

Calcium Carbonicum

Calcium carbonicum hahnemanni, or oyster shellchalk, is not analytically pure calcium carbonate but contains (as Hahnemann was well aware) important traces of other chemicals such as manganese. Its structural pattern is a six-pointed star with the rays touching the negative signs.

Taurus: Salivary glands, inflammation of the mucous membranes, tonsillitis, discharge from the ear, thyroid weakness.

Cancer: Hyperacidity of the stomach, sour or bitter taste in the mouth, heartburn, stomach cramps.

Virgo: Diseases of the digestive organs, acid diarrhea.

Scorpio: Gallstone colic, hemorrhoids, hard stools, intestinal cramps, diseases of the genitals.

Capricorn: Arthritis and muscular rheumatism, joint pains, skin complaints, poorly developed bones due to calcium deficiency.

Pisces: Cold feet, diseases from getting wet.

Planetary disorders:

Saturn: Debility of the cells and tissues due to a disturbed calcium balance, fragile bones, inhibited and depressed state, general fatigue, health failure due to overstrain, skin complaints, deadness of the limbs.

Venus: Chronic inflammation and swelling of the lymph glands and tonsils, tubercular glands, nasal catarrh, weakness of gonads.

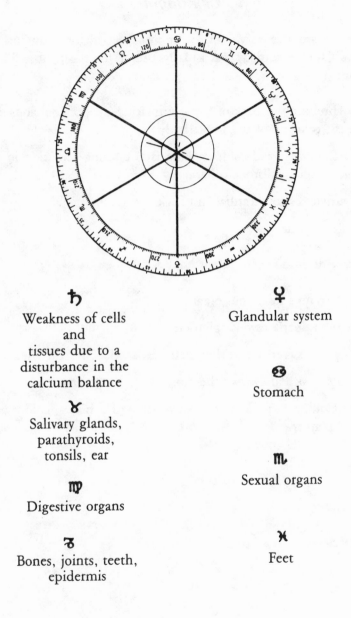

♄	☿
Weakness of cells and tissues due to a disturbance in the calcium balance	Glandular system
♉	♋
Salivary glands, parathyroids, tonsils, ear	Stomach
♍	♏
Digestive organs	Sexual organs
♑	♓
Bones, joints, teeth, epidermis	Feet

Figure 15. Cosmic remedy structure for Calcium carbonicum hahnemanni (Oyster Shell Chalk).

Camphora

Cinnamomum camphora, or Camphor Tree, yields camphor, an ancient Chinese remedy particularly useful for raising the blood pressure.

Aries: Throbbing at back of head, grimacing, loss of consciousness, giddiness, coldness of the whole body.

Taurus/Scorpio: Head cold, choking fits, burning sensation in the abdomen, colic, gallstone colic.

Leo: Cardiac distress, cardiac insufficiency, internal cold.

Libra: Renal colic.

Planetary disorders:

Uranus: Cramps in various organs.

Mercury/Uranus: Nervous agitation.

Sun/Neptune: General weakness and exhaustion, fearful visions.

Mars/Neptune: Paralysis of the muscles. A poison antidote.

Saturn: Coldness of the body, loss of strength, shivers, cold sweat, skin complaints.

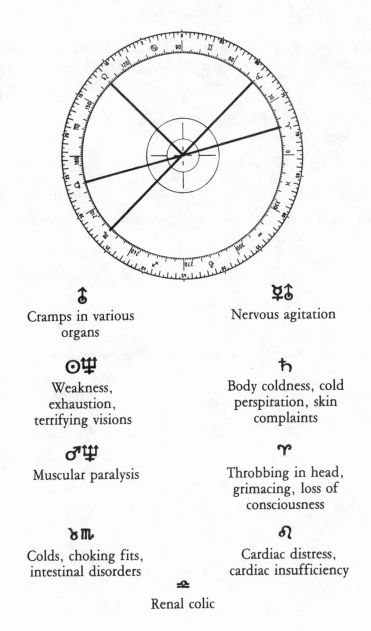

♂♁
Cramps in various
organs

☿♁
Nervous agitation

☉♅
Weakness,
exhaustion,
terrifying visions

♄
Body coldness, cold
perspiration, skin
complaints

♂♆
Muscular paralysis

♈
Throbbing in head,
grimacing, loss of
consciousness

♉♏
Colds, choking fits,
intestinal disorders

♌
Cardiac distress,
cardiac insufficiency

♎
Renal colic

*Figure 16. Cosmic remedy structure for Cinnamomum camphora
(Camphor Tree).*

Chamomilla

Chamomilla, or Chamomile, has a structural pattern based on the first quadrant of the zodiac and on the signs Scorpio and Sagittarius opposite it.

Aries: Teething-fever in children, headaches, hot perspiration and hot flushes to the head, red face.

Taurus: Cold in the head, paroxysms of coughing.

Gemini/Sagittarius: Pains in the extremities, muscular rheumatism.

Cancer: Bloated stomach after meals, pressure on the stomach, nausea, worse by anger or irritation.

Scorpio: watery or slimy stools, enteritis, colic.

Planetary disorders:

Moon: Organic disorders due to vexation or worry, sensitivity of the stomach, bitter and foul taste in mouth, sour eructations.

Uranus: Spasms and cramps, especially of the stomach and intestines.

Mars: Griping pains, inflammations, fever, neuralgias.

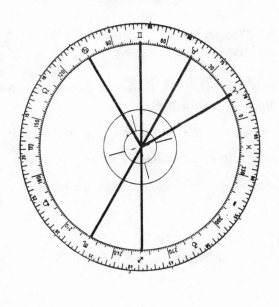

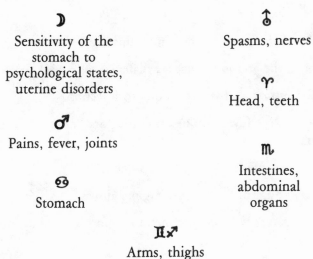

☽

Sensitivity of the
stomach to
psychological states,
uterine disorders

♂

Pains, fever, joints

♋

Stomach

♄

Spasms, nerves

♈

Head, teeth

♏

Intestines,
abdominal
organs

♊♐

Arms, thighs

Figure 17. Cosmic remedy structure for Chamomilla (Chamomile).

Eupatorium

Eupatorium perfoliatum, or Boneset, acts on the organs represented by the signs from Aries through Virgo.

Aries: Throbbing headache, hot flushes to the head with red face, giddiness, aching around the eyes.

Taurus: Sore throat, dry nose and throat, yellow-coated dry tongue.

Gemini: Bruised feeling, weakness of the limbs and joints.

Cancer: Pain in chest and stomach, especially when coughing; nausea.

Leo: Backache.

Virgo: Digestive disorders, pain in region of liver, nausea and vomiting.

Planetary disorders:

Mars: Head feels hot, fever, aches and pains everywhere.

Saturn: Every bone and joint aches, exhaustion and weakness.

Neptune: Exhaustion and weakness due to infection.

Mars/Saturn: Dry fever, bone lesions, dry nose and little perspiration.

Saturn/Neptune: Infectious diseases, epidemics.

Mars/Neptune: Susceptibility to contagious diseases.

Saturn = *Mars/Neptune*: Skin function suppressed, body full of toxins, malaise.

Eupatorium is a greatly prized remedy for influenza, being prescribed on its own and as an ingredient in many flu remedies.

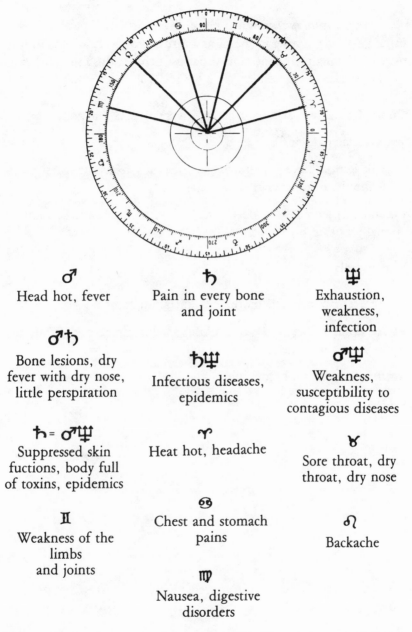

♂
Head hot, fever

♄
Pain in every bone
and joint

♅
Exhaustion,
weakness,
infection

♂♄
Bone lesions, dry
fever with dry nose,
little perspiration

♄♅
Infectious diseases,
epidemics

♂♅
Weakness,
susceptibility to
contagious diseases

♄ = ♂♅
Suppressed skin
fuctions, body full
of toxins, epidemics

♈
Heat hot, headache

♉
Sore throat, dry
throat, dry nose

♊
Weakness of the
limbs
and joints

♋
Chest and stomach
pains

♌
Backache

♍
Nausea, digestive
disorders

Figure 18. Cosmic remedy structure for Eupatorium perfoliatum (Boneset).

Hamamelis

Hamamelis virginiana, or Witch Hazel, has a structural pattern in the form of a cross pointing to the signs Taurus, Leo, Scorpio and Aquarius, with the main emphasis on Aquarius, because this folk remedy is very beneficial to the veins.

Taurus: Overactive thyroid, pharyngitis, exophthalmic goiter.

Leo: Cardiac pain and sacralgia.

Scorpio: Period pains, enterorrhagia (bleeding from the intestines), hemorrhoids, diseases of the sex organs.

Aquarius: Phlebitis, varicose veins, development of varicose veins — especially during pregnancy.

Planetary disorders:

Mars: Recent wounds, hemorrhages, inflammations.

Jupiter: Hemorrhages in tuberculosis of the lungs, and from the stomach and intestines, impure blood.

Saturn: Congestion, hardening.

Neptune: Ulcers, infections.

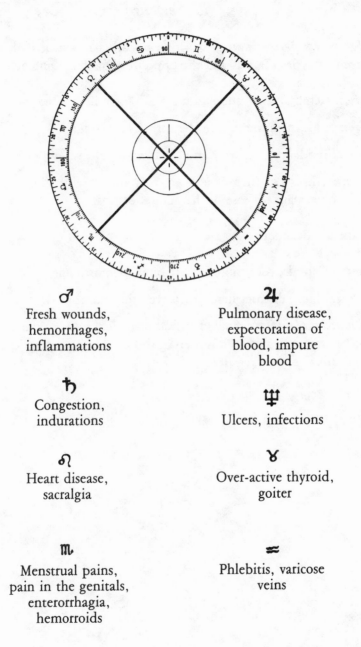

♂
Fresh wounds,
hemorrhages,
inflammations

♃
Pulmonary disease,
expectoration of
blood, impure
blood

♄
Congestion,
indurations

♅
Ulcers, infections

♌
Heart disease,
sacralgia

♉
Over-active thyroid,
goiter

♏
Menstrual pains,
pain in the genitals,
enterorrhagia,
hemorroids

♒
Phlebitis, varicose
veins

Figure 19. Cosmic remedy structure for Hamamelis virginiana (Witch Hazel).

Hypericum

Hypericum perforatum, or St. John's Wort, has a structural pattern based on Aries, Taurus and the opposite signs Libra and Scorpio.

Aries: Cerebral congestion with irritation of the cerebral nerves.

Taurus: Mucus formation in the throat, dry cough.

Libra: Tendency to kidney and bladder stone.

Scorpio: Epistaxis (nosebleed), gastritis and enteritis, hemorrhoids, abdominal pain, disease of the genital organs.

Planetary disorders:

Mars: Wounds, contusions, insect bites, hemorrhoids.

Jupiter: Lung disease, hemoptysis (coughing up blood).

Moon/Saturn: Melancholy, depression, anxiety states, mania, insomnia, extreme fatigue. In disorders of the psyche, high potencies (very high dilutions) are required.

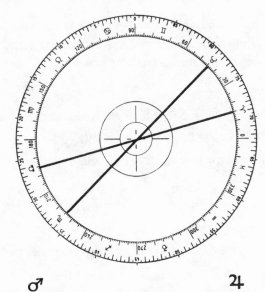

♂
Wounds, bruises, insect bites,
hemorroids

♃
Lung disease with coughing up
blood

☽♄
Melancholy, depression, anxiety states, mania, insomnia, lassitude

♈
Headache, facial neuralgia

♎
Kidney stone, toxins are
excreted via the urine

♉
Accumulations of
mucus in throat

♏
Nose bleeds, genital disorders

Figure 20. Cosmic remedy structure for Hypericum perforatum (St. John's Wort).

Ignatia

Strychnos ignatii, or St. Ignatius's Bean, exerts its main influence on the nervous system. Therefore, in the structural diagram, the emphasis is laid on Aries, with further effects from Taurus, Cancer, Scorpio and the planet Mercury.

Aries: Cerebral congestion with headaches and a flushed face, migraine.

Taurus: Tickling in the throat, irritating cough, coughing spasms, dry throat.

Cancer: Dyspepsia, stomach pains after smoking tobacco, flatulence.

Scorpio: Cutting pains in the anus and rectum, anal prolapse.

Planetary disorders:

Moon/Saturn: Emotional disturbance, melancholy, quiet grief, consequences of fear and terror, lack of self-confidence, vexation, fits of anger when contradicted, sensitivity to cold.

Uranus/Moon/Mars: Changeable mood, sobbing fits, convulsions, spasms, trembling of the whole body.

Mercury: Hypersensitivity of the nerves and sense organs.

Neptune/Pluto: Confusion, hysteria, ill-effects of toxic stimulants (tobacco, alcohol), psychological symptoms followed by functional disorders.

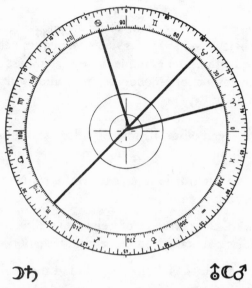

☽♄	☊☾♂
Emotional disturbances, melancholy, fear and terror, sensitivity to cold	Changeable moods, sobbing fits, convulsions, colonic spasms

☿	♅♆♀
Hypersensitivity of the nervous	Confusion, possession, injury by toxic stimulants

♈	♋
Cerebral congestion, headache	Stomach disorders due to agitation, gastric catarrh in smokers

♉	♏
Tickling in the throat, irritating cough	Prolapsed rectum, hemorrhoids

Figure 21. Cosmic remedy structure for Strychnos ignatii (St. Ignatius's Bean).

Iodum

Iodum, or Iodine, is a dark gray element belonging to the group known as the halogens. Its vapor is violet-colored. In nature, it occurs only in small quantities; for example, in sea water, in seaweeds and in salt springs. Its cosmic correspondences are mainly with Taurus, Leo, Scorpio and Cancer.

Taurus: Iodine metabolism, thyroid disorders, scrofulism, pharyngitis, hoarseness.

Cancer: Gastritis, intestinal ulcers, pancreatitis (inflammation of the pancreas), abdominal pain.

Leo: Goiter heart, constant sense of weight on the heart accompanied by worry, cardiac palpitation on the slightest exertion.

Scorpio: Diarrhea, duodenal ulcer, diseases of the genitals.

The influence of iodine should not be thought of as confined to the thyroid: it acts on all the connective tissues and on all the glands and lymph nodes.

Planetary disorders:

Venus: Iodine metabolism, the entire glandular system, scrofulism.

Mercury/Uranus: Inner unrest, nervous irritability.

Saturn/Neptune: Skin complaints, discolored yellowish skin with a red face, excretion of toxins through the skin.

Mercury/Neptune: Anxiety states, unbalanced behavior.

Mercury/Mars: Overexcitement of the nerves.

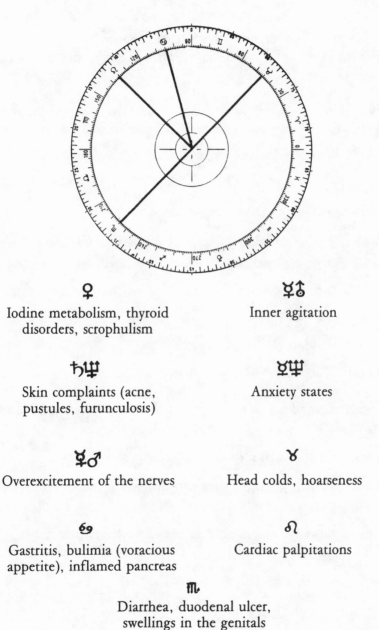

♀

Iodine metabolism, thyroid
disorders, scrophulism

☿⚴

Inner agitation

♄♅

Skin complaints (acne,
pustules, furunculosis)

☿♅

Anxiety states

☿♂

Overexcitement of the nerves

♉

Head colds, hoarseness

♋

Gastritis, bulimia (voracious
appetite), inflamed pancreas

♌

Cardiac palpitations

♏

Diarrhea, duodenal ulcer,
swellings in the genitals

Figure 22. Cosmic remedy structure for Iodum (Iodine).

Nux Vomica

Strychnos nux vomica, or Poison Nut, has a cosmic structure based on Aries (the head) and on the signs of the digestive organs, Cancer, Virgo, Libra and Scorpio.

Aries: Headache, giddiness, often due to stomach complaints which also cause bad breath, acute racking pains in the face, contraction of the face and jaw muscles.

Cancer: Capricious appetite, ravenous hunger, putrid condition of the stomach especially after indulgence in alcohol or tobacco, chronic gastritis especially in sedentary workers.

Virgo: Digestive disorders, alternate constipation and diarrhea. Liver region tender.

Libra: Kidney weakness, cystorrhea.

Scorpio: Liver disorders, colic, urgent need to relieve bowels or bladder, hemorrhoids, diseases of the genital organs.

Planetary disorders:

Mercury: Central nervous system, neuralgia, consequences of mental overstrain.

Venus: Cystorrhea, pain in neck of bladder and in urethra.

Uranus: Muscle cramps, rheumatism, facial spasms, menstrual disorders.

Moon/Saturn: Weariness of life, fear and anxiety, annoyance over trifles, connection between organic disorders and the mental state.

Moon: Stomach complaints, mental disorders.

Neptune: Consequences of abuse of stimulants (alcohol, tobacco, coffee).

Nux vomica will often quickly improve an upset stomach.

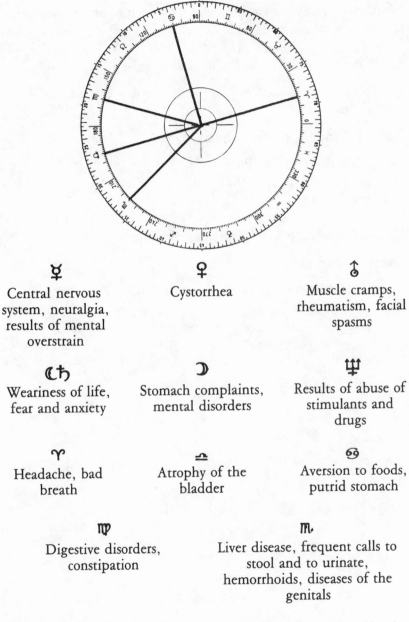

☿	♀	♂
Central nervous system, neuralgia, results of mental overstrain	Cystorrhea	Muscle cramps, rheumatism, facial spasms

☾♄	☽	♆
Weariness of life, fear and anxiety	Stomach complaints, mental disorders	Results of abuse of stimulants and drugs

♈	♎	♋
Headache, bad breath	Atrophy of the bladder	Aversion to foods, putrid stomach

♍	♏
Digestive disorders, constipation	Liver disease, frequent calls to stool and to urinate, hemorrhoids, diseases of the genitals

Figure 23. Cosmic remedy structure for Strychnos Nux Vomica (Poison Nut).

Passiflora

Passiflora incarnata, or Passion-Flower, has an unusual but symmetrical cosmic structure.

Aries: Mental disturbances due to addictions, e.g., to morphia.

Leo: Heart feels squeezed, angina pectoris, pain in left side and down left arm, insomnia.

Scorpio: Cramping pains in abdomen.

Pisces: Addiction, alcoholism.

Planetary disorders:

Mercury/Uranus: Nervous restlessness, insomnia.

Uranus: Spasmodic conditions.

Neptune: Addiction, especially to morphia.

Passiflora is much used to relieve pain and to induce sleep.

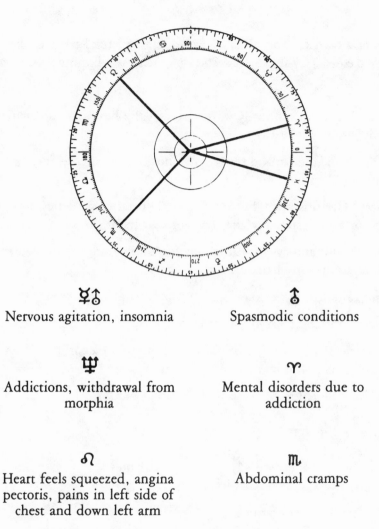

Nervous agitation, insomnia

Spasmodic conditions

Addictions, withdrawal from
morphia

Mental disorders due to
addiction

Heart feels squeezed, angina
pectoris, pains in left side of
chest and down left arm

Abdominal cramps

Addiction, alcoholism

*Figure 24. Cosmic remedy structure for Passiflora Incarnata (Passion
Flower).*

Pulsatilla

Pulsatilla pratensis, or Wind Flower, has a structural pattern like a Maltese cross and therefore has correspondences with quite a number of diseases.

Aries: Headache, especially in the back of the head, conjunctivitis, cloudy vision, ear diseases, migraine.

Taurus: Nasal catarrh and pharyngitis, hoarseness, intense tickling in throat.

Cancer: Gastritis with hypoacidity or hyperacidity (deficiency or excess of acid), especially after fatty or sour foods, stomach spasms.

Libra: Pyelitis and cystitis (inflammation of the outlet of the kidney and inflammation of the urinary bladder).

Virgo: Enteritis, some constipation, more frequent diarrhea.

Scorpio: Burning pain in the urethra.

Capricorn: Polyarthritis, stiff joints, itching of the skin, pimples in various parts of the body.

Aquarius: Phlebitis, varicose veins, varicose ulcers.

Planetary disorders:

Moon/Saturn: Weeps easily, inclined to depression, thirstlessness, dry lips and skin, poor circulation.

Mars: Irritability, inflammation, sore muscles.

Jupiter: Swellings and congestions.

Saturn: Colds and chills, skin diseases.

Uranus: Disturbed rhythm due to lack of movement.

Neptune: Infectious diseases, cutaneous eruptions (rashes).

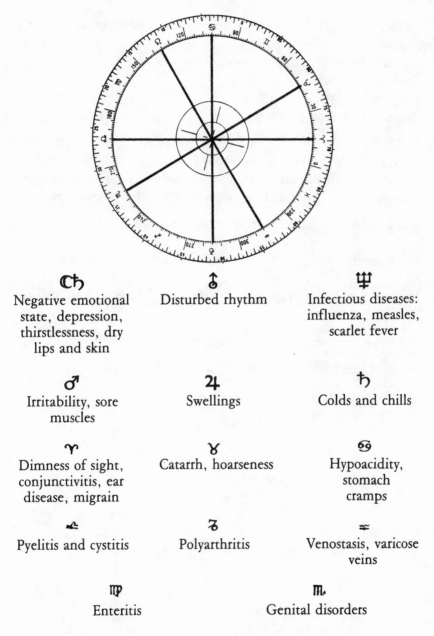

☽♄
Negative emotional state, depression, thirstlessness, dry lips and skin

☊
Disturbed rhythm

♆
Infectious diseases: influenza, measles, scarlet fever

♂
Irritability, sore muscles

♃
Swellings

♄
Colds and chills

♈
Dimness of sight, conjunctivitis, ear disease, migrain

♉
Catarrh, hoarseness

♋
Hypoacidity, stomach cramps

♎
Pyelitis and cystitis

♑
Polyarthritis

♒
Venostasis, varicose veins

♍
Enteritis

♏
Genital disorders

Figure 25. Cosmic remedy structure for Pulsatilla Pratensis (Windflower, or Pasque Flower).

Sulfur

Sulfur, or sulphur, has the structure of a rather irregular five-pointed star with its tips resting mainly on the signs representing the digestive organs, Cancer, Virgo and Scorpio, but also on the opposite signs, Aries and Aquarius.

Aries: Cerebral congestion with heat on top of the head, morbid fear of being out in the sun, conjunctivitis.

Cancer/Virgo/Scorpio: Bad breath, gastritis, swollen liver, loss of appetite for many foods, craving for alcohol and candies, heartburn, enteritis, constipation, itching of anus, hemorrhoids, diabetes.

Aquarius: Phlebitis, varicose veins, cramp in the calves.

Planetary disorders:

Saturn: Burning and itching of the skin, eczema, furunculosis through lack of hygiene.

Jupiter: Liver diseases.

Mars: Muscular rheumatism, polyarthritis, fever with dry heat and thirst.

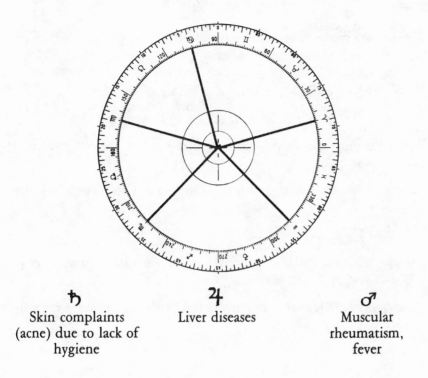

♄	♃	♂
Skin complaints (acne) due to lack of hygiene	Liver diseases	Muscular rheumatism, fever

♋ ♍ ♏

Portal vein system (stomach, intestines, pancreas, spleen, liver), many foods not tolerated, craving for alcohol and candy, diabetes, diarrhea or constipation, gastritis

♈	♏	♒
Aversion to light, conjunctivitis	Hemorrhoids, inflammed gallbladder, itching of anus	Phlebitis, varicose veins

Figure 26. Cosmic remedy structure for Sulfur (Sulphur).

Zincum Valerianum

Zincum valerianum, or valerianate of zinc, is indicated chiefly in sleep disorders from various causes.

Aries: Frontal headache, neuralgia, grinding of the teeth.

Cancer: Nervous dyspepsia, stomach cramps, continual eructation.

Libra: Burning and cutting pains in the urethra, urge to urinate, especially at night.

Aquarius: Fidgetiness in the legs, varicose veins, cramp in the calves.

Planetary disorders:

Mercury/Uranus: Restlessness, trembling of the limbs, nervousness, cramps associated with insomnia.

Sun/Neptune: Weakness, fatigue, nervous exhaustion due to mental overwork.

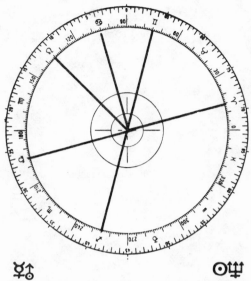

☿⚴

Restlessness, trembling,
nervousness, cramps, insomnia

☉♅

Weakness, exhaustion,
giddiness, faintness

♈︎

Frontal headache,
neuralgia, teeth
grinding

♋︎

Stomach cramps,
watery eructations

♌︎

Nervous heart
disorders,
palpitation of the
heart, backache

♎︎

Call to urinate, especially at
night

♒︎

Fidgety legs, calf cramp

*Figure 27. Cosmic remedy structure for Zincum Valerianum
(Valerianate of Zinc).*

CHAPTER FOUR

METALS AS HEALING AGENTS

KNOWLEDGE OF THE CORRESPONDENCES BEtween the planets and certain metals has been handed down to us from the remote past; and although metallic solutions are seldom used in medicine nowadays, we certainly read of cures being performed with metals in the ancient world. Thus it is related that when the youthful hunter Ilceus was suddenly robbed of his glowing health and fine physique by a pestilence, the nymph Lipare took him inside her underground cavern and bathed his body in liquid silver, that is to say, in quicksilver or mercury, and so restored him.[56]

The founder of the more modern use of minerals and metals for therapeutic purposes is Paracelsus. As he watched the work of his father, a mining engineer, and saw the metals being won from the ground, he was struck by the idea of using minerals and metals as remedies—and so became the father of the pharmaceutical industry. He went so far as to dissolve gold preparations in alcohol for medical use.

However, the relationships between diseases and metallic solutions will be best understood if we take a look at the homeopathic materia medica.

Gold—Aurum—the Sun

Gold is a normal constituent of the human body, being chiefly con-centrated in the brain, where it enters into the central nervous system and enhances its vitality. When it is deficient, we find symptoms of depression and even suicidal tendencies. Therefore, gold is an epit-ome of life. It has an affinity with the sense organs, especially the eyes. According to tradition, the Sun corresponds to the right eye and the Moon to the left. But, as ruler of Leo, the Sun has to do with the heart and circulation; consequently, Aurum is employed in cases of cerebral congestion with roaring and a sense of commotion in the head and ringing in the ears, also in palpitation of the heart, and a sensation of constriction round the heart compelling deep breaths to be drawn.

The dose is from the third to the twelfth decimal dilution. The number represents the number of zeros following 1; thus 3x is a dilution in the ratio of 1:10,000, 6x is a dilution in the ratio of 1:1,000,000, etc.

Various salts of gold are also prescribed, e.g., Aurum iodatum, Aurum sulfuratum, etc.

Silver—Argentum—the Moon

Silver is prescribed mainly in the form of Argentum nitricum. Since the Moon corresponds to the stomach and digestive organs, Argen-tum nitricum is a remedy for the stomach and the intestinal tract, especially in cases of nervous diarrhea before a journey, a public appearance, an examination, or whenever a person is tensed up over the future. The stomach is often distended and "feels like bursting," there is severe belching, and feelings of anxiety accompany the diges-tive disorders. If the Moon in the cosmogram is aspecting Saturn or Neptune, this can show a tendency to chronic stomach disorders, the cure for which can be found in Argentum nitricum, among other remedies.

Quicksilver—Mercurius—Mercury

The reason quicksilver is known as mercury is its relationship to the planet of the same name. In homeopathy, the preparation chiefly employed is Mercurius solubilis hahnemanni. Just as mercury corresponds to the central and peripheral nervous system, so Mercurius is administered for agitation of the nerves with fear and restlessness, hastiness, irritability, mental confusion, dread of losing one's reason, and for a lack of concentration and thought even bordering on idiocy. In addition, the preparation is recommended for facial neuralgia, conjunctivitis, suppuration in the ear, pharyngitis and bronchial catarrh.

Other mercurial compounds employed are Mercurius sublimaticus corrosivus, Mercurius iodatus flavus, Mercurius biniodatus (Mercurius iodatus ruber), Mercurius dulcis and Mercurius chromicus oxydulatus.

The dose is between 3x and 12x.

Copper—Cuprum—Venus

Copper is one of the essential elements found in the body; it occurs in blood serum and serves as a catalyst for a series of enzymes. It is a component of cellular protoplasm and controls the activity of the blood-building cells. Cuprum metallicum and Cuprum aceticum are particularly valuable in kidney diseases (Venus) when the latter are accompanied by spasms. Cuprum arsenitum can prove helpful in diseases of the urinary organs. The recommended dose is between 3x and 12x.

Iron—Ferrum—Mars

An old folk remedy for iron deficiency in weak, anemic people was to stick a clean nail in an apple in the evening and to eat it the following morning; the idea being that a certain amount of iron would be dissolved by the acids in the apple, to the benefit of the body.

Children suffering from a lack of iron show symptoms of growth disorders; adults have lack-luster rough hair, dry flabby skin and brittle nails. A lack of iron plays a part in feverish infectious diseases. Medicinal doses of iron act mainly to raise the hemoglobin content and the red cell count; they stimulate the bone marrow and accelerate the circulation of the blood. Ferrum is also used for sore muscles (Mars) and in rheumatic disorders.

In addition to Ferrum metallicum, we employ Ferrum collodiale, Ferrum aceticum, Ferrum carbonicum, Ferrum muriaticum, Ferrum arsenicum and others.

Tin—Stannum—Jupiter

Like Jupiter, the metal tin has a close connection with the respiratory organs and also with the digestive organs, especially the liver. The remedy is therefore employed in rawness and hoarseness of the throat, in a weak chest with shortness of breath, in obstruction of the air passages by phlegm (which is yellow or green and unpleasantly sweetish), in oppressive respiration and soreness of the chest.

The usual dose is 3x. Higher potencies are not always satisfactory.

Lead—Plumbum—Saturn

The most frequent application of Plumbum metallicum is in arteriosclerosis, a painful disorder in which fibrous tissue thickens the arteries so that some of the smaller ones may become blocked and lead to epilepsy, to kidney disorders, or even to apoplectic fits. It has proved its worth in spastic obstipation (complete constipation), in intermittent limping, in emaciation, and in a pale and muddy skin.

All the above come under Saturn. Since lead is a remedy that is not broken down in the body and is eliminated only with difficulty, only the higher dilutions from 6x should be employed.

In addition to Plumbum metallicum, we use Plumbum aceticum, Plumbum iodatum, and Plumbum collodiale.

With Saturn we come to the last of the traditional "seven planets" and therefore to the last of the traditional attributions of the
metals. The following relationships between planets and metals have
been worked out only within the last two centuries, as the more
distant planets were discovered.

Zinc—Zincum—Uranus

Zinc is still a relatively new metal, and was first extracted from its ore
in the middle of the 18th century, at the time when Uranus was
discovered.* The amount of zinc in the individual organs is higher
when cell growth is vigorous. Uranus chiefly relates to the function of
the cerebellum; it is therefore understandable that many physicians
regard zinc as a brain remedy and have used it in nervous twitching of
all kinds. Its main action is on the central nervous system when
tiredness and weakness alternate with restlessness and excitement. A
characteristic feature is that the legs can not be kept still when the
person is seated. In nocturnal insomnia, too, it is hard to keep the
limbs still. The typical diseases almost always have a nervous character, for example in digestive disorders. Zinc is valued as a tranquil-
lizer and as a remedy for neuralgia. Zincum valerianum is a good
soporific in doses between 3x and 6x. Zincum phosphoricum helps in
nervous exhaustion; Zincum sulfuricum in enteritis and eye
troubles.

---

*Uranus was discovered by Herschel in 1781. According to the *Encyclopaedia Britan-
nica*, 1947: "In 1597 Libavius described 'a peculiar kind of tin' which was prepared in
India. . . . From his account it is quite clear that this metal was zinc. . . . It is not
known to whom the discovery of isolated zinc is due; but we do know that the art of
zinc-smelting was practiced in England from about 1730." It is obvious from this that
the discovery of Uranus and the isolation of metallic zinc did not take place at exactly
the same time. However zinc production did continue to rise following the finding
of the planet.

Aluminum—Alumina—Neptune

Aluminum is one of those metals that have been discovered in modern times: pure aluminum was first successfully produced in 1827. Neptune was discovered in 1846. Aluminum is contained mainly in clay and loam. It is an essential trace element, but in soluble form can produce severe symptoms of irritation and poisoning (Neptune), possibly with paralysis (Neptune again) and muscular spasms. As a remedy it is used chiefly in infections, chronic nasal catarrh and pharyngitis, weakness of the vocal cords, clergyman's sore throat, mucus in the throat, aggravation of diseases by indulgence in alcohol (Neptune), general weakness of the whole body, unsteady gait, and weariness in the legs.

Since aluminum is used principally for constitutional disorders, the higher potencies from 12x and upwards are prescribed.

Baryta Carb—Barium Carbonate—Pluto

In all the astromedical writings known to me, there is no mention of any metals corresponding to Pluto, which was discovered in 1930. According to recent findings, Pluto is linked with unusual diseases and with disorders which develop until they are chronic and, like cancer, begin to disintegrate the body.

Barium does not appear to be essential to the human organism, and indeed is regarded as a toxin. To barium corresponds a type of child with impaired physical and mental development, who is clumsy, slow to learn to talk, stunted in growth, not interested in play, mentally dull and full of anxiety; in other words, it corresponds to the "backward children" on the care of whom vast sums are being spent today. Baryta Carb has given excellent results in retarded growth, since it has a specific influence on the endocrine system (pituitary and diencephalon).

Generally speaking, barium is also a remedy for disorders of the lymphatic and glandular systems. On the other hand, it is also a remedy for the elderly, being particularly good in arteriosclerosis accompanied by high blood pressure, in senile heart and in cerebral sclerosis. That this should be so is due to the fact that, in old age, the stunted growth sometimes found in childhood has its counterpart in a disharmonious involution (deterioration), possibly in the form of cancer.

The dose is from 3x through 12x and higher. In chronic cases the remedy is taken once a day at the most.

In addition to Baryta carb, Baryta muriatica, Baryta acetica and Baryta iodata are prescribed.

• • •

Whenever the use of metals in homeopathic form is being considered, the advice of a homeopathic doctor or qualified lay homeopath should always be taken. In speaking here of the correspondences between the metals and certain diseases, we have had to confine ourselves to disorders coming within the scope of the given planets. The range of application of the metals is much greater of course, and anyone who is particularly interested in this area of astromedicine would do well to consult Jaap Huibers's book, *Gesund sein mit Metallen* (How to Be Healthy with Metals).

PART TWO

COSMOBIOLOGY

CHAPTER FIVE

COSMIC PRINCIPLES FOR ASTROMEDICAL DIAGNOSIS

BEFORE TURNING TO QUESTIONS OF PRACTICAL diagnosis and prognosis, it is essential to discuss the fundamental working principles of cosmobiology. The term *cosmobiology* was coined several decades ago. All it means is that certain relationships exist between Cosmos and Bios, between the universal All and the All of living things. Once this concept had been given a special name, the need was seen to study such relationships much more closely than had been done in the past.

Astrology and cosmobiology are often wrongly treated as interchangeable expressions; sometimes for commercial reasons, often quite deliberately. But they are different, and the difference between them is that traditional astrology is largely built on a mantic basis, and is popularly resorted to for fortune-telling; whereas cosmobiology goes to work scientifically, collects empirical evidence of the relationships between the cosmos and the human race, sifts this evidence statistically, and endeavors to correlate it with and confirm it by the results obtained from other methods of investigation. While astrology is restricted mainly to making assessments of the native's character and prospects, cosmobiology, as I understand it, recognizes a cosmic factor which naturally co-determines the life-pattern and

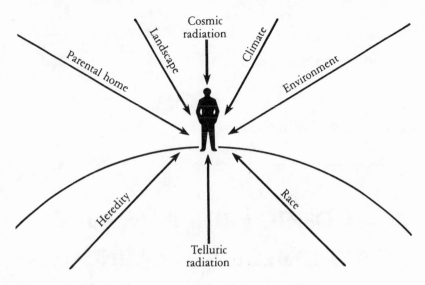

Figure 28. The influences considered in cosmobiology.

developmental possibilities, yet has a hand in other formative forces too. Figure 28 illustrates the following factors:

1) In heredity with its known strong influence on character, constitution and career;

2) In the parental home, where a special influence is exerted both by the relationship of the parents to each other and by that of the parents to their children (guiding images); also by the economic, social and educational background;

3) In the environmental setting of the parental home; in neighborhood, school and local community with their social, economic and cultural expectations;

4) In the landscape with its mountains and uplands, its plains and coastal regions;

5) In the climate, which is closely associated with the landscape and, as marine and inland, lowland and highland, produces distinct differences in the character of the inhabitants;

6) In the weather, which is produced both by cosmic and by terrestrial factors, and the appreciable influence of which on our mental and physical state has been highlighted by modern research (bio-climatics).

Clearly, among all these formative forces we are electing to take account of the cosmic factor represented by the planetary pattern at birth. But, since this factor is just one of many, cosmobiology— unlike traditional astrology—does not pretend to work out a total picture an individual's fate, but merely investigates the structural and developmental possibilities suggested by the factor.[57] And so it is imperative to stress once more that, in an astromedical study, we must obtain the supplementary information mentioned above and know the case history of the patient. Blind diagnosis is no more possible in a cosmobiological sense than it is possible in a scientific sense. (Which is not to say that blind diagnosis could not accidentally hit the mark on occasion.)

When working with an individual, I consider the following:

1) The astronomical positions of the planets: Sun, Moon, Mercury, Venus, Mars, Jupiter, Saturn, Uranus, Neptune, Pluto, the Moon's nodes, and perhaps Transpluto as well (I am not currently using the so-called transneptunian planets as none has yet been confirmed by astronomy);

2) The culmination point (Medium Coeli = Midheaven) over the birth place;

3) The Ascendant, or rising sign, where planets might just be coming up above the horizon at the birth place.

I do not employ the twelve houses; they are so speculative that fourteen rival house systems have been devised. However, the Ascendant and the Medium Coeli remain the same in each system and are therefore useable. What is more, I have abandoned the strengths and debilities; also the so-called points of fortune, love and death, since these are inaccurate unless the time of birth is known to within four minutes or has been rectified. But I do employ the half-

Table 10. Table of International Abbreviations of Cosmic Factors

Ap	= apex		N	= north		
Z	= galactic center		S	= south		
hel	= heliocentric		⚥	= nodes of Mer-		
⊕	= Earth (hel)	= ER		cury		
♃	= Cupid	= CU	(Planetary nodes are			
⊕	= Hades	= HA	symbolized by two small			
⚡	= Zeus	= ZE	circles as shown in the case of			
♄	= Chronos	= KR	Mercury above.)			
2♃	= Apollo	= AP	☉	= Sun		= SU
⊕	= Admetus	= AD	☽	= Moon		= MO
⚥	= Vulcan	= VU	☿	= Mercury		= ME
⚹	= Poseidon	= PO	♀	= Venus		= VE
p	= progressed		♂	= Mars		= MA
S	= solar arc directions		♃	= Jupiter		= JU
T	= transit		♄	= Saturn		= SA
r	= radical position		♅	= Uranus		= UR
R	= retrograde		♆	= Neptune		= NE
st	= stationary		♇	= Pluto		= PL
//	= parallel		♇	= Transpluto		= TP
A	= Ascendant	= ASC	☊	= Dragon's Head	= DR
M	= Medium Coeli	= MC	(Moon's ascending node)			
♈	= Aries	= AR	*Planetary Aspects*			
♉	= Taurus	= TA	0°	= conjunction	=	☌
♊	= Gemini	= GM	30°	= semisextile	=	⚺
♋	= Cancer	= CN	45°	= semisquare	=	∠
♌	= Leo	= LE	60°	= sextile	=	*
♍	= Virgo	= VI	72°	= quintile	=	Q
♎	= Libra	= LI	90°	= square	=	□
♏	= Scorpio	= SC	120°	= trine	=	△
♐	= Sagittarius	= SG	135°	= sesquisquare	=	⬚
♑	= Capricorn	= CP	144°	= biquintile	=	Bq
♒	= Aquarius	= AQ	150°	= quincunx	=	Qc
♓	= Pisces	= PS	180°	= opposition	=	∞

Table 10. Continued

GMT	=	Greenwich Mean Time
lst	=	local standard time
WEZ	=	West European Time (0°)
MEZ	=	Central European Time (15°)
OEZ	=	East European Time (30°)
st	=	summer time
DSZ	=	German summer time
DDSZ	=	German double summer time
zt	=	zone time
A.M.	=	ante meridiem (morning between 0 and 12 h)
P.M.	=	post meridiem (afternoon between 12 and 24 h)
l.a.	=	local ascendant
l.m.	=	local meridian

sums (midpoints), as they help me to gain a better idea of the cosmic state of a given planet and to identify many of the finer details in the complex pattern of modern life.

In order to keep our exposition compact and easy to follow, I shall make use of the standard symbols and abbreviations shown in Table 10.

Heaven and Earth, Yang and Yin

In the usual charts, the horizontal plane joins the Ascendant and the Descendant, and separates the visible from the invisible part of the heavens, the upper half being regarded as positive and the lower half as negative. Then again, a line dropped from the Meridian makes a division between East and West: the Eastern half being positive and the Western half negative.

The Chinese, relying on a five-thousand-year-old tradition, regard Heaven as Yang, as the generator of all phenomena and of everything that exists in the world, and regard Earth as Yin, the recipient of Heaven and the bearer of Heaven's progeny.[58]

The concepts Yang and Yin are aptly symbolized by a circular disc divided by a wavy line as shown in figure 29 on page 136.

Figure 29. The Tao, or Yin and Yang.

However, it is not implied that the two principles are antagonistic; rather they are complementary and flow into one another so as to form a unity. Of course, at some times the Yang principle preponderates and at others the Yin principle does so. If the balance is disturbed, it is possible, for example, to cure a Yin disease by Yang remedies (or treatment), which will restore that balance in the body. The two names are essentially distinguished by the vowels A and I, and it is helpful to look upon them as standing for the Ambient-oriented individual and the Interior-oriented individual, or, as C.G. Jung called them, the Extrovert and the Introvert. "A" is the initial of the word ambient (our external surroundings) and represents the centrifugal principle; "I" is the initial of the word interior and repre-

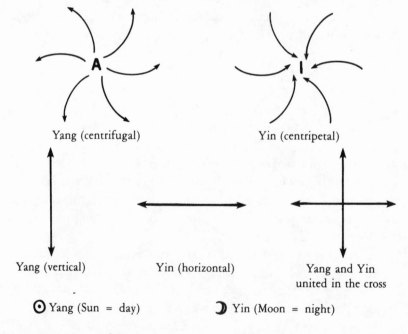

Figure 30. Yin and Yang energy.

sents the centripetal principle. In everyday life, ambient-oriented people are recognized by the way their whole being is focused on the outside world, by their lively behavior and their wish to do everything themselves; whereas interior-oriented people absorb everything into themselves and are very sensitive and reserved.

Yang corresponds to the vertical, Yin to the horizontal. When they are united they form the cross. Yang corresponds to the Sun and day; Yin to the Moon and night. During the day we walk erect in the Yang position, and at night we lie down and rest in the Yin position. When in the Yin position we are more exposed to cosmic radiation and take in energy which we give out again during the day. (See figure 30 on page 136.)

Yang can also be pictured as a triangle with its apex pointing upward, and Yin as a triangle with its apex pointing downward. When the two triangles are superimposed they make the six-pointed star symbolic of the union of positive and negative, of male and female.

As far as colors are concerned, Yang represents bright and warm colors; Yin represents dark and cold colors. Other colors are intermediate in value between Yang and Yin:

Yang — red, orange, yellow, green, blue, indigo, violet — Yin.

It should therefore be possible to adjust the balance between Yang and Yin by the color of our clothing. Thus people who need to contemplate do well to wear bright-colored clothing. And it is noteworthy that Buddhist monks observe this rule by dressing in saffron robes to offset their absorption in religious meditation.* Catholic monks, on the other hand (with the exception of those who wear white or colored cowls), have a negative effect in their black garb. (Some other contrasting pairs are shown in table 11.)

Yang and Yin are not clear-cut concepts or tendencies, but change into one another from time to time. Foods and medicaments play a big part in this. The content and strength of Yang and Yin

---

*Another explanation is that they wear yellow because they believe this color stimulates the mind.

Table 11. Contrasting Pairs

Yang	Yin
Male	Female
Fertilizing	Fertilized
Condensing	Dispersing
Concentrated, applied energy	Diffused, misapplied energy
Ordered	Disordered
Time	Space
Day	Night
Summer	Winter
Dry	Wet
Salt	Sweet, sour (sugar turns to acid in the body)*
Positive	Negative
Tight	Loose
Hard	Soft
Heavy	Light

*There is not the same simple polarity here as there is between hard and soft say; because salt and acid are part of one set of four—acid, base, salt, water—formed by the interplay of their components, another set of four—H, OH, M, X. *Tr.*

vary in them, as roughly indicated in the synopsis shown in table 12 on pages 139–141. The lists are intended to enable the reader to restore balance between Yang and Yin by eating the appropriate foods. A certain amount of guidance in this matter can be obtained from the birth chart, since a Jupiter-type, say, needs the balance to be restored by Yin foods, and a Saturn-type needs it to be restored by Yang foods.

The way in which foods are prepared can make them more Yang or more Yin, or can even convert them from one to the other. Heating, boiling, baking, roasting, drying, stewing, salting, or seasoning with bitter herbs makes food more Yang in character. Cooling, enriching with liquids, adding sour or sweet things, flavoring with spices containing strongly aromatic herbs or roots (provided they are not bitter), grating, crushing and fermentation makes foods more Yin in character. When cereals are soaked in water they become more Yin; when foods are sweetened with sugar, they too become Yin.

Table 12. Yang and Yin Foods

Yang Vegetables	Yin Vegetables
Cabbage lettuce, deep-rooted (1)	Artichoke (2)
Carrot (2)	Asparagus (3)
Celery root (1)	Butter beans (1)
Chicory (1)	Cabbage, red (1)
Coltsfoot root (2)	Cabbage, white (1)
Corn-salad, lamb's lettuce (1)	Cauliflower (2)
Dandelion leaves (1)	Celery leafstalk (1)
Dandelion root (3)	Cucumber (3)
Endive (1)	Fennel (1)
Garlic (1)	Jerusalem artichoke (1)
Horseradish (3)	Kale (1)
Leek (1)	Kidney beans, green (1)
Parsley root (1)	Kohlrabi (1)
Radish (1)	Paprika (5)
Radish, large, black/white (1)	Peas, green, dwarf (1)
Salsify (2)	Peas, tall (2)
Turnip (1)	Potato (1–4)
Turnip, early garden (1)	Sorrel (1)
	Spinach (1)
	Tomato (3)

Yang Fruit	Yin Fruit
Apple (2)	Banana (3)
Apricot (2)	Date (4)
Bilberry, whortleberry (1)	Fig, fresh (4)
Cherry (2)	Grape (3)
Gooseberry (1)	Grapefruit (2)
Raspberry, wild (1)	Lemon (2)
Red currant (1)	Melon (2)
Strawberry, cultivated (1)	Orange (3)
Strawberry, wild (2)	Peach (2)
Sweet chestnut (2)	Pear (3)
	Pineapple (4)

Continued

Table 12. Continued

Yang Meat, Fish, Poultry	Yin Meat, Fish, Poultry
Beef (3)	Carp (1)
Caviar (3)	Eel (4)
Chicken (1)	Lobster (1)
Crab (1)	Octopus (2)
Egg, fertilized (3)	Oyster (3)
Hare, rabbit (1)	Pork (4)
Herring (3)	Sausage (4)
Lamb (1)	
Mackerel (2)	Invalids should avoid the
Pheasant (3)	above foods if possible.
Pike (1)	
Reindeer (3)	
Salmon (2)	
Sardine (2)	
Shrimp (2)	
Sprat (3)	
Tuna (1)	
Veal (1)	
Venison (2)	

Yang Fats, Oil	Yin Fats, Oil
Beech kernel oil (1)	Beef suet (5)
Rapeseed oil, pure (1)	Butter, natural soured (3)
Rice oil (1)	Butter, dairy cream (4)
Seasame oil (2)	Coconut oil (2)
Soybean oil (1)	Coconut oil, hardened (3)
Sunflower oil (1)	Groundnut oil (1)
Wheat-germ oil (1)	Lard (4)
	Margarine, solidified (3)
	Olive oil (1)
	Palm oil (2)

Table 12. Continued

Yang Beverages	Yin Beverages
Alcohol, medicinal (3)	Beer (2)
Birch-leaf tisane (2)	Champagne (3)
Centaury tisane (2)	Cocoa (5)
Ginseng tisane (3)	Coffee, ground (5)
Mugwort tisane (3)	Fruit juice, sweetened (4)
Rhododendron tisane (2)	Fruit juice, unsweetened (2)
Sage tisane (2)	Mineral water (2)
Thyme tisane (2)	Soda water (2)
	Spring water (2)
	Tea, Chinese or Indian (2)
Yang Milk Products	**Yin Milk Products**
Camembert cheese (2)	Buttermilk (1)
Goat's milk cheese (3)	Cream, fresh (3)
Gruyère cheese (2)	Cream, sour (3)
Quark, skimmed (1)	Kephir (a Caucasian milk
Roquefort cheese (2)	drink) (2)
Soft cheese (2)	Milk, full-cream (12)
Whey cheese (2)	Milk, sour (2)
	Whey (2)
	Yoghurt (2)
	Miscellaneous Yin Foods
	Honey (3)
	Sugar, raw cane (4)
	Sugar, refined white (5)
	Syrup (3)

The Human Body

A human body is an entity composed of Yang and Yin. The right side of the body is Yang and the left side is Yin since, in most people, the right side is the more active. When a person is defending himself, he holds his left hand (Yin) in front of his face and raises his right arm (Yang) to push or strike.

According to Rilling there are obvious anatomical differences between the two sides. For instance, the left side of the heart is more powerfully developed, the left of the portal vein is longer than the right, the left kidney is larger than the right, the left ureter is the longer of the two, the left apex of the lungs is more frequently attacked by tuberculosis than the right, etc.

Rilling has also found experimentally that the left side of the face is changed less by events than is the right. "Stamped on the right side of the face are the various impressions made by life, and it hints to us, moreover, concerning certain traits hiding in the unconscious. . . . It has been shown empirically that there is a genetic connection: the father's ancestry being embodied more strongly in the right side and the mother's in the left." Rilling lists the Yang and Yin meridians as shown in table 13.

The gallbladder is seen as particularly important. It is the organ that is noted for its purity, since it contains nothing but bile; whereas waste products are contained in or pass through the other organs. There is a Chinese proverb that says that a brave man has a strong gallbladder but a timid man has a weak one. As we shall see later, the bile is assigned to Mars; so that it would not be strange to find a well-fortified Mars going with a strong gallbladder and vice versa.

Table 13. Yin/Yang Meridians

Yang	Yin
Large intestine	Lungs
Stomach	Spleen and pancreas
Triple warmer	Circulation-sex
Small intestine	Heart
Gallbladder	Liver
Urinary bladder	Kidneys

The relationship between the large intestine and the lungs is confirmed by the frequency of constipation in pulmonary disease brought on through taking a chill. If heat is generated in the large intestine, this is often revealed by a dry irritating cough. Similar relationships exist between the other organs.

Types of Character and Constitution

The Yang/Yin principle also turns up in the modern theory of types, which recognizes the contrast between those who are thin and fat, or tall and slim, short and stout.

Table 14 on page 144 contains a small excerpt from the very detailed "Synoptic Constitution Table" of Schulte-Kuhlmann as given in Rilling's book.[39] A brief synopsis such as the one in our table can give no more than a general impression; anyone who wishes to go deeper into the subject needs to make a thorough study of Rilling's fact-packed volume.

Whatever theory of types we study, we shall find that there is really no such thing as a pure type: individuals tend to favor one type or another, that is all. We shall find also that a person who was unusually thin when young may well fill out with fatty tissue in old age. And, in any case, it is possible to alter the size of the body by a suitable diet, sporting activities, massage, etc.

Yang and Yin in the Zodiac

Although the same names have not been used of course, Yang types and Yin types have long been recognized in the zodiac. Even Claudius Ptolemy in his *Tetrabiblos* wrote of some signs being male and of some being female:

> Apart from these definitions (of the various types of sign), six signs are male and day signs and an equal number belong to the female and to the night. Their succession is unbroken; just as day follows night and just as the union of male and female beings is a natural necessity. We shall adopt Aries as our starting point on the grounds, which I

Table 14. Constitutional Types

Origins, Authors	Broad Type	Narrow Type
Ancient Chinese medicine	Yang type	Yin type
Ancient Indian concepts ca. 500 B.C.	Cow elephant (used of females)	Gazelle type
Cervantes (1605)	Sancho Panza	Don Quixote
Carus (1865)	Plethoric constitution with preferential development of the digestive organs	Cerebral, sensitive, asthenic constitution
Huter (1880)	Alimentary temperament	Sensory temperament
Kretschmer (1921)	Pyknic, cyclothymic	Leptosome (asthenic), schizothymic
Stockard (1923)	Lateral type	Linear type
Curry (1949)	Warm-front sensitive type	Cold-front sensitive type
Rilling (1957)	Plus type	Minus type

have already mentioned, that the male lord must always go first since the active energies invariably rush ahead of the passive. Thus Aries and Libra are male and belong to the day. This arises from the circumstances that the equator on which they lie produces the most original and most powerful motion of all living things. From these follow a male and a female sign in a continuous series.[60]

Figures 31 and 32 on page 145 illustrate the positive and negative signs and show you how the yang energy and yin energy manifest.

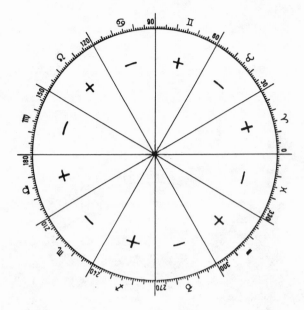

Figure 31. Distribution into positive and negative signs.

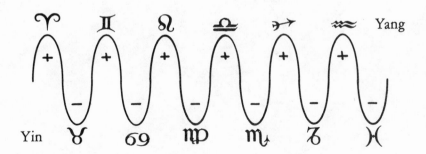

Figure 32. The alternation of Yang (+) and Yin (-) signs in the zodiac.

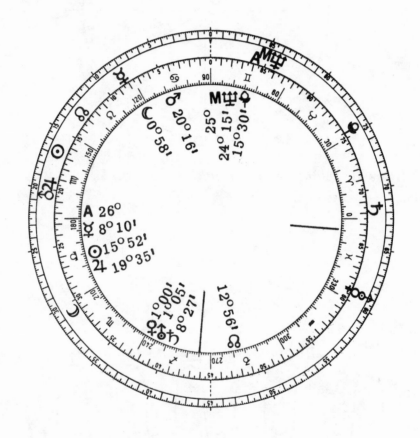

Figure 33. Cosmogram for October 9, 1898, 4:30 A.M. at
50° N36'/17° E02'.

Yang and Yin in the Cosmogram

Figure 33 on page 146 is a sample cosmogram for the 9th October 1898. The Ascendant is on the horizontal line dividing the circle into an upper Yang half and a lower or Yin half. The Meridian (MC) is on the vertical line dividing it into an eastern Yang half and a western Yang half.* A scrutiny of the placements shows that Pluto, Neptune, MC, Moon, Mercury, Sun, Jupiter, Venus, Uranus and Saturn all occupy positive (or Yang) signs, while Mars, ASC and the lunar nodes are in negative (or Yin) signs. Therefore Yang predominates in this cosmogram.

Cosmosophic Principles

As Boll tells us, "Prechristian astrology made an admirably valiant attempt to explain the world as a whole — as a single great unity; it also fitted the human race into this commonwealth which binds all living things together by its laws."[61] Now what can be the implication of this, except that the connection between the Cosmos and the Bios is not open to complete understanding by scientific means and lies deeper than science, in the realm of philosophy and religion, linking us with our Creator, with God? Here is an outlook that used to be the common property of mankind: its traces being found among the healing, and survives, if only unconsciously, in all religions that share a common cosmic basis.

The Three Humors

In Tibetan and Indian medicine, physiological processes are categorized according to a threefold division, which can hardly be purely empirical but must have been the consequence of a preconceived metaphysical view of the threefold nature of being.[62]

---

*Readers new to the subject should note that here, unlike in an atlas, east is on the left-hand side of the chart and south is at the top. *Tr.*

The first of the three principles is *Chi* = air, wind. This is not ordinary air, however, but Reason which upholds and penetrates the All; it is Idea and Law.

The second principle is *Schara* = bile (yellow), which is not ordinary bile, either, but the principle that governs and moves the cosmos and underlies each impulse and force: the Doer or principle of action.

The third principle is *Bagdan* = water (phlegm). As we might expect, it is not ordinary water, but the transporting principle or Vessel, which is passive in character and is codetermined and shaped by the other principles.

It would take us too far afield to give a proper account of these principles here; especially as we are more interested in the theories worked out in the Mediterranean region. The basis of humoral pathology, the concept that all disease can be traced back to a faulty condition of the body humors, was laid in the astrology of ancient Greece. The fundamentals of the theory were developed by Greek philosophers and physicians.

Elements—Temperaments—Humors

The wide acceptance of the age-old doctrines of Yang and Yin, of the elements and humors, and of the constitutions based on these, is obvious from the fact that the doctrines have survived for five thousand years and are still being endorsed today. (See figure 34 on page 149.) Thus they find a place even in the *Psychologie* (Psychology) of Dr. Anschütz, from whose book the following lines are taken:

> Whereas, in its beginnings, psychology goes back to the classification of men and women according to the predominance in them of one of the four elements (fire, air, water and earth). Hippocrates and Galen explain the temperaments in terms of the postulated four main fluids of the human body: yellow bile (cholos), black bile (melas cholos), blood (sanguis) and phlegm (phlegma). Later on, the temperaments were attributed to the condition of the blood, and the choleric temperament was called hot-

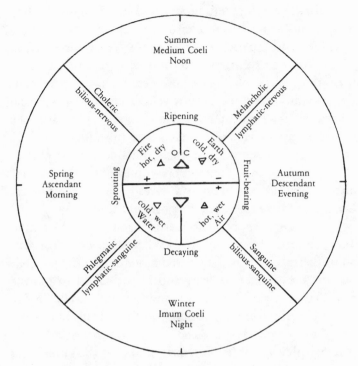

Figure 34. Cosmopsychological diagram.

blooded, the melancholic thick-blooded, the sanguine thin-blooded, and the phlegmatic cold-blooded.

1) *The choleric temperament* expresses itself by touchiness and, at times, by displays of strong emotion, which do not persist at a high level for long, however, and therefore occur by fits and starts rather than for any length of time. The expression of the feelings is often bitter and wounding. There is a tendency to irascibility, rather than to adoring love, but not to implacability. The choleric person has great self-confidence, and has no time for minor details or slavish adherence to rules and regulations. He easily becomes overbearing and ambitious, and can act decisively. He can be broad-minded and loyal, but also proud and egotistic. In the main he is serious-minded and is seldom seen indulging

in boyish high spirits. His negative traits are arrogance, bad temper, insolence and recklessness.

2) *The phlegmatic temperament* is seen in the person who is fussy and difficult over everything and obstinately sticks to his guns. He likes repose, leaves things to happen, and is traditional and conservative. Because being punctual makes life easier, he is punctual in his affairs, provided they are relatively undemanding. He is free from illusions, does not fret, and is sensible, practical, reliable and peaceable. He is content to let others get on with things if they do not disturb him, and he always preserves his inner composure. On the negative side are indolence and sloth.

3) *The sanguine temperament* is characterized by a high degree of excitability, which lacks depth however. The sanguine person is easily impressed, interested and pleased; but he loses interest quickly and is not suited to routine work. He is forgetful, given to impulse, and unreliable. He enjoys cheerful company and likes to be helpful, but makes promises without keeping them. He gets into trouble for playing silly tricks, says he is sorry, and does the same thing again at the earliest opportunity. He is a complete optimist, treats everything lightly, but knows as little of deep happiness as he does of deep unhappiness. Frivolity, thoughtlessness, absent-mindedness and superficiality are his bad points.

4) *The melancholic temperament* is not open to slight and superficial impressions, but anything that does affect one who possesses it will do so inwardly for a long time. Whatever stirs his emotions will put down deep roots in him and will determine his frame of mind. Outwardly he is pretty cautious, often mistrustful. He is serious, almost dismal, worries about the future and is often avaricious and mean. In love and friendship he is true, but prone to jealousy. He is marked by industry, punctuality and conscientiousness, and expects others to be so, too. When embarking on a project, he does so thoughtfully and deliberately and then stays with it. He avoids noisy entertainments and seeks solitude, communion with nature and the society of

just one or two good friends. In extreme instances, he can become misanthropic and depressed.[63]

· · ·

By the term *temperament* readers should understand the style in which the mind and (in particular) the will and emotions operate in an individual. The term *constitution* indicates the quality of a person displayed in body form and function, in executive ability, power of resistance, and reflexes. Psychology and medicine have now joined forces, and our conception of the body-soul combination has been expanded to include everything which through inheritance and experience has become part of the psychophysical basis of the personality. We must also include proneness to certain diseases, the state of vitality and functioning of the entire organism and, finally, all physical and mental abilities.

In summarizing the traditional view mentioned above, we can recognize in figure 33 on page 146, the divisions into Yang and Yin, day and night, summer and winter, and the various elements. The circle is successively divided into halves, quarters and eighths to give the basic aspects of opposition, square, semisquare and sesquisquare. What is more, according to Retschlag,[64] the traditional elements of the signs have an affinity with certain of the chemical elements as follows:

Fire signs with oxygen (O)
Earth signs with carbon (C)
Air signs with nitrogen (N)
Water signs with hydrogen (H)

Cosmobiological Types

As is shown in the book *Grundlagen der kosmobiologischen Heilkunde* (The Fundamentals of Cosmobiological Medicine),[65] various sorties have been made into the field of typology (from Kretschmer, Pfahler, Jaensch, Jung and others). For the purposes of cosmo-

Table 15. Cosmopsychological Types

Aries, Leo, Sagittarius	tense outer	= SA type
Taurus, Virgo, (Scorpio), Capricorn	tense inner	= SI type
Gemini, Libra, Aquarius	relaxed outer	= LA type
Cancer, Pisces	relaxed inner	= LI type

biology, it has been found helpful to borrow the graphological types of Christiansen-Carnap.[66] In these we have both a relaxed and a tense type and, following Jung, an outer type and an inner type (or extrovert and introvert).

Scorpio has been placed between brackets and put with signs belonging to the SI type in Table 15, since we do not see how it can possibly be equated with the LI signs Cancer and Pisces — it lacks their tenderness and composure.

As Baron von Klöckler[67] pointed out some time ago, the Scorpion has quite a different nature from the Crab and the Fish. In a private conversation, Professor Gerhard Krüger explained this as follows: "Cancer may be likened to a water-spring, Scorpio to a stagnant pool, and Pisces to the sea — because Scorpio has a more settled and unbending character like the matter-of-fact SI types. Then again, Scorpio is ruled by the positive planet Mars, whereas Cancer is ruled by the Moon and Pisces by Neptune, both of which are negative."

Assessment of the various features of the cosmogram can not be carried out on a single level since, as will be appreciated, the slow-moving planets often remain for years in a single sign and so make the same impression on very many individuals, while other planets transit a sign within a month and the very quick-moving points ASC and MC pass through one zodiac degree in about four minutes. The swifter the cosmic factor, the fewer the people who can share any of its positions.

If we were to rate planetary positions based on the following scale of values, the individuality factors (Sun, Moon, MC, ASC) would be valued at 3 points, the quick-moving planets (Mercury, Venus, Mars) valued at 2 points each, and the slow-moving planets (Jupiter, Saturn, Uranus, Neptune, Pluto) plus the lunar nodes valued at 1 point each. Therefore using our chart for 9th October 1898, the planets would rate as follows:

SA signs have:

Moon in Leo	3 points
Venus in Sagittarius	2 points
Uranus in Sagittarius	1 point
Saturn in Sagittarius	1 point
Total:	7 points

SI signs have:

Ascendant in Virgo	3 points
Dragon's Head in Capricorn	1 point
Total:	4 points

LA signs have:

Pluto in Gemini	1 point
Neptune in Gemini	1 point
MC in Gemini	3 points
Mercury in Libra	2 points
Sun in Libra	3 points
Jupiter in Libra	1 point
Total:	11 points

LI signs have:

Mars in Cancer	2 points
Total:	2 points

All told, this amounts to a total of 24 points. When the results are displayed graphically, the material shown in figure 35 emerges.

A bar chart such as figure 35 is useful for statistical research. For example, Dr. Rolf Reissmann carried out some studies on epileptics in Leipzig and found:

SA types	=	37 points
SI types	=	95 points
LA types	=	53 points
LI types	=	53 points

It seems, therefore, that epileptics belong mainly to the SI type, although this needs verification by further work.

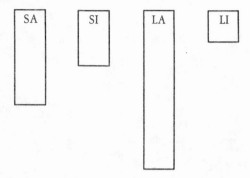

Figure 35. Type composition.

Character and Disease

The reason character types have been mentioned in the present treatise is that character and disease go together and exert a reciprocal influence on one another. Anyone who has studied homeopathy will know the homeopathic "drug pictures." One speaks, for instance, of the nux vomica type who, with wide mouth and full lips, seeks sensual enjoyment, but also is predisposed to disorders of the stomach and intestines, has taunt features and is slightly nervy. Or of the phosphorus type with slender figure and eagerness to do his best, but with little interest in sport or practical activities. Since these homeopathic types have so much in common with the cosmobiological ones, doctors who have been trained in cosmobiology take readily to prescribing homeopathic remedies.

Nevertheless, it must not be forgotten that it would be worse than useless to attempt a diagnosis from a cosmobiological standpoint alone. The standard physical and psychological clinical methods are also necessary. The main value of cosmobiology lies in its power to detect a disease which is still latent, thus enabling preventive measures to be taken. It will also warn us of likely relapses or recurrences and will say whether we should treat a given disorder as chronic or acute. The following material is an overview of the cosmic correspondences to diseases and remedies, as types relate to temperament and constitution. The remedies should be taken on the advice of a homeopathic practitioner.

1) The Tense Outer type = SA type

General characteristics: Practical, unimaginative, understanding of the outside world, plenty of determination, good powers of observation, enterprising with clear-cut aims and plans, often out for personal advantage, little empathy or flexibility, enjoys a contest, likes to be seen to be superior.

Temperament: Choleric, bilious-nervous.

Constitution: Athletic, ectomorphic.

Physique: Lean or stream-lined with powerful muscles, often prominent veins, hirsute body, strong, expressive face, sparkling eyes.

Diseases: In many instances the diseases originate in a disordered function of the liver and gallbladder. If too much bile is secreted, combustion increases and there is a tendency to feverishness. With the spread of bile through the body, the organism becomes poisoned and the individual suffers from jaundice, and from a painful and swollen liver. The stomach, intestines, kidneys and urinary bladder are often implicated as well. Nervous disorders, such as so-called nervous indigestion, can occur as well. Sometimes there is a predisposition to neuralgia, sciatica and rheumatism.

Around middle life, between the ages of forty-five and fifty, there is a possibility that the choleric temperament will turn melancholic, especially if the set goals have not been achieved by this time or if there have been severe reverses.

Prophylaxis (preventive measures): Any overactivity or excess should be avoided. The tendency to eat highly-seasoned foods, to take alcohol, tobacco and poisonous medicaments, etc., should be curbed, because stimulants activate the choleric temperament and upset the digestive organs. Foods should be more Yin than Yang. Especially recommended are oat and barley gruel, rice, green vegetables, plenty of fruit, little milk and few eggs. Good to drink are soda water with a dash of wine, orange juice, lemons, red currants, cherries and raspberries.

During convalescence long excursions are beneficial. Vacations should be spent in resorts with a temperate climate.

According to Herlbauer, suitable homeopathic remedies are Belladonna, Chelidonium, China, Hyoscyamus nig., Nux vomica, Phosphorus, Veratrum vir., Natrum nitr. Obviously, these remedies need to be taken under the supervision of a qualified practitioner.

2) The Tense Inner type = SI type

General characteristics: A cautious, reflective nature, usually on guard, not very outgoing, given to thoughtful, planned and systematic behavior, reserved, often shy and embarrassed, many times inconsiderate and unsociable, in all projects patient, tenacious and obstinate, conservative, sometimes fanatical and narrow-minded.

Temperament: Melancholic, lymphatic-nervous.

Constitution: Solid, endomorphic.

Physique: Slim to stout with soft outlines, sometimes rather puffy; a lax, often stooping posture; not many prominent veins, normal hairiness, dark eyes.

Diseases: The causes of disease can lie in the condition of the blood; especially in a deficiency of red blood corpuscles, by which the resistance is lowered. Common complaints are insomnia, and digestive troubles—especially constipation or diarrhea. The appetite is capricious and oscillates between ravenous hunger and no desire to eat at all. Headaches are frequent, particularly if the diet is faulty. There is a tendency to hysteria and hypochondria. A sedentary occupation plus an unsuitable diet lead to vein troubles and hemorrhoids. Autotoxins (uric acid) are often excreted via the skin. The throat is sensitive with a likelihood of tonsillitis.

Prophylaxis: Illnesses are frequently brought on by a lack of exercise; the circulation should be constantly stimulated. The consumption of fats and sour things (acids) should be cut down as much as possible.

Since the temperament is liable to incline to Yin, the diet should incline to Yang. Care should be taken that drinks are not overly sweetened artificially.

Convalescence is aided more by a cold than by a hot climate.

According to Herlbauer, suitable homeopathic remedies are Aesculus hippoc., Arsenicum alb., Aurum met., Calcarea carb., Graphites, Pulsatilla, Veratrum alb.

3) The Relaxed Outer type = LA type

General characteristics: Quick reactions to all impressions from outside. The individual is content to be borne along by the stream of life, rises to every occasion, readily makes contact with others, displays no inhibitions of any kind, easily brushes difficulties aside, takes people and things for what they are, is neither dogmatic nor mystical, adapts to any situation, seldom makes a commitment to fixed principles or tenets. The LA type is most clearly seen in dancing, musicianship and rhythmic movement.

Temperament: Sanguine, bilious-sanguine.

Constitution: Slender, ectomorphic.

Physique: Slim, medium height to tall, mobile body with lively gestures. Often a supple and sporty type. Light eyes, fine teeth, veins visibly bluish.

Diseases: The diseases are mostly acute rather than chronic, and often arise from plethora with a tendency to nosebleeds, congestion of the blood, hemorrhagic effusions. There can be a predisposition to inflammations of the throat and chest, or to inflammations as a consequence of injuries. Illnesses are quite frequent but usually run a rapid course.

Prophylaxis: A mixed diet which is not too soggy, hot, or salty is recommended. The key to preserving the health is moderation in all things. This animated temperament needs to be balanced by Yin foods, dried fruit and fruit juices; new light wines are usually well tolerated.

For convalescence rainy regions are best.

Herlbauer's suggested homeopathic remedies are Sulphuricum acidum, Aconitum, Belladonna, Hyoscyamus nig., Pulsatilla, Rhus tox.

4) The Relaxed Inner type = LI type

General characteristics: Whereas the LA type is uninhibited enough to get those around in tune with himself or herself and has the knack of "managing" them by being adaptable and flexible, the LI type is more self-contained, makes no demands on the outside world and bases his or her activities on hard necessity or on maintaining the balance of the inner life. People of this type are often dreamy and meditative and not always equal to all demands; at times they are unpractical and irresolute. They seek to bridge over conflicts, avoid dissensions, try to empathize with others, and are considerate and easy-going. In a negative sense, they can be driven to and fro by their appetites and by pleasure seeking. They are full of strong emotions, helpful and tolerant, but never inclined to take a risk.

Temperament: Phlegmatic, lymphatic-sanguine.

Constitution: Endormorphic.

Physique: Short to medium height, roundish outlines, lackadaisical posture, scant body hair, inclination to baldness, slow pulse, flabby muscles (because any exertion is avoided), little physical strength, inclination to fatness.

Diseases: The diseases of this type arise mainly from a deficient metabolism and from reduced secretory activity of the glands and skin, the main cause of which is avoidance of exercise. When illnesses are neglected they can become chronic. Glandular diseases are the chief problem. The healing fever is usually slow to make its appearance and therefore the cure is delayed.

Prophylaxis: The diet should be on the dry side, and should be light whenever the body is sluggish. Drinks containing bitter principles are to be preferred. Indulgence in poisons such as alcohol, tobacco and strong sleeping pills should be avoided. In order to stimulate the metabolism, plenty of fresh air, exercise, toughening, and sporting activities are required.

Herlbauer says that the appropriate homeopathic remedies are Belladonna, Capsicum ann., Magnesium chlorat., Natrum carb., Natrum chlorat., Natrum sulph., Pulsatilla nigr., Abies canad., Argentum nitr., Lilium tigr., Populus trem., Sepia, Calcium carb., Carbo anim., Carbo veg., Phosphorus, Phytolacca dec., Silicea.

• • •

The individual types have now been described in sufficient detail as regards character, physique, temperament and constitution to enable the reader to determine the type to which he or she belongs. However, the picture is not always a simple one because there are quite liable to be interfering factors. If, for example, in a radix of the LA type, the Sun is conjunct Saturn, the vitality of the type will be drained and the individual will not be so animated. On the other hand, if Mars is conjunct and Sun in an SI type, the native will be much more energetic and positive than we should normally expect.

Zodiac Signs—Organs—Diseases

In medieval almanacs there was always a blood-letting manikin showing when the Moon was in the right sign for blood-letting in cases of disease; the theory being that each part of the body was governed by a sign of the zodiac. These correspondences of the signs to body parts are not authoritative, however, and do not have the degree of reliability needed for diagnostic purposes. A great deal of research is still required in this field. Nevertheless, experience has shown that there are certain sectors of the zodiac, and even certain degrees, that provide amazingly precise indications. Some of the evidence is contained in the *Anatomischen Entsprechungen der Tierkreisgrade* (Anatomical Correspondences of the Zodiac Degrees) and in Brandau's Organuhr.

As it turns out, we have to take into account not only a given sign but also, as a secondary influence, the signs that are in square and opposition to it. Thus there is often a connection between the signs of the fixed cross, Taurus/Leo/Scorpio/Aquarius. For example, vein trouble (Aquarius) is often associated with heart trouble (Leo) or

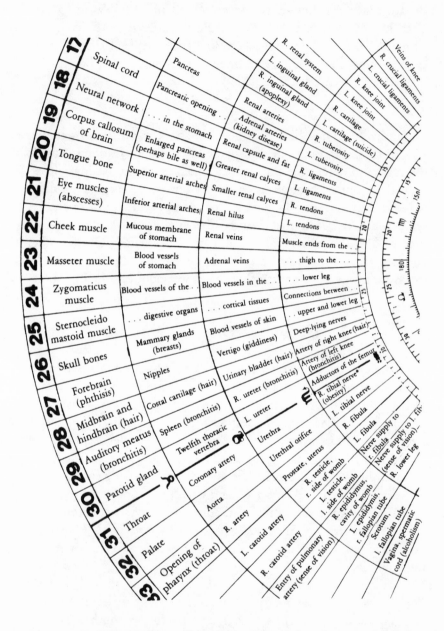

Figure 36. From Fritz Brandau's Organuhr der anatomischen Entsprechungen *(Aalen, 1978).*

even with abdominal disorders (Scorpio). Then again, Taurus may not be implicated in throat problems but in abdominal disorders corresponding to its opposite sign, Scorpio. Taurus and Scorpio correspond to the various secretory organs, including the nose and tonsils. Therefore we need to take due note of the reciprocity of the individual organs.

Mutual Relationships Between Organs of the Body

As has just been pointed out, the anatomical correspondences concern not just signs taken singly but their opposite signs as well. The situation is comprehensible in terms of the homology of organs which

Table 16. Relationships between Organs of the Body

Adrenals—thymus	Mammary glands—ovaries
Beard—pubic hair	Mouth—vulva and vagina
Bladder—trachea	Nostrils—rectum
Breasts—ovaries	Ovaries—thyroid, breasts
Bronchii—ureters	Pancreas—liver
Cecum—stomach	Pituitary—endocrine glands
Cervix of uterus—tonsils	Prostate—tonsils,
Chin—pubic region	thyroid, larynx
Clitoris—tongue	Pubic region—chin
Endocrine glands—pituitary	Rectum—nasal concha
Genital mucosa—salivary	Small intestine—ileum
glands	Spleen—liver,
Genital organs—thyroid,	internal secretion
endocrine glands	Stomach—cecum
Glans of the penis—tongue	Testicles—thyroid
Heart—uterus (womb)	Thyroid—ovaries,
Intestines—esophagus	prostate, spleen, testicles
Kidneys—lungs	Tongue—clitoris, glans
Larynx—heart	Tonsils—prostate, uterus
Larynx—uterus	Trachea—bladder, urethra
Liver—pancreas, spleen	Upper lip—perineum
Lungs—kidneys	Ureters—bronchii
	Urethra—trachea

are connected or alike in some way. For instance, there are the mouth and the vulva and vagina, the tongue and the clitoris, the tonsils and the uterus or prostate as the case may be. It is observable in young women, for example, that a vaginal discharge or infection often follows a tonsillectomy.

These relationships were published many years ago by the French physicians, Dr. Adrien Peladan and Dr. Duz, and by the Viennese physician, Dr. Feerhow. They are listed in Table 16 in alphabetical order.

Dr. Feerhow cautioned that he would not vouch for the absolute accuracy of this list, which is meant merely to serve as an incentive to further investigation.

Planets—Body—Diseases

Experience over several decades has convinced me that for diseases of individual organs the planets are often more decisive than the signs in which they are posited. Consider, for example, the aspects between Venus and Saturn which often evoke kidney trouble or female diseases, between the Sun and Neptune indicating cardioasthenia (a weak heart), or between the Moon and Saturn indicating disturbances of the fluid balance, etc. Interested students should refer to table B and table C in Appendix I on page 359 for sign correspondences and planetary correspondences.

CHAPTER SIX

THE COSMOGRAM

THERE ARE VARIOUS METHODS USED IN ASTROL-
ogy, differing mainly according to the house system
favored. Originally, the houses were nothing more than the
twelve signs of the zodiac. These signs were each allotted to
a planet or planetary deity known as the ruler of the house. Presumably, the feast of a planetary deity was celebrated in the month
belonging to the given sign or house. But then, in imitation of the
twelvefold division of the zodiac, another division of the heavens was
made into twelve sections beginning with the Ascendant, or rising
sign.

Originally, these sections were counted clockwise, that is to say
in the natural order consisting of Ascendant, MC (culminating
point), Descendant (setting point), IC (midnight point), and back to
the Ascendant. It is said that the Egyptian god Hermes Trismegistus
brought about a reform in which the houses were counted anticlock-
wise, because "the individual, on entering the world, has his whole
destiny lying in the night of the future; therefore, the planets that are
still in the dark lower hemisphere are those that must indicate what is
to come." This absurd method of counting the houses is still used
everywhere today.

The uncertainty that is a feature of using houses arises from the
fact that fourteen houses systems have been devised, agreeing on only

two points: the Ascendant (ASC) and the Medium Coeli (MC). Now, in certain house systems, the ASC and MC practically coincide when the birth place is in the far north, and some houses are only a few degrees wide, whereas others span several signs. My own response has been to abolish this unsatisfactory state of affairs by making do with the ASC, the MC and the aspects. So no house divisions will be found in my examples. The two authentic points, ASC and MC are written A and M respectively, in order to mark their positions as accurately as possible, especially when other factors are crowded into the same region.

In order to work with the cosmogram, the zodiac has been surrounded by a 90° outer wheel to facilitate locating the aspects. (See figure 37.) I have reduced the number of aspects that I use to those that are based on a continuous subdivision of the cross; that is to say, to angles of 0°, 180°, 90°, 45°, and 135° as shown in figure 38.[68]

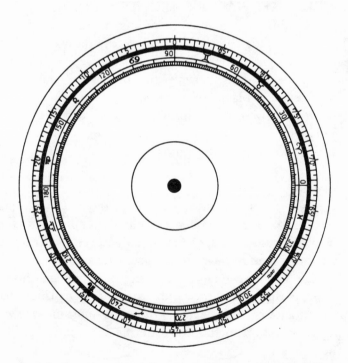

Figure 37. Composite chart showing the 360° circle of the zodiac, and the outer 90° circle (or dial) that we work with in cosmobiology.

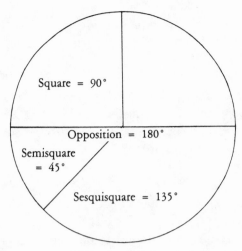

Figure 38. Progressive subdivision of the circle into aspects.

For efficient study of the cosmogram, a 90° dial or at least a slide rule is necessary to help determine the aspects, the midpoints, and the solar arc directions. To get the timing right, I have developed the Life Chart,[42] and will use this a number of times in the examples that follow. The Annual Chart can be taken from graphic 45° ephemerides.

In recent years the declinations of the planets[69] have been much neglected by astrologers, even though—since a point is always defined by two intersecting lines—the position of a planet can never be located by its zodiac longitude alone. Reference to any atlas will illustrate this. For instance, Hamburg in North Germany and Tunis in North Africa both lie near longitude 10°E, but the latitude of Hamburg lies between 53°N and 54°N, while that of Tunis lies more

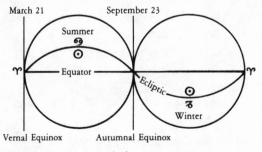

Figure 39. The declinations of the Sun.

or less on 37°N. No one could consider these positions to be the same. Equally, the distances of the planets from the celestial equator are significant too.

The declinations of the Sun have a profound influence on the seasons, as can be seen in figure 39 on page 165. The other planets more or less follow the path of the Sun. The declinations will be often mentioned in the following examples, and the reader will soon come to appreciate their importance.

The Aspects

Individual planets in the cosmogram are related to one another by aspect. Especially significant are the aspects arising from the cross and its successive divisions, i.e., conjunction, opposition, square, semi-square and sesquisquare. The trine and sextile, and the rest of the aspects belonging to traditional astrology play hardly any part in disease unless they form half-sums as in the case of an exact trine.

The next thing to do is to combine the meanings of the aspecting planets. Recommended reading on the subject is my book *Kombination der Gestirneinflüsse* (The Combination of Stellar Influences).[70]

The Sun always symbolizes the whole body, the vitality, the will to live, the heart and the circulation. In its combinations with other planets, we get such effects as cardiac deficiency from Sun/Neptune; inflammations from Sun/Mars; blood diseases from Sun/Jupiter; cell deposits, indurations, and stone formation from Sun/Saturn; irregularities of the heart beat from Sun/Uranus, etc. Lunar aspects are involved with the body's fluid balance and with the fluid balance of individual organs. Thus with Moon/Venus we may expect disorders relating to glandular products and hormones; with Moon/Mars unconsciously activated muscle movements, or mental reactions to the outside world, e.g. blushing or blanching.

Further information is obtainable from the half-sums (midpoints) when there are planets at equal distances on either side of a given planet.

In figure 40, Jupiter is shown in the middle of and equidistant from Saturn and Neptune. This is written Jupiter = Saturn/Neptune

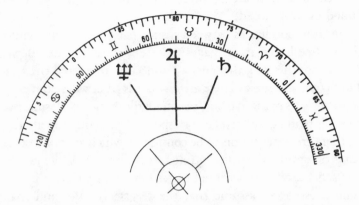

Figure 40. Jupiter at the midpoint of Saturn and Neptune.

or, in brief, JU = SA/NE. Another way of putting it is to say that Jupiter is at the half-sum of Saturn and Neptune. In calculating the half-sum, it is helpful to count from the first point of Aries in each case.

Thus, Saturn at 28° Aries = 28°; Neptune at 14° Gemini = 74° (30° Aries + 30° Taurus + 14° Gemini = 74° from the first point of Aries). Their sum is 102°, and therefore their half-sum is 51° = 21° Taurus, the position of Jupiter. Such a laborious calculation as this will seldom be performed, however, since it is easier to use our special calculator (the 90° dial) and slide rule.

JU = SA/NE is a direct midpoint. Now, if the Sun were at 21° Aquarius, it would be square SA/NE, and the latter would be an indirect midpoint. At one time, we made a distinction between direct and indirect midpoints, but this has turned out to be unnecessary, as numerous examples will show.

The Ninety-Degree Dial

The usual piece of equipment is made of plastic and has a screw in the center of the inscribed zodiac in order to secure it to the rule. The half-sums are measured on the rule, as are the distances between the positions of the planets, in order to determine at what age the various combinations are activated. The handling of the equipment will be explained as we proceed.

The correspondences between cosmic patterns and the symptoms of disease (see Table A on pages 359–368) must not be allowed to delude us into thinking that cursory inspection of a natal chart can be used to diagnose disease. There are cases, it is true, where the evidence immediately strikes the eye but, generally speaking, the cosmic pattern of disease is made up of several correspondences acting together. Then again, there are other factors to be considered which are not susceptible of being determined cosmically (e.g., telluric rays). Whenever a disease presents itself, the essential correspondences will also be found; but one must never assume that the reverse is true, and that the correspondences will always materialize in the form of disease. They should be treated more as indications of what to avoid or prevent. If the life-style is natural and healthy, individual aspects will do little harm; it is only through persistent wrong feeding, stimulant and drug abuse, or over-indulgence in sport, that trouble starts. Further information will be found in my comprehensive work, *Kosmobiologische Diagnostik* (Cosmobiological Diagnosis).[71]

The disease correspondences have been numbered for easy reference. DC followed by a number stands for the given disease correspondence. For example, if you see (DC 17) in the text in the following sections, this means that you should refer to Table A, number 17 and see the disease correspondence.

Determining the Predisposition to Disease

On leafing through the relatively few books on astromedicine, one finds numerous rules but no advice on how to proceed systematically. Now, although an experienced practitioner will often recognize the significant patterns at first sight, the novice can easily go wrong. An endeavor must therefore be made to start from the general situation, from the picture presented by the chart as a whole.

In order to do this I have prepared a table to make this work as easy as possible. (See Table 17 on page 170.) As the reader no doubt remembers, we have already used this scheme in our sample chart. In this particular case, the positive (or Yang signs) contained nine factors, as against three factors in the negative (or Yin) signs. Using the key for type composition already supplied (see page 153), we obtain eighteen points for Yang but only six points for Yin.

On coming to the aspects, we must also distinguish between planets with positive and those with negative characters. Finally, we have to list the midpoints and underline those having a particular bearing on disease.

When all these findings have been tabulated, the following synopsis is obtained:

1) The individual belongs to the Yang type, which is very active and lively and, when ill, tends to suffer mostly from acute diseases associated with fever, sudden spasms and colics, etc.

2) The heavy occupation of air signs points to a sanguine or LA type with a bilious-sanguine constitution. Since Gemini and Libra are especially strongly tenanted, and the planets in them exhibit close mutual aspects, there could be a predisposition to diseases characteristic of Gemini and Libra, such as pulmonary disease, nervous disorders or diseases of the kidneys, bladder and lumbar region.

3) Among the strong aspects, we note those between the Sun, Jupiter, and Mars giving warning of blood diseases, and of disorders of the circulation, liver and gallbladder. The Venus/Uranus aspect points to glandular problems, especially where the kidneys are concerned. Neptune/MC hints at professional disappointments and at limited opportunities for development, so that the mental reaction could have a deleterious effect on the weaker organs.

4) Of midpoint aspects listed in Table 17 on page 170, those underlined are particularly important. For full details, my book *Kombination der Gestirneinflüsse* should be consulted, although the essential correspondences have already been given here. MA = VE/SA, which was not set down in our list, suggests suppression of the internal secretions, and glandular problems (kidneys).

Table 17. Cosmobiological Table of Predispositions to Disease

Name: *XY, civil servant*			Disease: *Renal colic*		
Date of birth: 10.9.1898			Hr.: 4:30 A.M.		
Place: 50°36′ N/17°12′ E					
Sign occupation:					
Aries		0	Taurus		0
Gemini	♇♆M	5	Cancer	♂	2
Leo	☾	3	Virgo	A	3
Libra	☿☉♃	6	Scorpio		0
Sagittarius	♀⛢♄	4	Capricorn	☊	1
Aquarius		0	Pisces		0
Elements:					
Fire		7	Earth		4 (11)
Air		11	Water		2 (13)
Positive total:		18	Negative total:		6
Yang (+)		18	YIN (–)		6
Aspects:					
			Lunar nodes		
Sun	☌♃□♂∠♀∠⛢		Moon	∠♇	
Mars	□☉□♃⚼♀		Venus	☌⛢∠☉⚼♂	
Jupiter	☌☉□♂		Neptune	☌M□A	
Uranus	∠☉☌♀		Saturn	–	
Pluto	∠☾		Mercury		
MC	☌♆	13	ASC	□♆	7
Midpoints:					
SU =	♃/☊–♂/☊–♀–⛢		MO =	♇–♄/♆–♄/M–♄/A	
MA =	♃–☽/☿–♀/♄–♄/⛢		VE =	⛢–☉–♃/☊–♂/☊	
JU =	♂–☽/☿–♀/♄–♄/⛢		NE =	M–A–☿♄–♂♃/♀⛢	
UR =	☉–♃/☊–♂/☊–♀		SA =	♀/♇–⛢/♇–☽/♃	
PL =	♄/♆–♄/M–♄/A–☉/♀⛢–☾		ME =	♂♃/♆M–☾/♇	
MC =	♆–A–♀/♄–♂♃/♀⛢		AS =	M–♆–♄/☊–♂♃/♀⛢	
Remarks:					

If a certain midpoint aspect can not be found in Table A in the Appendix, we take the meaning of the midpoint itself — in the above instance this was DC 59 = VE/SA.

The midpoints listed below are those we would be concerned with. The disease correspondence comes from Table A.

MA = SA/UR : Injury, accident, operation (DC 113)
PL = SA/NE : Serious disease, chronic suffering (DC 123)
PL = SA/MC : Ego disorders, lack of perseverance (DC 132)
PL = SA/AS : Suffering from repression
MC = MA/UR : Injury, accident, operation (DC 88)
MO = SA/NE : Depression (DC 117)
MO = SA/MC : Mental suffering, depression (DC 134)
SA = MO/JU : Disease of liver or gallbladder (DC 29)
ME = MA/NE : Nervous debility, abuse of vital energy (DC 91)

Tendencies to develop certain diseases cannot manifest themselves until activated by directions or transits. This principle, which hardly receives a mention in most textbooks, is very important since it supplies a general key to the history of a disease. In our example chart, everything depends on the activation of the following essential configurations:

Venus/Uranus/Sun
Jupiter/Mars
Pluto/Moon
Neptune/MC/ASC

The quickest and shortest way of making a synopsis is as follows: consult the ephemeris for the year in question, in this instance 1898, and see if there are any significant aspects to the radix made 30 and 60 days after birth. These are the progressions, or secondary directions, and are based on the day-for-a-year system. Thus the 30th day after birth represents the 30th year of life and the 60th day represents the 60th year of life.

On the 30th day after birth, or October 9th, there is nothing of much interest. Mars is 3° Leo and has therefore made a conjunction with the natal Moon, which could affect the years leading up to age 30. The native did not recall anything particularly worth mentioning for this period however.

The 60th year of life is represented, near enough, by the 8th of December. Uranus is at 4° Sagittarius, having just made a semisquare to Jupiter, and is approaching a sesquisquare to Mars.

Saturn is 14°57' Sagittarius and will soon be in opposition to Pluto = Saturn/Neptune! At the same time, it is approaching a sesquisquare to the Moon. Jupiter is 2° Scorpio and has just made a square to the Moon. Now we have to remember that the effects of such progressed aspects become apparent many years before they are exact; so that SA_p-180-PL = SA/NE can make itself felt long before the 60th year of life.

The second method for pinpointing events or diseases is by using solar arc, which amounts to ca. one degree for each year of life. The special rule can be used to discover whether there are any special aspects for the 30th year of life. It will be found that, at age 32, Pluto reaches the Sun on the 90° dial, and so therefore does the SA/NE midpoint with which Pluto is already in aspect. At around 35 years of age, the AS, MC, NE complex approaches the Moon. Around 30 years of age, the Moon joins Venus and Uranus in a semisquare to the Sun, and Saturn transits Mercury. Thus, within the compass of a few years, there are a number of possibilities of disease.

So what actually occurred? In 1932 the native suffered from an attack of renal colic, which is signified in the cosmogram by the heavy tenancy of Libra and by the conjunction of Venus and Uranus. The colic persisted until 1938.

In 1959, at age 69, the native became ill with jaundice and, in the end, a gallbladder operation was required. As has already been seen, progressed Saturn approaches Pluto in opposition in this year; also the progressed Sun has transited Pluto while making a sesquisquare to the Moon. Therefore significant patterns were activated during this period. What is more, Saturn$_s$ (s = advanced with solar arc) and Mars$_s$ link up with the AS, MC, NE complex. On the 24th of September 1962, the native suffered from heart failure initiated by Mars at 20° Cancer conjunct Mars square Jupiter, and to Mercury being stationary in 21° Libra after making a square to Mars.

This, then, should give the reader some idea of how to work out the indications of disease. In Part Three, we will go in depth into the elements of cosmobiological practice, and provide several case studies for further study.

PART THREE

COSMOBIOLOGICAL PRACTICE

CHAPTER SEVEN

CHART DIAGNOSIS AND CONSULTATION

T HE PLANETARY PATTERNS SHOULD BE RE-
garded as no more than an aid to diagnosis, because a full
diagnosis and prognosis are not possible on a cosmobiological basis alone. An anamnesis, or case history, must always
be available for reference, since the radix (or natal chart) tells us
nothing about heredity, environment, family and contemporary life,
etc. A chart diagnosis may hit the bull's-eye but may also be wide of
the mark. During a consultation, significant facts can emerge which
are important for advice and treatment and, to drive this home, I am
going to let the reader sit in with me, so to speak, at a typical
consultation.

Following a recommendation from a doctor friend of mine, I was
visited by a lady who had already consulted several physicians and
had taken various tests without positive results. She explained that
she was partly well but, then again, quite unwell.

I pencilled in the planetary positions for her day of birth without
making an exact calculation for the moment. This took no more than
five minutes. I at once noticed a Mercury/Sun/Saturn complex with
an opposition from Venus. The lady certainly did not give the
impression that she felt in any way inhibited by the aspect of the Sun

and Saturn, but the fact did emerge that she had not been able to develop as she would have liked. She had a husband considerably younger than herself (Venus/Saturn can mean a big age difference) who left her much on her own and did not behave very affectionately toward her. This was fully in line with the Venus/Saturn aspect; which was only a semisquare of the sort that is often disregarded, yet is highly significant in my work, as I have already pointed out.

Since Pluto was at the midpoints Sun/Moon = Moon/Uranus = Venus/Mars, and Mars was at Venus/Saturn, I inquired whether she had any children, knowing that these planetary patterns either deny a birth or else correspond to very difficult births. I also asked if she had undergone any major surgery. In reply, she mentioned four miscarriages and an abdominal operation.

The husband's chart had a Venus/Mars conjunction which was aspected by the wife's Pluto. From this and other constellations, it could be concluded that he was not only very passionate but also brutal and inconsiderate. It emerged during the interview that he never took his wife with him on business trips because he liked to enjoy himself with other women.

The consultation revealed that, apart from the usual problems associated with the change of life, there was nothing wrong with this lady, but that there was an urgent need to take the stress out of her relationship with her husband, by arranging for a doctor to have a frank talk with him or by referring the couple to a marriage guidance counselor.

● ● ●

On another occasion, a man brought his 27 year old daughter to me. The latter was unsure of herself and was dissatisfied with her occupation; what is more she did not seem able to find the right partner. A glance at the aspects in her chart showed a Jupiter/Saturn/Moon stellium in Taurus square Mars. The degrees of Taurus involved were 16° and 17°, which can have a lot to do with the thyroid gland. My first question, therefore, was whether she had had any problems with her tonsils or thyroid gland. She answered in the affirmative. My next question was, "Weren't you under treatment during 1962 and 1963?" She confirmed this as well. The inquiry was prompted by the fact that in the years concerned, Neptune had made an aspect to the points mentioned, thus giving the possibility of ill-health. Careful and judicious interrogation helped to confirm other surmises.

Since there was apparently none of the reticence often associated with Moon conjunct Saturn, I thought their conjunction might imply some disorder of the digestive apparatus, especially the stomach. The young lady admitted that she had already suffered from gastric ulcers and that her digestion left much to be desired.

She told me that a number of her friendships had been broken, this being further evidence of the effect of the Moon/Saturn conjunction, which is liable to bring estrangements and separations together with a sense of isolation. I learned that this scientific assistant was deskbound much of the time; this was not good for her since the above mentioned aspects are a sign of digestive disorders brought on by underactivity.

This example illustrates how use of the cosmogram can provide an opportunity to ask pertinent questions and to elicit answers that many clients might otherwise hold back.

The potential value of these studies to the physician and lay practitioner may be seen in the following case. An elderly physician with whom I had been associated for many years, and who was conversant with my methods, phoned me one evening with some very interesting news. Before saying what it was, I must mention that this doctor owned a small sanatorium and that whenever a patient applied for admission he immediately prepared their Cosmogram and Annual Curve.

Well, to return to our story, one day a patient was brought to him in whose chart he found a severe crisis indicated for the next few days. He therefore declined to accept the responsibility and had the man admitted to hospital. Three days later he received news that the man died. If the death had occurred in his private clinic, he might easily have become embroiled in litigation. His cosmobiological knowledge had saved him from this.

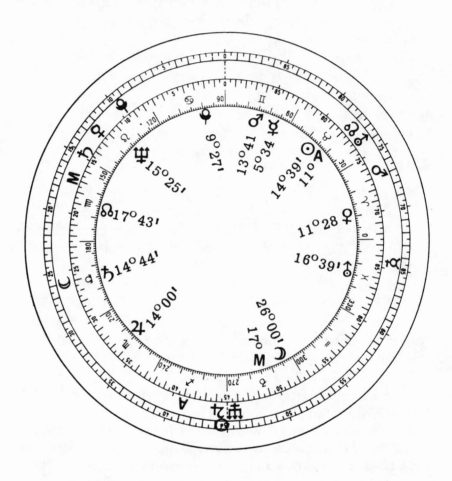

Figure 41. Cosmogram for Inge Lehmann, born May 6, 1923. Birth data withheld for confidentiality.

Calculating a Nativity

In the Federal German Republic, some forty thousand handicapped children are born every year. They are a heavy mental and financial burden on their parents and require costly assistance from the state. Professor G. Wendt of Marburg, at a convention of the Evangelical Academy, Loccum, in November 1975 spoke on the topic of "Genetics and Health" and said, "In our eagerness to help the handicapped, we have failed to consider the possibility of preventing people being handicapped in the first place."

This possibility is put on a cosmobiological basis when procreation is undertaken at a certain time. (Further light on the subject can be found in a memorandum of the Cosmobiological Academy, Aalen, on "The Prevention of Down's Syndrome." Researcher Erich Modersohn of Lippstadt did much of the spadework for this.) The point can be illustrated by the birth of a handicapped child and the cosmobiologically calculated birth of a healthy one.

The children's mother, whom I shall call Inge Lehmann, was born on the May 6th, 1923 (see figure 41 on page 180). She married at the age of 27 and two years later bore a child who, because one of the parents was Rhesus negative, did not develop normally, and had to be placed in an institution. When the child was 4 years old the father died and it was a long time before the mother could bring herself to remarry. She eventually did so at the age of 38. The man was not completely healthy but he did want to have a child. "A marriage without a child is not a marriage at all!" he said. But his wife had a nagging fear that a second child would also be abnormal. The family had had great confidence in me for many years and asked whether it would not be possible to calculate a propitious conception date. The first task was to investigate the cosmograms of the mother and of the handicapped child. The mother is of the Yin SI type. Using the 90° dial, we immediately recognize the association of Venus with Pluto and Saturn, and of Saturn with the MC. The Jupiter/Sun-Neptune complex is not good either, and there is a distinct possibility of difficult or defective births (VE = SA/PL) and of disappointments in love and marriage. Doubts are also raised by UR = DR = SA/NE and MA = SA/NE and by VE/NE.

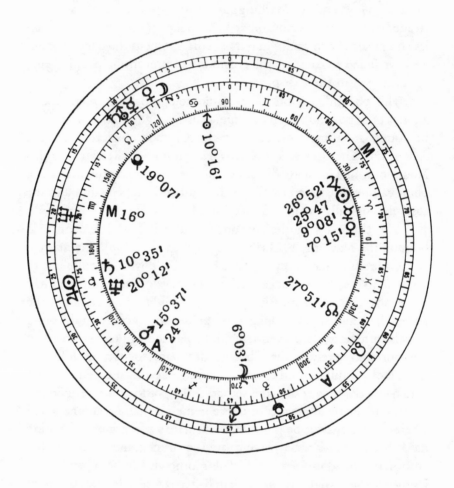

Figure 42. Cosmogram for Marta, born April 15, 1952. Birth data withheld for confidentiality.

When Marta was born on the 15th of April 1952, the progressed Sun in the mother's cosmogram had reached the place of Mars, which was a critical place in the chart. In Marta's own cosmogram (see figure 42 on page 182), we are struck by the fact that on the 90° dial, the Moon/Venus/Mercury/Uranus/Saturn complex coincides with the Pluto/Venus/Saturn/MC complex of the mother. UR = ME/SA signifies diseases of the nerves in the child (DC 46). In *Kombination der Gestirneinflüsse* (*The Combination of Stellar Influences*), we read for ME/SA, "Nerve-block, affections of the organs of speech and hearing." At the time of this writing (1978), the child, though fully grown, is still living in an institution, has not been able to learn anything and can do only simple manual work. At the 45th degree, the child's Mars is covered by the mother's Jupiter, Sun and Neptune. At the 76th degree, the child's MC stands at the midpoints MA/UR = SA/NE. It is easy to see that extraordinarily critical constellations affected both mother and child at the time of birth. No wonder the mother feared to bear another child. Nevertheless, the life diagram looks hopeful.

The Life Diagram

On the 90° dial all the conjunctions, squares and oppositions come together in the same place. Yet it has been found that the 45° and 135° aspects (the semisquare and sesquisquare) are also very significant. Because they are harder to recognize, they used to be ignored. But if we substitute a 45° dial for the 90° dial, they will leap to the eye just as clearly as squares and oppositions do in the latter. When the zodiac is divided into eighths, the starting point for the 45° dial will lie at 0° Aries, Cancer, Libra and Capricorn, and at 15° Taurus, Leo, Scorpio and Aquarius. In the Life Diagram, this partition will be shown on the left of the diagram. In our example (see figure 43 on page 184), the first column is the key to the positions of Venus, Pluto, Saturn, MC and the Moon, the second column to those of the Sun and Neptune, the third column to those of Mercury, Mars, Uranus, and lunar nodes, etc. These positions are plotted on the graph and the planetary curves are drawn from left to right.

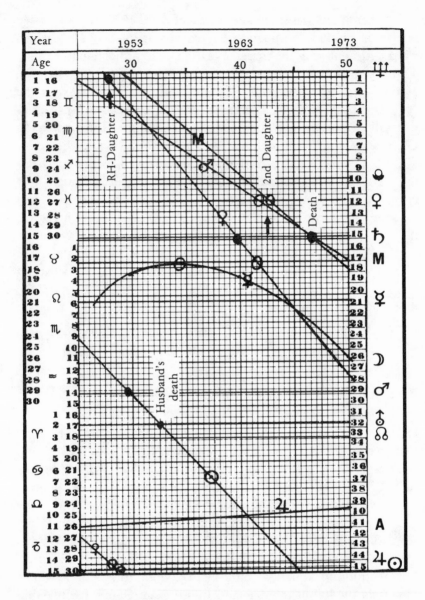

Figure 43. Life Diagram for Inge Lehmann. Note the birth of her first daughter, who was handicapped, the death of her first husband, the birth of her second daughter, and her own death.

It would be unwieldy to reproduce more than a short section of the Life Diagram here, so we will commence at the 30th year of life. The paths of the planets are plotted from the 30th day after birth, i.e. June 5th, 1923, and their positions are marked for every ten days (representing years). See figure 43. The positive constellations are identified by small open circles, the negative ones by black dots. In this way a survey of the entire life can be made.

A small orb must always be allowed for the individual constellations. Usually these constellations begin to make their influence felt before they are exact. With the swiftly moving planets, this can happen one or two years in advance. When the slow moving planets aspect one another, the effect can appear as much as ten years or more ahead of time.

At the birth of the first daughter, the path of progressed Venus is crossing the line of radical Neptune at the place of a critical midpoint between Mars and Saturn in the mother's radix. (The paths of the progressed planets take the form of curves or sloping lines and are labeled inside the graph with the symbols of their planets; the positions of the radical planets are shown by horizontal lines and are identified by their respective symbols in a separate column to the right of the graph.) Already the contact of Venus with Neptune underscores the disappointment in love and marriage created by the birth of a handicapped child. Lower down the chart, the Sun is crossing the position-line of Mars, which is also the disease midpoint of Saturn and Neptune. Finally, at the very bottom of the chart, Venus is crossing the position-lines of Jupiter and the Sun. This represents the birth, but Neptune gives it a negative character.

Now the couple was thinking of having a second child. This is shown around 1965/1966 by the passage of progressed Mars and MC over the position-line of Venus; a direction that was influential on the following investigation into the possibility of calculating a suitable time for another conception and birth. What was required was to find, within the years mentioned, a point in time that would favor conception and birth—a time that would be troubled by as few negative aspects as possible during pregnancy.

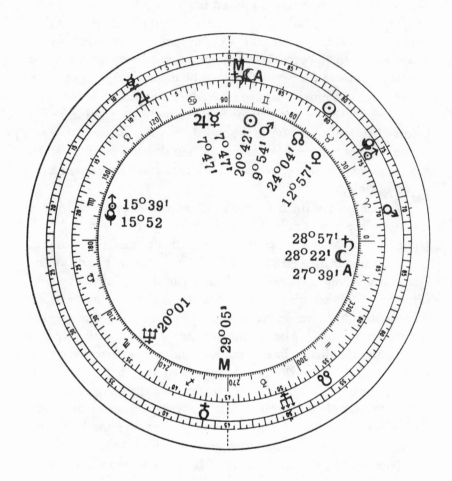

Figure 44. Cosmogram for Sabine, born June 11, 1966. Birth data withheld for confidentiality.

The Annual Diagram

During World War II, I carried on quietly and developed the graphic 45° ephemerides, which has been improved a number of times since. The graphic 45° ephemeris has proved particularly useful in recent decades.[72]

To return now to our married couple, after I had reviewed the year using the Annual Diagram, September, 1965 seemed to be the most favorable month, since on September 11th the paths of Mars and Jupiter would meet on the position-lines of Jupiter and the Sun taken from the mother's radix. (See figure 45 on pages 188–189.) In addition there were overlappings, such as Mercury on Venus and the MC, Venus on the Moon, Venus on Mars, the midpoint Venus/Mars on Uranus, and the Sun on the North Node. Saturn's path had already intersected the position-line of the Moon, and Uranus and Pluto were approaching the position-line of Uranus.

I warned the couple to remain continent before this date, as the time was one of great procreative energy. After exactly 273 days, the normal period of gestation, the second daughter, Sabine, was born on June 11, 1966. (See figure 44.)

When this child's chart is superimposed on that of her mother, quite another picture emerges from the one seen with the first child. The girl's Jupiter and Mercury coincide with the mother's Pluto, the child's Venus falls on the mother's Sun and Jupiter, and (less favorably) the child's Uranus and Pluto are in the same place as the mother's Uranus and North Node. The parents were overjoyed at the birth of their daughter.

Now you probably have already noticed in the life diagram of the mother that the progressed movements of Mars and the MC to the position-line of Saturn presaged her own premature death. In Sabine's cosmogram, the early separation from her mother is indicated by the Moon/Saturn conjunction. The child's cosmogram is not without its problems, but the wish of the parents was fulfilled.

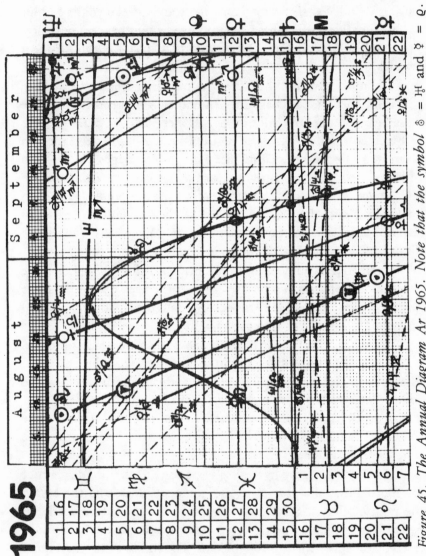

Figure 45. The Annual Diagram Ar 1965. Note that the symbol ♅ = ♅ and ♇ = ♀.

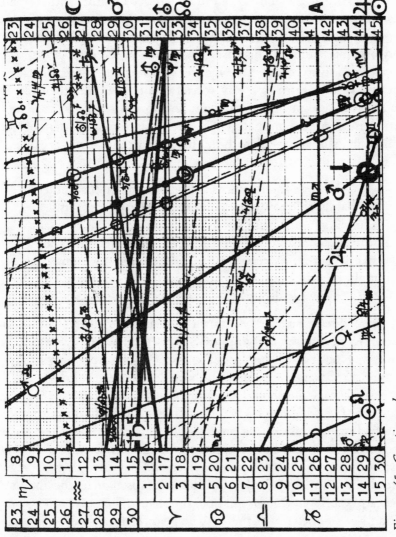

Figure 45. Continued.

Smoking Mother, Ailing Child

Anyone who was present at the 29th Conference for Cosmobiological Research held at Aalen in 1977 will remember a mother with a small deformed boy. The mother gave me a long account of her troubles together with a photo of the child, so that it was possible to make a very accurate study of this case. (Incidentally, the case shows how important it is to consider the mother's natal chart as well as that of the child, for a birth is a very special event for the mother and is bound to figure in her cosmogram; and this fact will facilitate any birth-time rectification that may be needed in the cosmogram of the child.) So in order to work with this problem we can learn a great deal from the mother's statements.

> The boy's abdomen has become so swollen that his legs are hardly able to support him. He is always tired, listless, and whimpering, and sleeps a great deal; he has frequent stomachaches and pains in the head and bones. He is constantly perspiring, his arms and legs often go numb, at night he tosses and turns, moans and talks gibberish. During the day his sleep is more peaceful.

The disease he had is known as Gaucher's disease and is a deformity in children that implicates the central nervous system. It is a rare metabolic disorder thought to be incurable. According to conventional medicine, the child had been "no longer clinically viable" for several years and should "scientifically speaking" have been long dead. For five years he had ben treated by a lay medical practitioner and had made considerable progress. The main worry was the huge abdomen, 32 inches in circumference at the navel. All the organs were displaced by tumors of the liver and spleen. His heart had already been lifted to the level of the third costal arch, and the boy constantly suffered from respiratory problems. The cause of his condition was a deficiency of the enzyme glycocerebrosidase, which was down to fourteen percent. Consequently, an aliphatic saccharide in the body was not broken down and accumulated in the spleen, liver, bone marrow, lungs and brain. Its main storage place was the spleen. The lungs still seemed to have been spared. The marrow had almost disappeared; at least it had not been possible to extract any by puncture the previous summer. Obviously the disease was genetic, but the mother imagined that the child had been injured at birth and that she had—unwittingly—poisoned him over the years.

She wrote:

When my son was due to come into the world, some other mother was getting most of the attention. The midwife just let me lie there and told me to hold back the contractions, but I did not quite manage it; the baby's head kept bumping against my pelvis. I was totally exhausted and must have fainted. Suddenly a doctor lay across my tummy and pressed with all his weight, while a second doctor forced my head into the pillow and then pulled me up so that my neck and spine nearly snapped. All at once I was still. One of the doctors wanted to perform a cesarean section, the other was against it. The process began again. Once more I lost my strength. Then I heard the sister say that the heart had stopped beating and I thought the child was dead. At that instant I had no more pain and I saw myself lying in the bed while hovering over myself [apparently she experienced an OBE in which her spirit left her physical body]. Then I returned. A doctor said I had a son. However, I did not manage to see my child; he was so feeble that they had wasted no time in transferring him to another ward. When I did see him, he was bright red and would not stop crying; every now and then he had a fit of convulsions. The lady doctor said that the boy was not red but was suffering from a severe rash. Bottle-feeding did not suit him. It was then that I must have started poisoning him with the milk from my breasts. When he was three years old he started hemorrhaging, two years later he became mentally disturbed and, when he was 6, no longer knew his name. A year later the naturopath started treating him. The boy had to enter the class for handicapped children. He had to be kept on a strict diet. When, in the summer of 1976, he ate some sausage and pork again, the rash broke out once more. His abdomen swelled by about four inches.

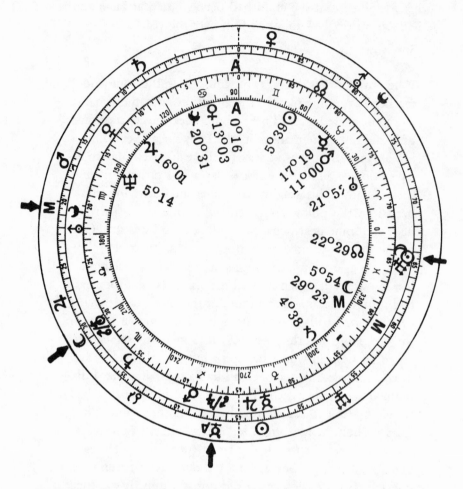

Declinations			
☉ = 21°16N	☾ = 10°49S	☿ = 15°07N	♀ = 25°48N
♂ = 14°40N	♃ = 16°54N	♄ = 19°24S	☊ = 7°58N
♆ = 10°20N	♇ = 22°31N	M = 11°41S	A = 23°27N

Figure 46. Cosmogram for mother, born May 27, 1932, at 6 A.M. in Munich, W. Germany.

Before we start investigating the cosmograms for mother and son, the report must be analyzed. The facts described imply that the causes of the disease lie in the mother and also that mistakes were made when the baby was being born. We have the following dates for the mother: born May 27th, 1932, at 6 A.M. according to the Munich registry. On October 12th, 1948, she had her first period. On December 1st, 1952, there occurred the suicide attempt of a boyfriend. She said, "I was so upset that for three days I smoked so much that I became an addict. I did not feel I was to blame, but I was the reason for the attempt; I suffered greatly over it and was anxious about him." (Here is where the cause could lie for everything that happened later.) On July 18th 1962, she had an appendix operation and several attacks of shortness of breath. (The child suffered from these, too, later on.) On February 24th 1966, she had a tonsillectomy and suffered more breathing problems. She married in 1966 as well. On August 14th 1966, she went on a mountain trip without realizing she was pregnant. The child was born on May 8th 1967. On August 6th 1976, she was short of breath and became exhausted but refused to take valium (very wisely, since valium can have serious side effects).

When looking at the mother's consmogram, we are immediately struck by the Neptune/Sun/Moon complex opposite Uranus and Pluto on the 90° dial (SU-90-NE-90-MO-45-PL-45-UR, or SU = UR/PL = MO/NE). At the same time, among the declinations, MO/NE is approximately MO-180-NE. Aspects between planets having the same declinations, i.e., between those that are equidistant from the equator, must be regarded as particularly powerful. (See figure 46 on page 192.)

The crucial constellations have been set out in a 90° wheel on their own (see figure 47 on page 194). We take the following notes from *Kombination der Gestirneinflüsse* (*The Combination of Stellar Influences*) and from the disease correspondences: affliction through mental suffering, sudden upsets, cramps and convulsions, sudden events in the circle of friends (the suicide attempt!) and in the marriage, sensitivity, susceptibility to influences, etc. The blows of fate early on are also indicated by MA = JU/SA.

These constellations begin to take effect at age 20 in 1952, when PL$_s$-90-MA becomes exact. It is not only Pluto that is involved near

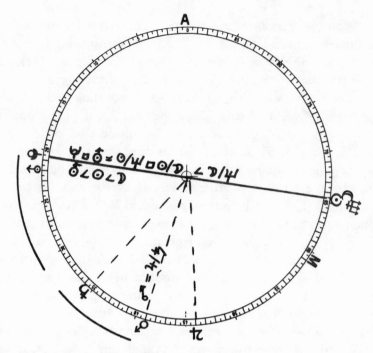

Figure 47. Cosmogram for the mother on the 90° dial.

this 20th degree, but the whole complex in which the planet is found. PL-90-MA points to some act of violence, in this instance the suicide of the friend. NE$_s$-135-MA means addictions (according to No. 722 in *The Combination of Stellar Influences*). The addiction and its consequences are also indicated by SU/NE (COSI No. 266),* SU = NE/PL (COSI No. 999) and ME = MA/NE (COSI No. 725). The last-mentioned constellation is valid because ME$_t$ — almost stationary — activates the entire complex at 6° Sagittarius. The various constellations also point to disorders of the body's fluid balance and to blood disease (through addiction). The likelihood of there being foci of infection in the body due to the strong Neptunian constellation is confirmed by the appendix and tonsil operations.

The powerful disease complex, which is especially noticeable in the life diagram (see figure 48 on page 195), is ever menacing. Around 1967, Mars$_P$ transited the complex, so that a severe setback

---

*COSI from now on refers to *The Combination of Stellar Influences*.

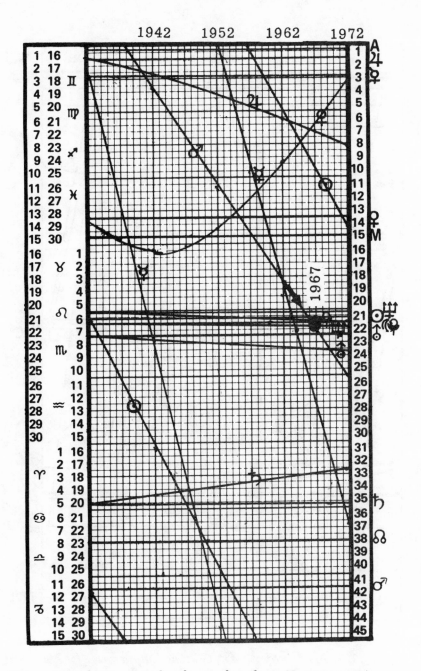

Figure 48. Life Diagram for the mother (born May 27, 1932).

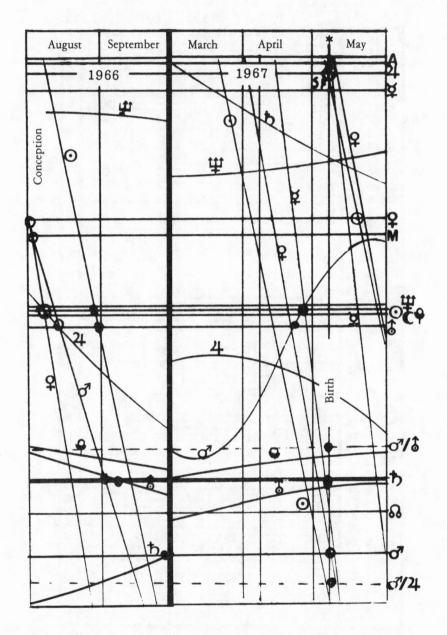

Figure 49. A portion of the 45° Graphic Emphemeris for 1966 and 1967. This shows the conception.

would be expected at that time. There is a link, too, with the 1952 direction of Mars to the complex. To judge by the planetary pattern, this was no occasion for risking conception.

The crisis becomes even clearer when you examine the 45° graphic ephemeris for 1966/67. Our excerpt shows the constellations for the times of conception and birth (see figure 49 on page 196). Presumably, conception took place under the transits of Venus and Mars over the position-lines of Venus and the MC. In the days that followed, thus during the strenuous mountain holiday, Venus, Jupiter, and Mars transited the disease complex. It will, of course, be remembered that the birth was activated by Mars$_p$ over this complex in the Life Diagram. At the end of April, shortly before the birth on May 8th, Mars again transited the disease complex. Uranus, which contacted Saturn just after conception, now approached Saturn's position-line. The Sun on Jupiter would be regarded as positive, if a solar eclipse had not been due at the same time. Also moving over the disease complex is the MC, although the graphic ephemeris does not show this.

Now it is particularly interesting to note the declinations at birth. The only way to get a good view of them is by using the scheme I devised. See figure 50 on page 198. Here we have, firstly, MO/NE reinforcing MO-180-NE, then ME/MA = SU/UR = UR/PL and JU = NE/PL (impure blood). At the birth, we have MO$_p$//VE and VE$_T$//VE, so that VE has the same declination in both mother and child; SU//PL//ASC, MA$_p$//SU and JU$_T$//SU; JU$_p$//ME and ME$_T$//ASC$_T$//ME, so that ME, too, corresponds in mother and child. In the parallels of the child, the disease constellations SU//NE, SA = SU/NE and MA = UR/NE preponderate. Their evidence points to low powers of resistance, misapplied energy, paralysis, handicap and misery.

In the radix of the handicapped child there are many critical constellations, in which there are indications of two tumors. (By a tumor we mean a swelling or growth at a place where it is not supposed to be. It can be a malignant, cancerous growth from the size of a pea to the size of a human head.) We should therefore look for constellations associated with cancer, constellations which will be examined in more detail later. The relevant aspects (shown in figure 51 on page 199) are between PL, NE, SA and the personal points

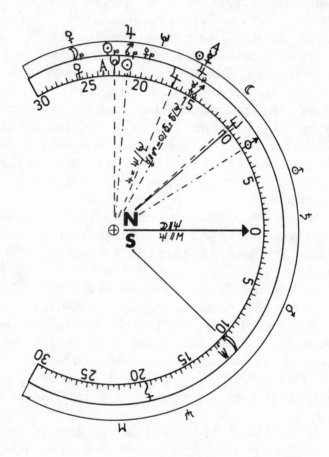

Figure 50. Declination Diagram of the mother. On the declination midpoint dial, the inner circle registers the natal positions, and the outer circle shows the current positions of the declinations.

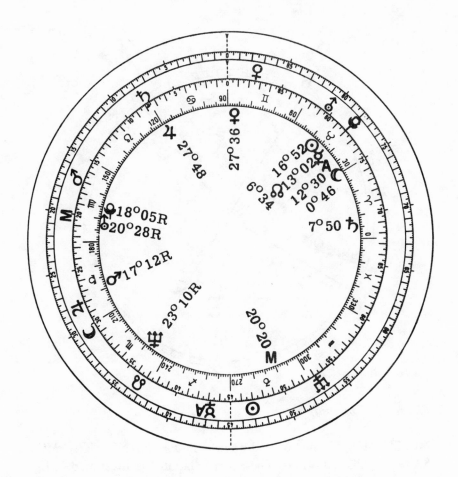

Declinations			
☉ = 16°53N	☾ = 11°38N	☿ = 15°08N	♀ = 25°41N
♂ = 5°43S	♃ = 21°10N	♄ = 1°08N	☊ = 4°30N
♅ = 16°50S	♇ = 18°43N	M = 21°55S	A = 15°36N

Figure 51. Cosmogram for unhealthy child born May 8, 1967, at 4:40 A.M., Munich, W. Germany.

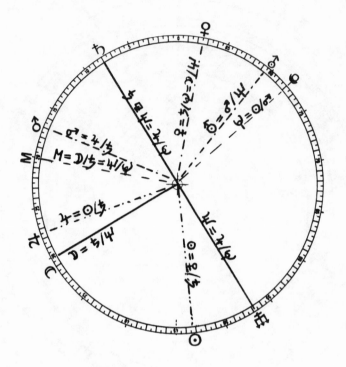

Figure 52. The midpoints.

MC, SU, MO. On the 90° dial we have MO = SA/NE, MC = MO/
SA = NE/PL and others. These constellations are illustrated in figure 52.

From an inspection of the planetary positions on the day of birth
as shown on the graphic 45° ephemeris (figure 53 on page 201) it
appears, to begin with, that the nativity coincides with an aspect
between Venus and Mercury shortly before an eclipse of the Sun. In
the first days of life, corresponding to the first years of life, the paths
of Saturn and Neptune cross, but luckily move off in different directions. Pluto remains for a whole week at SU/MA, where it indicates
inflammations and heart trouble. What is more, for a whole week
(interpreted as a decade), Uranus does not leave the midpint MA/
NE, signifying continual weakness and the consequences of poisons

derived from the mother—seen initially in a rash covering the entire body. (If expectant mothers smoke immoderately or take too many medicaments, the baby's body is often covered in a rash.) There is some hope of improvement in the years after puberty when Jupiter$_p$ squares MO, although, of course, MO = SA/NE is unfavorable here.

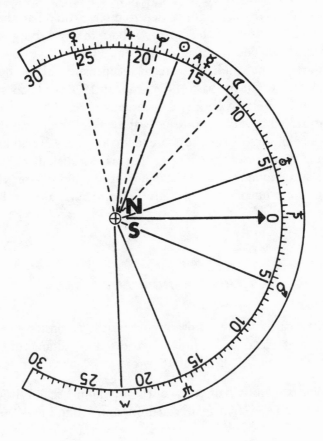

Figure 53. The unhealthy child born May 8, 1967, on the 45° Declination Midpoint Dial.

Since toxins were present in the child's body right from the start, the best course of action would have been to try and eliminate them; instead of which, wrong treatment seems to have made matters worse. A physician or naturopath schooled in cosmobiology would have immediately recognized the fundamentally toxic condition and would have adopted the appropriate measures. Better still would have been to start treating the mother before she became pregnant. Top priority should be given to persuading women to give up smoking, since the habit always loads the body with poisons which can be transferred to the child.

As was subsequently discovered, the boy's father, too, was unhealthy, so that a predisposition to disease could have been inherited from him as well. The father was born to Regensburg on October 25th 1934, at about 11:30 A.M. On August 6th 1965, two years before the birth of the child, he suffered a concussion of the brain and a double fracture at the base of the skull. In 1970, he had a severe rash which started on his back and eventually covered his body; this was accompanied by chills and fever, watery, fetid stools, ear discharges, nausea, vomiting, loss of appetite, and thirst. In 1971 all his hair fell out and he had to wear a toupee. He became diabetic. Even though the last-mentioned diseases did not appear until after the child's birth, the tendency to suffer from them must already have been there.

"I Don't Want a Dead Child!"

The next case also shows how important it is to consider the mother's natal chart if we are to judge a diseased condition correctly. The mother, whom I shall call Mary, wrote in a letter dated July 1975:

> For two-and-a-half years, our son [whom I shall call John] has suffered from anxiety neurosis and compulsions. He has received medical treatment a number of times. Six weeks ago, we were informed that there is little chance of improvement. However, we have refused to give up hope, seeing he is our only child. We have already spent a small

fortune on treatment and have now consulted a hypnotherapist. Our son was always a nervous child, and frightened of anything new.

Three years ago, in 1972, an accident gave John a shock; since then he developed a desire for cleanliness which has degenerated into a terrible obsession. The life he leads, owing to his condition, is almost unbearable. We could certainly do with some hope of his recovery.

A second letter, in reply to a request for further information, contained the following:

The accident occurred on July 2nd 1973. Four weeks later, my husband and I visited a spa; all John wanted to do was to stay at home. On the day in question, the cellar of our house was under water following an electric storm. The house was flooded. When everything was tidied up, John set out after us. A slow change began to take place in him.

John was very independent and liked to try and get his own way. But when he was 10 years old he had to go into hospital to have his testicles adjusted. His nurse was unsympathetic to children; she treated him roughly and used to hit him and smack him. As a result he developed an anxiety neurosis. She was later dismissed from service.

During my pregnancy, I had a stone in the kidney, and for this reason my child was born six-and-a-half weeks early. The doctor told me that I must be prepared for the child to be stillborn—after we had been thrilled to be having a child! I had endured so much pain in the kidneys that I could not imagine that my child was not alive. I became hysterical and screamed, "I don't want a dead child!" I was fearful for a long time that I might end up losing it. However, the birth—with the exception of a pelvic displacement*—was perfectly normal.

---

*SA at 1° Sagittarius, corresponding to the pelvic bones!

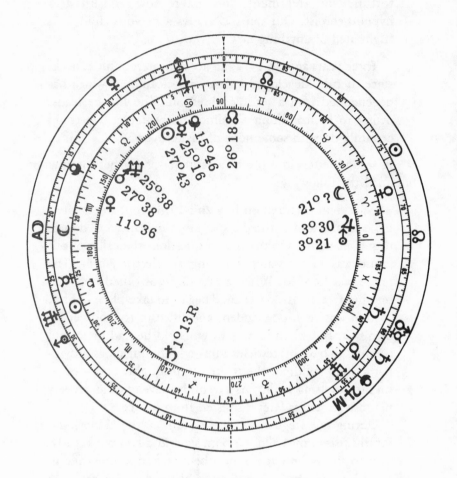

Declinations

☉ = 20°38N	☽ = 5°51N	☿ = 16°14N	♀ = 6°31N
♂ = 13°22N	♃ = 0°0 7N	♄ = 18°31N	☊ = 0°39N
♅ = 13°25N	♇ = 21°23N	M = ° '	A = ° '

Figure 54. Mary, born July 21, 1927. Birth data are incomplete for we have no birth time.

Throughout the whole of May 1975, John was in a psychiatric hospital where he was put on drugs to help him overcome his fear of dirt. But every time he was given the medication he suffered a nervous and circulatory collapse and remained unconscious for three hours. After the third attempt, the treatment was discontinued because he could not tolerate it. The doctors wanted to try something more drastic such as is used on children who are out of control but, rather than submit to that, John left the hospital.

Our cosmobiological investigation must start with the mother's cosmogram (see figure 54 on page 204). As it happens, we have to make do with the planetary positions for July 21st 1927, without knowing the exact time of birth. It is probable that she was born before noon and that the position of her Moon more or less coincides with that of her Sun, because the Moon at 21° AR-180-LI would be appropriate for kidney disease.

When the directions are calculated, we find that SU (on August 19th, 29 days after her birth) is 25° Leo 30' and conjunct Neptune. (See figure 55 on page 206.) This means that in the corresponding year the mother was particularly susceptible to disease and ought not to have considered having a child. In any case, MA-0-NE and MA//NE in the chart show a constant risk of infection. If conception occurred in or around November 1955, then this would be the time when NE_T-90-SU was due.

For the period preceding the birth, we reproduce a copy of the graphic ephemeris for 1956 (see figure 56 on page 207) showing the main planetary paths. It is obvious from this how NE_T moves to SU at the very time of birth, UR having already contacted the position-line of SU. SA cuts the position-lines of SA and PL more than once, and PL moves between the position-lines of MA and NE. The causes of the kidney disease, so far as they are not decided by directions, lie especially in the year-long passage of Neptune through the ME/VE/SU complex. Just prior to the birth, MA crosses the position-line of MA and, on the day of birth, crosses the lines of PL and SA. Disease correspondence No. 126 reads, "Undergoing ill-treatment, having to fight for one's life, catastrophe, operation." The danger of a stillbirth

is evident, and the mother's cry: "I don't want a dead child!" need
not surprise us.

The birth positions for John, the son, are noted in the outer 90°
wheel of the mother's cosmogram. First of all, it is characteristic that
the birth took place when MO and ASC were linked with the mother's MO. NE = SU denotes weakness, SA = MA and MA = SA
reveal the danger to the child's life.

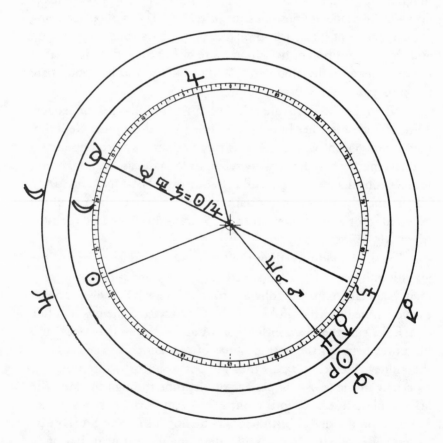

Figure 55. Mary's directions on the 90° dial.

A Life Diagram for the Declinations shows that SU reaches the joint MA/NE line and that the same line is also directly activated by MA_T in the day's constellation. The birth is indicated by MA_P over VE and MO, and JU_P = UR represents to a certain extent the happiness that the child is still breathing. Finally, the agitation accompanying the birth is shown by UR_T = SU on the day in question. Thus one can approach the birth constellations from various angles but will always run into Neptunian aspects, which turn out to be decisive.

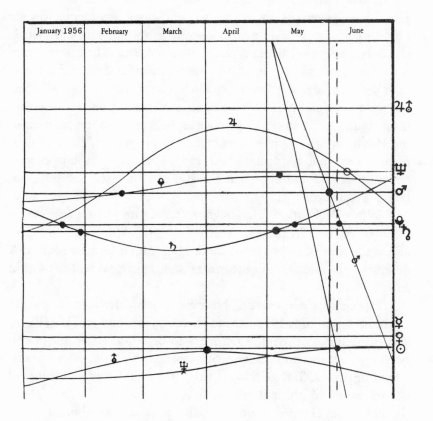

Figure 56. A portion of the Graphic Ephemeris for 1956.

The terrible anxiety over his life was probably communicated from the mother to the child (See figure 58 on page 210.) On extracting the essential constellations from the child's radix (see figure 59 on page 211); we have MO = ASC = SU/SA, which according to COSI No. 243 signifies "depression, anxiety, inferiority feelings." SU = UR/NE corresponds, according to DC No. 137, to "little will to live, sensitivity, disease."

If John's Life Diagram (figure 60 on page 212) is used to study his progressions, we can see when the above mentioned constellation MO = ASC = SU/SA was activated. The first time was when, at age 10, he had an operation on his testicles and used to dread the rough hands of his nurse.

Corresponding to age 17, Mercury crosses MO and ASC = SU/SA. This was when the doctors began their wrong treatment and were keen to perform radical tests on a sensitive and nervous individual. Of course, we would be hard put to it to tell, from the cosomogram alone, that the case is one of obsessional cleanliness. But if we consider SA/ME/MA in the inner circle, we find MA = ME/SA. According to COSI No. 494 this signifies nervous disorders; and that these result from a troubled psyche can be seen from the position of the Moon. Even if there is a temporary improvement, the Life Diagram shows that a further crisis can be expected approximately between ages 22 and 24, when ME and MA_p intersect the position-line of Neptune.

John's Declination Life Diagram (see figure 61 on page 213) is informative, too. In the first years of life JU//MA is still forming, and at the time of the accident shock MA//MO is forming. ME//SA designates the alteration in the mental state, while SA//MC is within an orb of 1°.

Especially characteristic, however, is the declination picture around the July 2nd, 1973. As in the case of the mother, SU //PL, so that in both cases there is a tendency to be self-assertive and domineering. At this time SA and SU move to SU//PL. This means, according to COSI No. 284, firstly "the ruthless overcoming of obstructions and hindrances"—such as occurred when the cellar in the house was flooded—and secondly "physical impediment," i.e., disease. SA//ASC produces difficulties in the environment (ASC). The mother's report contained nothing that would correspond to

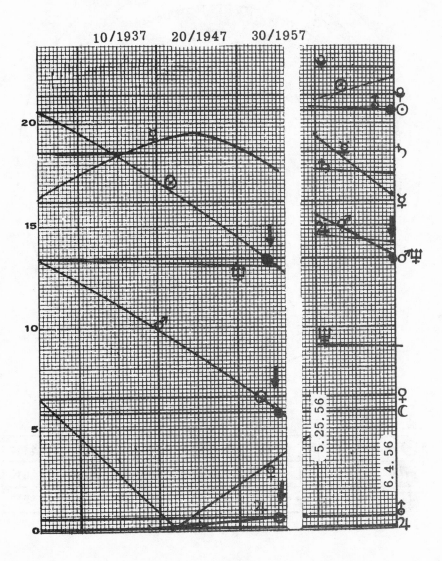

Figure 57. Directions for Mary.

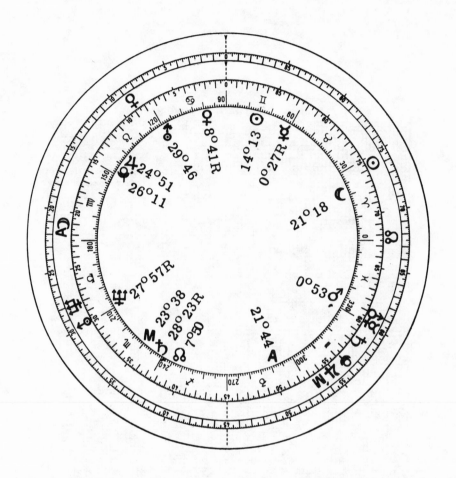

Declinations

☉ = 22°30N	☾ = 11°50N	☿ = 16°33N	♀ = 24°41N
♂ = 13°47S	♃ = 14°11N	♄ = 17°39S	⚷ = 20°45N
♅ = 9°05N	♇ = 22°50N	M = 18°40S	A = 21°45S

Figure 58. John's cosmogram. He was born June 4, 1956. Birth data withheld for confidentiality.

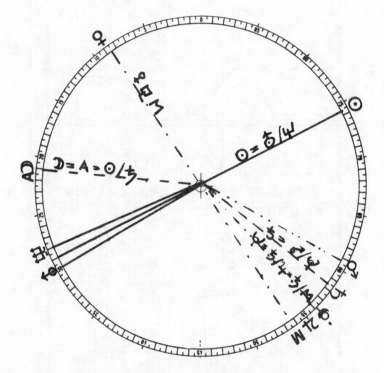

Figure 59. John's essential constellations.

VE//UR; but ME//SA corresponds to the Mercury constellation in the planetary-longitude cosmogram and, in this instance, points to a nervous disorder affecting the structure of the personality (SA//MC). We should also take note of ME = SU/NE = NE/PL in the declination diagram, since these also indicate nervous disorders. The declination midpoint discs (figures 62 and 63) are shown on pages 215 and 216.

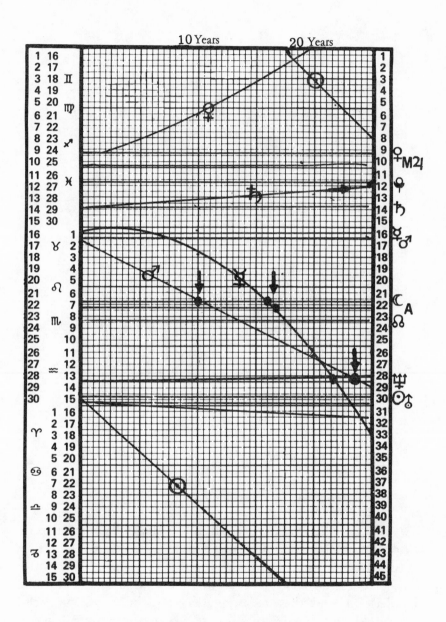

Figure 60. John's Life Diagram.

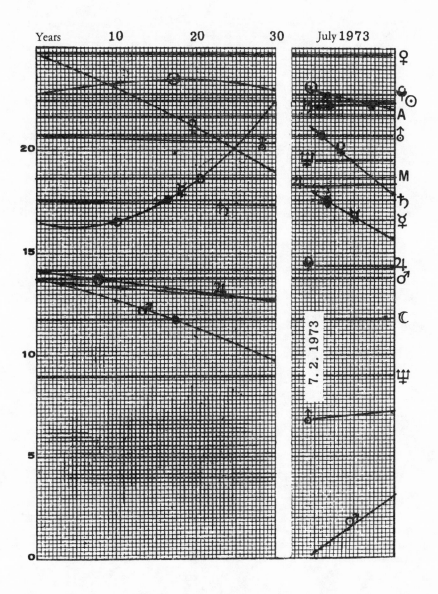

Figure 61. John's Declination Life Diagram.

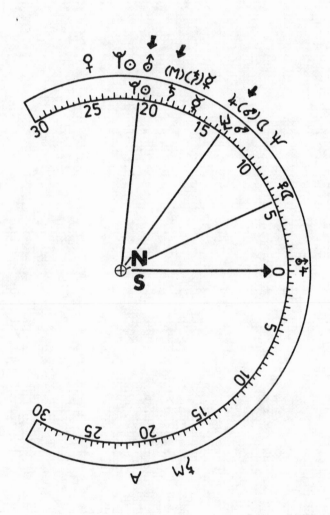

Figure 62. Mary's Declination Midpoint Disc for July 21, 1967.

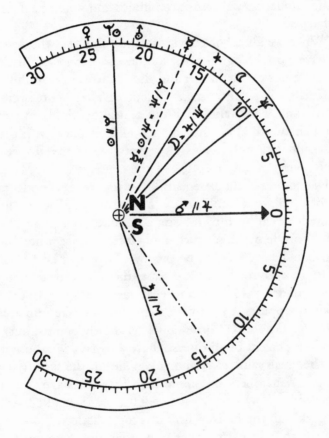

Figure 63. John's Declination Midpoint Disc for June 4, 1956.

How Can Cosmobiology Help in Cases of Disease?

A whole book could be devoted to a single case, but enough has been said to demonstrate how a cosmobiological investigation can be conducted without recourse to the traditional houses, to sign rulers, or to speculative transneptunian planets which have not been confirmed by astronomy. The question now arises: how can cosmobiology help?

In the examples discussed, the cosmic correspondences were shown to match the facts. The various treatments mentioned were handled under critical cosmic conditions and were therefore far from satisfactory.

When we are involved with treating children who have diseases that have a psychological basis, it is necessary to look at the planetary configurations of the mother and also to involve her in the treatment so that she will avoid mistakes in looking after her offspring.

Anyone who wants to bring a healthy child into the world should choose the best time for sexual intercourse with the spouse, and should definitely not leave the matter to chance. To see the sense of this, one has only to think of the consequences of conceiving a child when one of the parents is ill, or the father is under the influence of drink, or the mother is a heavy smoker! The parents should prepare for each birth by making a suitable adjustment to their way of life. This demands sacrifice, and abstention from life's little pleasures, but the rewards can be the joy of having a healthy child.

In the event of illness or disease, the best treatment ought to be applied under favorable constellations; then the trouble should quickly disappear. A treatment that does not take into account the psychological state is of little value. As already pointed out, between 40 and 60 percent of all diseases have a psychological origin.

The great value of cosmobiology lies in the facility it gives for timing. I remember how, more than fifty years ago, when I was a teacher, one of my pupils was a very backward small boy who would not speak. On the basis of his birth constellations I looked for days when the child might be more responsive and there was a chance of getting through to him.

Over twenty years ago, a mother consulted me about her girl. The child was far too fat and frequently fell ill. Little Asta, born May 7th 1953 (see figure 64 on page 217), had a cosmogram from which a

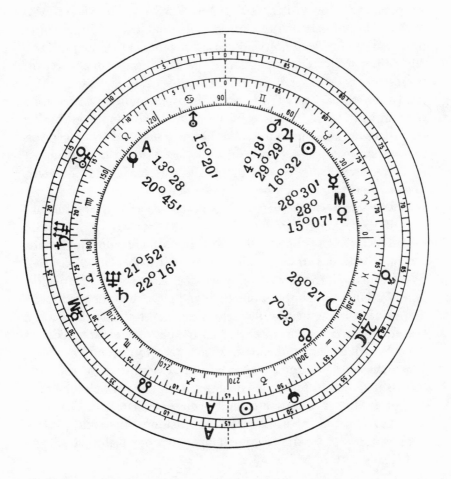

Figure 64. Asta, born May 7, 1953. Birth data withheld for confidentiality.

disposition to disease can be instantly recognized, since SA and NE in Libra are scarcely half a degree apart. This is a sign of chronic (SA) diseases (NE) affecting the kidney region (LI), possibly accompanied by rashes and patches of redness on the skin because the kidneys are not functioning properly.

And so it is not surprising that a severe cutaneous eruption made its appearance shortly after birth. MA = VE/SA = VE/NE and ASC = MA/NE are part of the pattern. VE/SA (DC No. 59) signifies inhibited internal secretion and glandular problems (kidneys); MA/NE points to infectious diseases. The child was often feverish, because her body was trying to rid itself of its toxins. She also suffered from a sore throat every few weeks. The latter condition is shown by the Sun in 16°–17° Taurus, which are the degrees representing the thyroid gland and the tonsils. A constant watch had to be kept on these weaknesses; the diet had to be modified (to exclude all animal fat and especially any type of pork), and the child had to be given plenty of exercise in the open air to harden her.

When she was $3^1/2$ years old, she developed a cough and pharyngitis. If Mars is progressed by $3^1/2$°, it is 135° away from the disease midpoint SA/NE. When, in 1958/59 she suffered from chickenpox (varicella), measles and whooping cough (pertussis), UR_s-90-SA/NE was forming and the disease midpoint was activated again. In addition, SA/NE_s was in opposition to ME and MC. Then the predisposition to disease was successfully kept under control. The child was a late developer, as is shown by SA/NE, and her progress at school was slow. Vocational and other tests gave satisfactory results however. When she failed to enter high school, I advised that for the time being she should be sent to a school that would let her develop at her own pace. Higher education could be considered later on. Thanks to a natural diet and the avoidance of inoculations, the child steadily improved, passed various examinations, went on to technical college, and finally entered university.

This example demonstrates the possibility of countering quite ominous constellations, and that it is worth while to watch how an individual is developing in the light of the cosmic correspondences so that the knowledge may be used to advantage.

CHAPTER EIGHT

CASE STUDIES

THIS CHAPTER WILL EXAMINE INDIVIDUAL CASE histories in considerable detail, although our discussion will be confined to really significant features in order to leave space for as many examples of cosmobiological diagnosis as possible. We will look at a preponderance of examples dealing with cancer first.

The scourge of cancer is on the increase. Nearly every fourth or fifth person dies of the disease. Therefore it is natural to ask whether a predisposition to cancer can be recognized in the cosmogram. Well, I have used the statistics to identify the following groupings, each composed of three factors, and conclude that these are mainly responsible for the cancer diathesis:

1) SU-PL-MC
2) SU-SA-MC
3) SU-NE-PL
4) SU-SA-PL
5) SU-SA-NE

We can speak here of a cancer syndrome. By a syndrome is meant the simultaneous appearance of a group of symptoms characteristic of a certain disease—all of which need not be present, however. Usually we find several of these three-factor groupings, but it must be emphasized that they do not doom the native to become a cancer sufferer; all they do is to warn of the possibility. They are generally present in the charts of sufferers however.

When Wilhelm König lectured on a certain cancer pattern during one of our conferences, many of those present were alarmed to find this pattern in their own cosmograms although they were free of cancer at that time. They were over-reacting; but anyone who discovers a cancer constellation in his or her chart ought to take preventive measures at the slightest hint of trouble in this direction.

The three-factor groupings mentioned do not usually show up except in the 90° wheel. In the following examples we shall try to illustrate the forms taken by the cosmic indications of cancer.

A Case of Unrecognized Cancer

The following lines are taken from a letter written to me:

> After my wife's death, I went over things in my mind so thoroughly that, if you would like to study it, I can paint you a detailed picture of her illness right up to the day she died. About two or three months before her death she began putting her affairs in order and expressed the opinion that things would have to take their course. She had always looked after her health: throughout the year she would tread dew in our garden and in winter went barefoot in the snow. Her blood pressure was always very high and she visited the doctor for regular checkups. In October 1968, the doctor said to her, "Your blood sedimentation rate worries me." However, a preliminary examination for cancer was negative. On April 14th, 1964, she had had an operation on her ear to remove a small tumor which was supposed to be benign. Presumably the family doctor attributed the bad sedimentation rate to this. Anyway, he arranged for her to see the ear specialist every two weeks in order to have her ear examined.

On June 13th, 1969, my wife noticed something wrong and went to the doctor, who rushed her into hospital. On June 30th, 1969, she had a hysterectomy. The operation was a success but, on July 10th the surgeon who had operated on my wife announced that there was no more hope of saving her because the disease had spread to other parts of her body. Treatment was given to control the disease as much as possible. On 11th September, my wife was allowed to come home; in any case she no longer wanted to stay in hospital. On 10th October, we took a trip to the North Sea, where my wife could still enjoy the beauties of nature, while I was constantly oppressed with the knowledge that nothing could help the one who was dearest to me in the whole world.

From this time on, the patient steadily deteriorated. By the end of October she could hardly eat anything. She asked the doctor when the end would come, and he answered that her sufferings would be over before the year was out. She died December 8th, 1969.

If we now take at the radix (figure 65 on page 222) and at its essential structures as given in a separate illustration (figure 66 on page 223), we shall recognize the cancer syndrome MC = SU/PL, SA = PL/MC, MA = SA/MC, NE-PL-MC. These structures emerge as part of larger groupings. The solar arc directions at the time of the hysterectomy are marked in the outer circle. UR_S = MA represents the operation, NE_S = MA represents the spread of the cancer by metastasis, and ASC_S = MA is a further pointer to the operation. It will be noted that MO_S = SA and MC_S (in opposition) = PL are particularly critical in their effect on the constellations in the inner circle—an effect for which we must always allow.

The extract from the declination life diagram (figure 67 on page 224) is very striking. As has already been said, the directions usually take effect ahead of time. Here we see how MA_P rises, and then dips to cross the entire complex UR/VE (ovaries!)/MA/NE. The adverse movement of Mars covers the period from 1964 through the time of death.

Our extract from the Annual Diagram for 1969 (figure 67) highlights the final stages of the disease. Unfortunately, the operation was

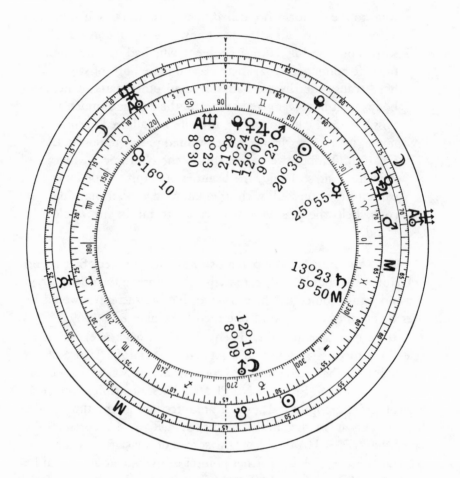

Declinations

☉ = 18°03N	☽ = 19°35S	☿ = 7°34N	♀ = 23°06N
♂ = 22°30N	♃ = 21°50N	♄ = 8°05S	☊ = 23°30S
♆ = 22°17N	♇ = 15°24N	M = 9°23S	A = 23°11N

Figure 65. Female who died from cancer. Born May 12, 1906. Birth data withheld for confidentiality.

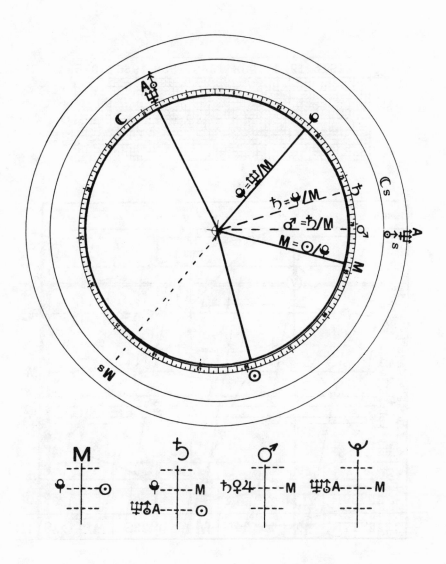

Figure 66. The major constellations from figure 65. The solar arc directions for the time of the hysterectomy are marked in the outer circle.

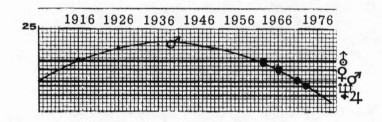

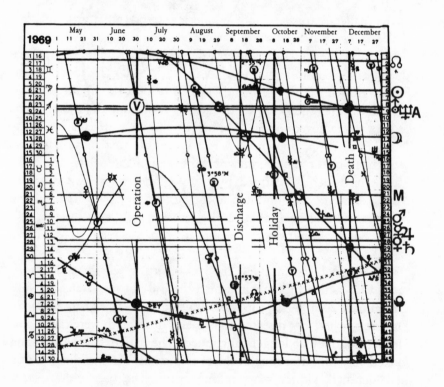

Figure 67. Sections of the Declination Diagram and the Annual Diagram for 1969.

performed on a full moon and with SA over PL (= NE/MC). Under
JU = MO, the wife was very glad to be discharged from hospital.
But, on the occasion of the trip to the North Sea, we find very critical
adverse constellations: UR = SA, NE = MO, SA = PL. Death
occurred when UR_T = UR = NE was activated by MA. The release
from suffering is represented by JU_T = VE = SA. In this case, the
doctor should have been alert to the danger of cancer when a growth
had to be removed from the ear.

Recovery from Cancer

The following case, as described by cosmobiologist Erich Modersohn
of Lippstadt, is a good example of the help to be derived from a study
of the planetary constellations. Modersohn reported: "I can't stand it
any longer; my appendix will have to be removed and so will the cyst
in my abdomen!" said the female patient in August, 1969. The
operation was performed on September 8th, 1969. There was a cancerous growth the size of a child's head behind the uterus and this
was taken out together with the uterus itself and the ovaries. The
rectum was removed too and was replaced by an artificial anus on the
left side of the abdomen. It was not feasible to remove daughter
growths from the right kidney and the wall of the pelvis. The findings, which were confirmed by histological tests at two different
institutes, were communicated to the patient's relatives. The surgeon
said that he had been able to alleviate her condition for the time
being but that her life expectancy was in the region of only six
months.

In the autumn of 1969, the patient was given the usual treatment with radioactive cobalt, which she did not tolerate at all well.
On January 20th, 1970, she was admitted to the Ringberg Clinic of
Dr. Issels, where her diseased tonsils and dead teeth were taken out.
Her right kidney no longer functioned. The patient was bloated and
looked very ill. After four weeks of treatment, she was slimmer and
her "defunct" kidney was working again. The patient took fresh
courage and hoped to improve.

She was discharged on April 10th 1970. Her family physician
continued to treat her on the lines laid down by Dr. Issels. A thor-

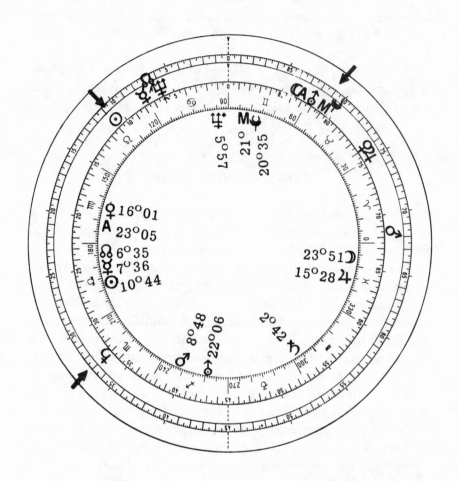

Declinations

☉ = 4°19S	☽ = 0°44S	☿ = 3°30S	♀ = 0°14S
♂ = 23°06S	♃ = 7°09S	♄ = 20°14S	☊ = 23°22S
♅ = 22°15N	♇ = 14°26N	M = 23°09N	A = 2°49N

Figure 68. Cancer patient, born October 5, 1903, at 5 A.M., Dortmund, W. Germany.

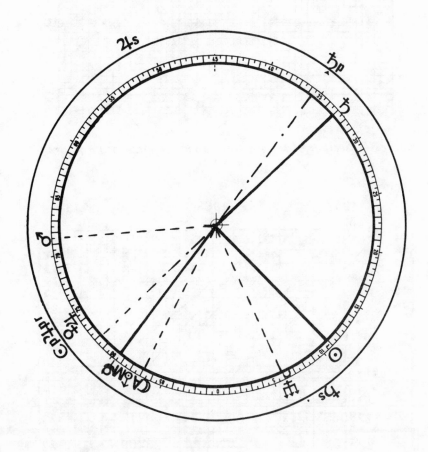

Figure 69. The major constellations for figure 68.

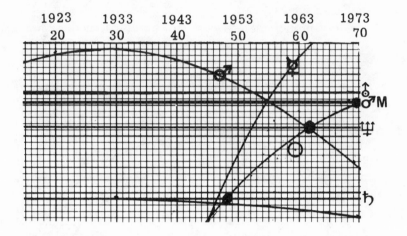

Figure 70. Section of the progressed Life Diagram from figure 68.

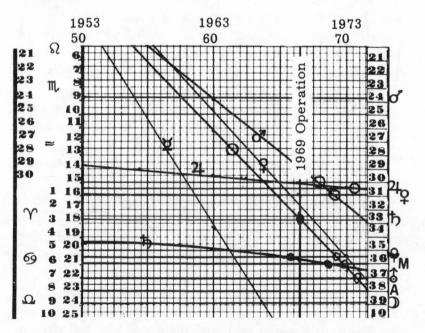

Figure 71. Section of the Declination Life Diagram.

ough examination at the hospital where she had had her operation revealed no trace of the secondary growths. The woman felt better than she had done for years; she resumed her normal activities and started eating proper meals again. She returned to the Ringberg Clinic for a course of preventive therapy and was confident that she had beaten the disease. See figures 68 and 69 on pages 226 and 227.

The following points are of special interest in the cancer syndrome: $SU = SA/PL$, $SU = SA/MC$, $NE = MA/SA$. In this person's Life Diagram SA_P approaches the position-lines of PL and MC and reaches them around 1968 through 1970 as shown in figure 70 on page 228. At the time of the operation $SU_P = SA$ is due. What is so helpful for the recovery, however, is the movement of JU and MA over JU with VE.

In the extract from the Declination Life Diagram, you'll notice some things in common with the previous example. (See figure 71 on page 235.) In both cases MA_P runs up to its highest (most northerly) position and then moves down over a complex to activate the disease. What is more, SU_P and MA_P cross the position-line of NE simultaneously. In many instances we see time and again how clear is the connection between the junction of MA and NE and a gradual poisoning of the body. In cancer this happens through metastasis (by which cancerous cells travel from the original site of the disease to other parts of the body via the bloodstream, the lymphatic system, etc.). At birth the critical declination was $4° 19' S$; but 60 days = 60 years had to elapse before the declination line of NE was reached.

Turning now to the sections from the Annual Diagram (figure 72 on page 230), we find that the operation was performed under $NE = SU$ and PL with SU over MO. After the patient was transferred to the Ringberg Clinic, it was fortunate that JU joined $PL = MC$ stationary. $JU = PL$ signifies organic regeneration, that is to say, the production of healthy new cells. Among other benefits, the kidneys started functioning properly again. $PL = MC$ signifies an internal change, self-assertion, the overcoming of a crisis in the life.

The patient was discharged when SA had crossed the PL, MC, UR, ASC, MO complex and UR had crossed the $ME/NE/DR$ complex. The worst was now over, and the doctor who had given our example patient six months to live was proved wrong.

We hope that this example will restore hope to many cancer sufferers, and that they will realize that it is possible for them to recover; especially if they can find a physician who knows what he or she is doing and is not so dazzled by the wonders of modern medicine that he or she forgets the healing powers of nature.

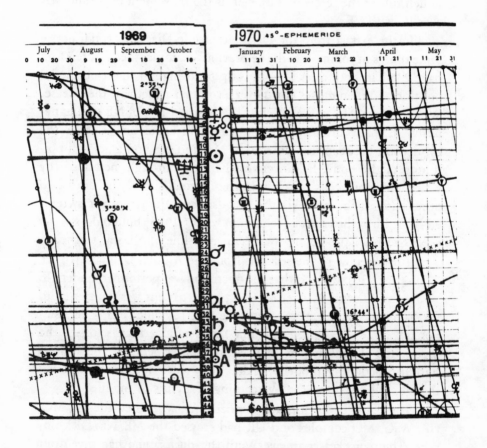

Figure 72. Annual Diagram for our cancer patient.

Günther Lüders' Death from Cancer

Günther Lüders, the popular German actor, was born in Lübeck on March 5th 1905, at 6:30 A.M. He died on March 1st 1975, of liver cancer, after suffering from kidney disease for a long time. Apparently he was completely unaware he had cancer, for it was only at the time of his operation that secondary growths were discovered in various parts of his body.

The significant planetary formations in his cosmogram can be seen at a glance: MC = SA/NE, MC = SU/PL, and SU = MA/NE = VE = JU. In addition, MA and NE form a sesquisquare. Since the liver and kidneys were chiefly affected, it is significant that JU and VE are in aspect with SU = MA/NE. See figures 73 and 74 on pages 232 and 233.

On consulting the *Organuhr* devised by Fritz Brandau, we find that the degrees occupied by PL and MC are associated with liver trouble and that the degree occupied by MA is associated with kidney disease.

It is noteworthy how decisive the above mentioned constellations are at the time of death. NE_S coincides with SU and opposes MA_S with VE = JU. Therefore the disease formation SU = MA/NE = VE = JU was activated at death. What is more, SU_S is moving over the midpoint between MA and SA, or over the "death axis." MC_s coincides with SA.

In the section from the progressed life diagram (see figure 75 on page 240), NE_P had cut the position line of MA several decades earlier. Shortly before death, SU cuts the position-lines of NE and MA, SA approaches the position-line of MO, and SU approaches that of SA. As has already been said more than once, an event can be triggered by progressed aspects years before the latter are exact. The direction MC_S = SA was activated at the time of death by transiting UR.

Cancer of the Kidneys

The famous rocket engineer, Wernher von Braun (with the "atom formula" SU-PL-MA), was born at 9:15 A.M. on March 23rd, 1912, in

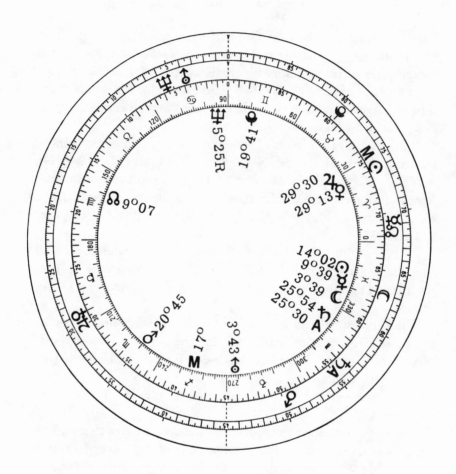

Declinations

☉ = 6°18S	☽ = 9°42S	☿ = 9°00S	♀ = 14°54 N
♂ = 16°24S	♃ = 10°25N	♄ = 13°57S	↑☊ = 23°37N
♆ = 22°21N	♇ = 14°47N	M = 22°49S	A = 13°02S

Figure 73. Günther Lüders, born March 5, 1905, at 6:30 A.M., in Lübeck.

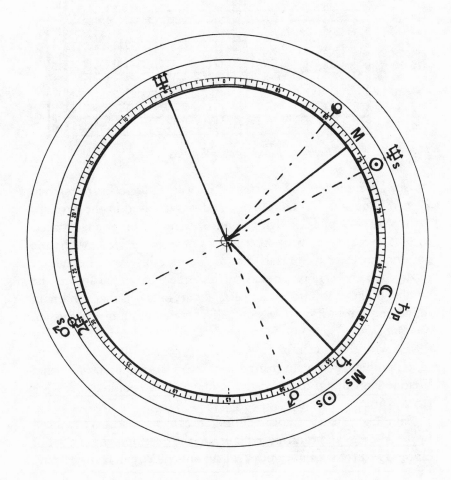

Figure 74. The significant factors in Lüders' cosmogram.

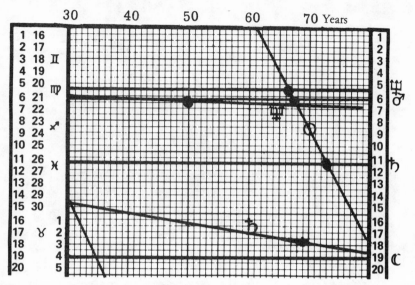

Figure 75. Life Diagram for Günther Lüders.

Wirsitz bei Bromberg, W. Germany. He worked on rocket research in Peenemunde with Dr. Dornberger and was involved in the development of the V-1 pilotless flying bomb and the V-2 long-range rocket. In 1945 he was taken with other top scientists to the USA, where the government offered him facilities to continue his work. Because of rivalry between various services of the American armed forces, the satellite program was frozen for years, a state of affairs that von Braun found very frustrating. It was only after the triumph of the Russian *Sputnik* that he came into prominence again, and he enjoyed his first success with the launch of *Explorer I* in February 1958. In 1972 the rocket problem was again treated as of secondary importance, so that Wernher von Braun returned to Germany a disappointed man. See figure 76.

It is likely that the repeated hindrances and setbacks experienced by the inventor and contributed much to the development of a major cancer. He died of kidney cancer in Alexandria, Virginia, at age sixty-five.

Looking now at the anatomical correspondences of the individual positions of the planets, we find that ME/DR/NE/MC points to kidney disease. The prominent cancer syndrome is NE = SA/PL, and the fact that it is connected with VE is another sign of glandular

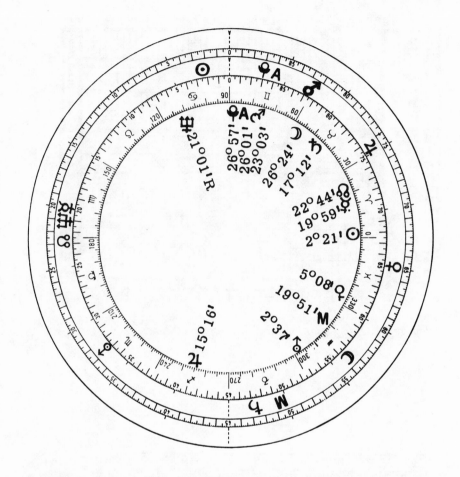

Declinations

☉ = 0°57'N	☽ = 22°30'N	☿ = 9°19'N	♀ = 10°38'S
♂ = 25°13'N	♃ = 21°51'S	♄ = 15°02'N	☊ = 20°07'S
♅ = 21°16'N	♇ = 17°08'N	M = 14°52'S	A = 23°23'N

Figure 76. Wernher von Braun, born March 23, 1912, at 9:15 A.M. in Wirsitz.

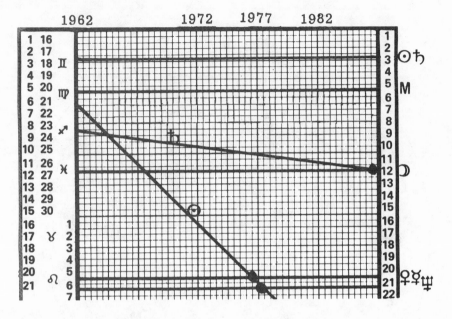

Figure 77. *Life Diagram for Wernher von Braun.*

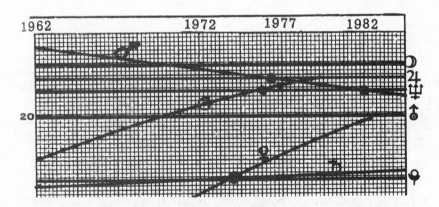

Figure 78. *Declination Diagram for Wernher von Braun.*

disorders in which the kidneys may well be implicated. PL = VE/NE and MO = VE/SA = SU/NE point in the same direction.

The life diagram (see figure 77 on page 243) provides the clearest indications of the development of the disease. The radix shows a platic (wide) conjunction between SA and MO. In a case like this, it is essential to determine if SA moves toward the position-line of MO, as it does here. However, as we have already discussed, it is possible to pick up advance warnings of a disease of this nature years or even decades before it manifests itself.

The kidney disease is indicated by VE-135-NE. This constellation was activated in the year of death.

The invariable close association of NE with cancer emerges once again from the Declination Diagram. See figure 78 on page 236. Here SU and MA move to NE while the paths of VE (kidneys) and SA cross the position-line of Pluto.

Intestinal Cancer

The case of W.G. fits in well in our series of cancer patients because the Life Diagram presents the same picture as that presented by the Life Diagram of Wernher von Braun. See figure 79 on page 238. SA_P goes to meet the position-line of the Moon and death occurs when it eventually does so. Now, whereas in the previous example the cancer affected the kidneys and here it affects the intestines, we are led to conclude that we are unable to make an exact diagnosis of the disease but have to content ourselves with weighing up the probabilities. In both cases the fluid balance, represented by the Moon, is involved. And in both cases Saturn leads to disorders, tightnesses, hardening, swellings or secondary growths. See figure 80 on page 239.

Many years before SA_P = MO is exact, SU/NE and MA_S cross the position-lines of SA and MO. NE is involved as usual and MA is the activator of the illness. SU-135-NE in the cosmogram already warns of a predisposition to disease.

Apparently this lady used to "take everything to heart" without bringing herself to talk about it; and the tendency to bottle things up was easily transmitted to her entire digestive system, which became clogged. This is characteristic of a MO/SA conjunction. But, when a

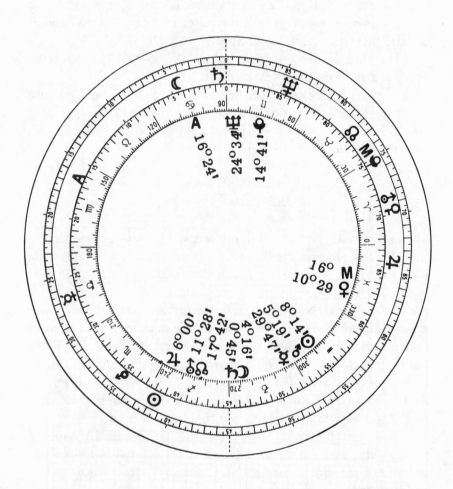

Figure 79. W.G., born January 28, 1900.

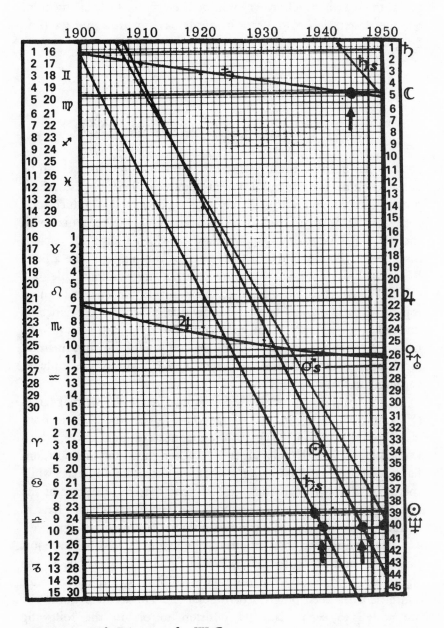

Figure 80. Life Diagram for W.G.

constellation of that kind is seen in the cosmogram, it is possible to take preventive measures. If the person concerned does not have the power to take them, relatives can do wonders with a little loving help. See the description of the case in my book *Lebensdiagramme* (Life Diagrams).

Lung Cancer Visible on the 90° Dial

So far it has been taken for granted that most chronic diseases can be detected on the day for a year system. However, there are cases where progressions prove difficult. Then it is necessary to introduce solar arcs into the Annual Diagram. Solar arcs are easy to recognize with the 90° dial. The dial is a square plate on which a large 90° circle is inscribed. A hole is bored in the center of the plate to take a bolt. What we do is to prepare two forms—with a larger and a smaller 90° circle. The larger form is placed on the dial with the smaller form on top of it, each marked with the individual positions. 0° Cancer is marked by a dash or with the Aries sign. The outer circle can now be moved through the solar arc for any desired year of life, and the solar arc directions can therefore be determined straight away simply by turning the dial manually.

Lying in front of me is a report from a reader of my magazines (H.G.D.), who was born at 3:34 P.M. on October 5th, 1923, in Breslau (figure 81 on page 241). For the diagnosis of lung cancer, which was made in 1976, the solar arc is 53°. When the individual positions have been marked, the smaller cosmogram disc is held in place while the larger disc is turned through 53°. The fifty-third degree of the smaller disc is marked with a dash and the Aries sign. We now have to consider a further degree-circle beginning with this Aries sign.

Two immediate observations can be made: JU and NE have just passed SU and PL on the left side and SA$_S$ has reached UR on the right side. The addition of minuscule "s" indicates that the factor concerned has been progressed by solar arc. For accurate work, 53° are added to each planetary position to obtain the following progressions:

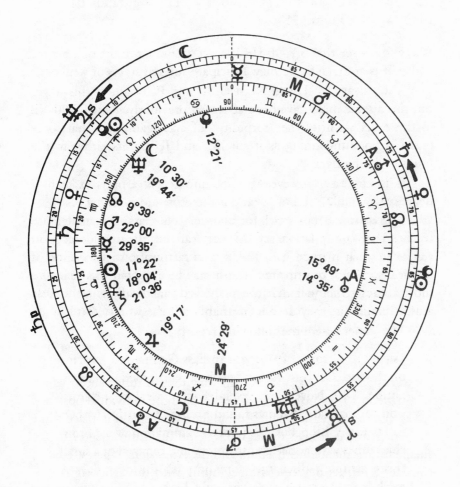

Figure 81. H.G.D., born October 5, 1923, at 3:34 P.M. in Breslau, W. Germany.

MO	=	3° Libra 30'		MC	=	17° Aquarius 29'
DR	=	2° Scorpio 39'		PL	=	5° Virgo 21'
MA	=	15° Scorpio 00'		NE	=	12° Libra 44'
SU	=	4° Sagittarius 22'		ASC	=	8° Taurus 49'
SA	=	14° Sagittarius 36'		ME	=	22° Scorpio 35'
JU	=	12° Capricorn 17'		VE	=	11° Sagittarius 04'
UR	=	7° Taurus 35'				

We can now see that SA_s-90-UR is exact within a minute of a degree and, UR is at SU/NE, we may anticipate sudden states of weakness.

The passage of JU and NE over SU and PL occurs at this stage, but the disease must have been activated previously. Now JU-90-NE in the radix signifies the "torpidity" of an organ, i.e., that some organ is not functioning as it should, and JU points either to the lungs or to the liver.

It is not easy, however, to find progressed aspects exact to a degree. SA_P is in 27° Libra 28' and is therefore approaching SA_P-135-UR. The aspect is not exact for another ten years, but experience teaches that constellations of this sort can be effective decades in advance. What is more, SA_s-90-UR is in fact exact; so some kind of physical weakness or impaired health may be expected this year. We must always remember that the planetary constellations are simply aids to diagnosis; they do not invariably tell the whole story.

The patient gave the following report:

> 1st to 6th October, 1976: visit to East Germany; I felt fine on the trip. On 16th November chest pains; medical examination. 18th November: several X-rays, weakness, admission to hospital. Shadows found on lungs. 8th December: full narcosis, bronchoscopy (visual examination of the bronchial tubes with a special instrument and removal of a small tissue sample), discharge from hospital the next day. A week later the result came through: lung cancer.

The patient guessed that the lung cancer had been activated by NE_s = SU.

On the 28th December he was admitted to the hospital, and on December 29th the right lobe of the lungs was surgically removed. The operation was successful.

Suddenly, for two days in succession, I along with other patients in the ward felt very ill; suffering from fluctuating, low blood pressure, physical weakness and digestive difficulties on the 5th and 6th of January 1977. I later discovered that there had been a full Moon, with the Sun at 16° Capricorn; both aspecting the SU-PL constellation. When at midnight on January 6th, the Moon entered Leo, I felt an immediate improvement. I was discharged on the 12th of January, and have since been at home, still not able to do very much and rather short of breath.

If, in the light of the above report, we look at the constellations in the Annual Diagram (figure 82 on page 244), we find that the beginning of October was positive, with PL over SU indicating energy and the ability to get things done. SA = ME signifies travel. At the end of October events took a critical turn when UR crossed the MA position-line, but there was still a residue of positive energy left over from JU over PL early in the month. On the 16th of November, the patient suffered from chest pains. At this time MA, SU and ME were crossing the position-lines of SU and PL. This constellation is certainly consistent with pains (MA). According to COSI No. 218, SU and MA combine to give "inflamed cells." Then came a New Moon (the circled N in the graphic ephermeris) and this is characteristic of weakness. When the diagnosis of lung cancer was announced, UR was approaching the MC; MA over UR apparently produced the corresponding hectic activity.

NE crossed the position-line of UR and UR crossed that of MO. These can hardly be called good constellations for surgery, but the operation was a success. Shortly afterward, however, came a relapse on the 5th of January. But MA over JU and NE saw the patient being discharged from hospital. Nevertheless, he remained an invalid and was very short of breath, since critical constellations continued to be operative, for example UR = MO and NE = UR. Also, in the middle of January SA = ME intervened. The reader will recall that for the trip to East Germany we equated this constellation with travel; now, however, it does not have the same meaning but signifies negative (SA) thoughts (ME), because in someone aged fifty-three, the powers of recuperation are not as good as might be wished and

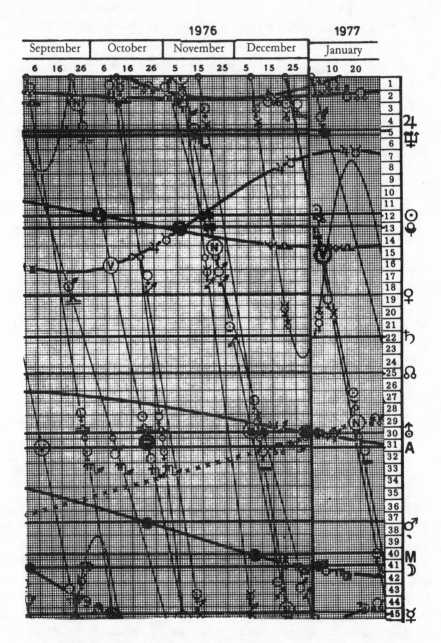

Figure 82. Annual Diagram for H.G.D.

the outlook was rather gloomy. Without knowing how urgent the operation was, it is hard to say whether a more favorable day could have been scheduled for it.

Inge Egger Died of Cancer

Inge Egger was one of Germany's best-loved actresses. She entertained her public in films like *Hochzeit im Heu* (Wedding in the Hay), *Auf der Alm, da gibt's ka Sünd* (All's Well in the Alps), *Eva im Frack* (Eva in Evening Dress), and *Der eingebildete Kranke* (The Imaginary Invalid). She preferred schmaltzy music to classical music, and had an unaffectedly natural style of playing. Her father, who had been an Austro-Hungarian officer, placed her in a young ladies' boarding school and would not countenance her dream of becoming an actress. But fate was kind to her.

In her own words: "Every Sunday we were taken for a walk somewhere like a flock of sheep. On one occasion we visited the race track at Freudenau an die Reihe. And what do you think happened? A man suddenly came up to me and introduced himself as a talent scout for Wien-Film (Vienna Films). It seems that he and his staff were looking for young hopefuls. I was given a screen test that very morning."

At this time JU_S-90-VE and MC_S-180-VE were due. Her parents gave in and agreed to her entering the Reinhardt-Seminar, as she had already passed the test.

Nevertheless, her radix (see figure 83 on page 246) does contain a number of critical points. Following her initial successes in 1944, a glandular disease (VE = SA/PL) made her put on so much weight that for some time she was unfit for filming (JU_S-90-SU). All the money she had started earning encouraged her to indulge in big meals with plenty of rich foods and wines. However, her appearance quickly changed after an appendix operation (SU at 3° Virgo corresponding to the caecum); she became and remained slim.

In 1956 she unexpectedly ran out of work: actresses of her type had gone out of fashion. This was when SU_P, JU_P and ME_P were crossing the position-line of Neptune in the Life Diagram, Neptune being the planet of disappointment and disillusion, which, in the

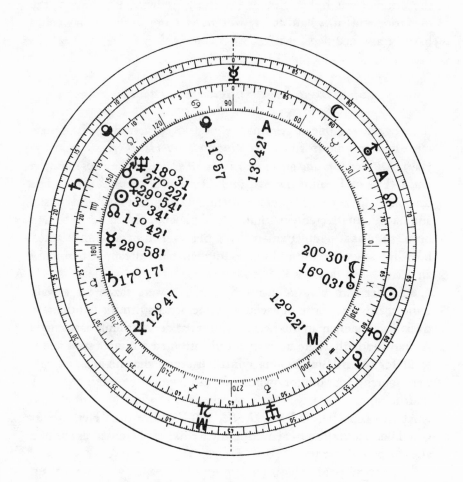

Declinations

☉ = 10°05'N	☽ = 4°30'S	☿ = 1°35'S	♀ = 12°32'N
♂ = 13°33'N	♃ = 14°50'S	♄ = 4°39'S	☊ = 6°15'S
♆ = 15°28'N	♇ = 20°23'N	M = 17°06 S	A = 22°27'N

Figure 83. Cosmogram for Inge Egger, born August 27, 1923, 10:45 P.M.

radix, holds a critical position at MO/SA. See figure 84 on page 248. This constellation points to constitutional depression. The actress became so depressed, in fact, that at the end of March 1958, she slashed her wrists in a bid to end it all. However, she was saved in the nick of time. MA and PL are semisquare in the radix, and it will be noted how close their position-lines are in the Life Diagram. At the period in question, PL_P was within one minute of a degree of making an exact semisquare with MA. This constellation can indicate suicide.

There were additional upsets too. Her friend Richard Haüssler had left her, and another friendship, with Willy Birgel, had turned sour. This is mirrored by VE_P crossing the position lines of MA and PL.

Further insights are provided by the Declination Life Diagram. Here, MO/SA and NE = SU/PL immediately spring to the eye. At the time in question, ME, VE and SU cross the position-lines of MO and SA in quick succession. It is obvious that the seeds of cancer were sown at this time. The interplay of planetary longitudes and declinations can be seen in the death constellation at the beginning of September 1976 where, as in 1958, SE, VE, and MA cross the parallel of MO//SA. UR_T moves over MO just before the death axis MA/SA. See figures 85 and 86 on pages 249 and 250.

To sum up: the following disease constellations were present in this case: PL = SU/NE = MA; SA = UR/NE = SU; NE = MO/SA; MO = VE/PL (= MA/SA); MO//SA; NE//JU = SU/PL.

Cancer of the Colon

Now we shall discuss the cosmogram of a male cancer patient who had a malignant growth in the colon which was surgically removed on July 12th, 1976. In the cosmogram (see figure 87 on page 252), the predisposition to cancer may be seen in the formulas MC = NE/PL and SU = SA = MA/NE. Whenever SU and SA are in exact aspect, there is always a tendency to the thickening and hardening of tissues and to growths. However, whether or not the SU/SA combination will lead to a serious illness depends on the native's life-style and on what happens to him. But we do advise that, if anyone has either this

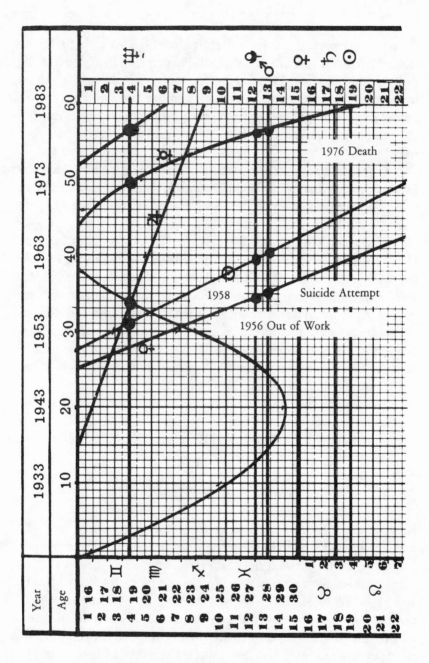

Figure 84. Life Diagram for Inge Egger.

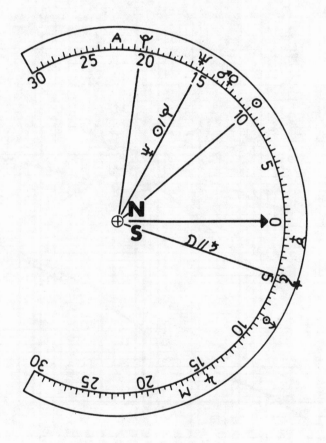

Figure 85. Declination Midpoint Disc for Inge Egger.

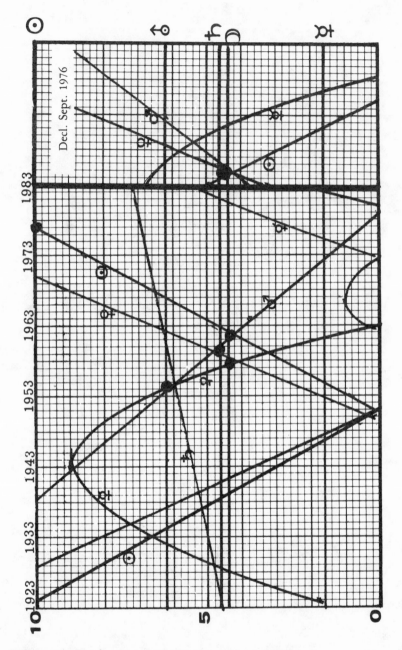

Figure 86. Declination Life Diagram for Inge Egger.

constellation or MO = SA in the cosmogram, he or she ought to take prophylactic measures in good time and, above all, should avoid any form of psychological stress. One might assume from JU = MC that this individual would enjoy considerable success and good fortune in life, but MC = JU = NE/PL must not lie overlooked. What is more, according to the *Anatomischen Entsprechungen der Tierkreisgrade*, the Ascendant at 7° Sagittarius indicates intestinal disorders. The Ascendant is also afflicted by SA/MC = SA/JU = SU/JU.

The excerpt from the Life Diagram (figure 88 on page 253) reveals that, between ages fifty and sixty, NE_P-135-ASC was forming, and JU_P at this place encouraged the development of a growth. The predisposition to cancer was activated by SU_P and MA_P over the MO/MC/JU/DR/MA complex. In addition, ME and VE meet on the position line of PL.

The Annual Diagram (figure 89 on page 254) shows that the operation was initiated by MA_P crossing the entire complex; fortunately, JU_T was transiting this complex and the operation was a success. Of course, PL = MA/ SA = SA/SU and UR = SA, SU added to the problem.

The directions which fell due are marked in the outer circle of the cosmogram, and we may single out as specially characteristic SU_S and SA_S over MC = JU, and UR_S with VE_P and ME_P at PL, which are indicative of the operation.

Since the patient was a student of astrology, he felt it was significant that SA_S would reach the cusp of the 8th house in 1980, and that there had been similar constellations in the case of his wife. On this basis, he calculated that he would die in the summer of 1980.

From a cosmobiological point of view, a prognosis of this kind must be positively discouraged; particularly when made on the basis of house cusps. The danger is that the invalid will convince himself that Saturn on the cusp of the 8th house, traditionally known as the house of death, must signify the end of life and that this idea will take such a hold on him that it will bring about his demise regardless of any constellations. Thoughts are extremely potent. Negative thoughts produce negative events; positive thoughts fortify the life energy and are capable of overcoming very grave crises.

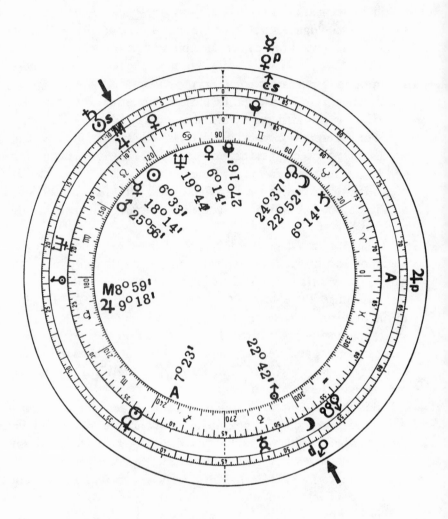

Figure 87. Male cancer patient, born July 30, 1910, 4:15 P.M., Central European Time at 53°N51', 12°E. The time of birth has been rectified based on events in the life.

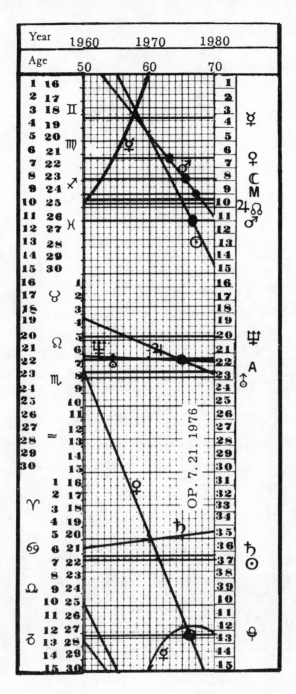

Figure 88. Life Diagram for male cancer patient in figure 87.

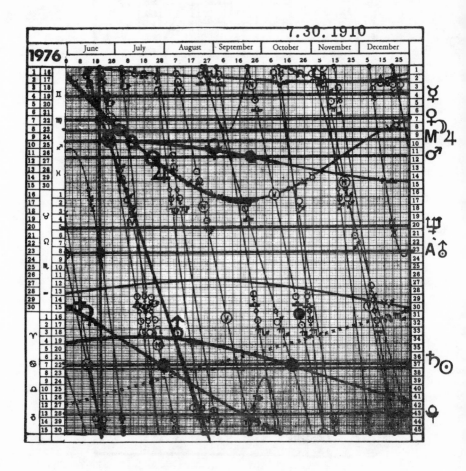

Figure 89. Annual Diagram for male cancer patient (figure 87) showing surgery done in July, 1976.

Testicular Tumor

For this young man, born on September 12th, 1945, as for his parents, the diagnosis of a tumor was a heavy blow. Karl was the only son, and already the head of an international company. See figure 90 on page 256. His parents did their utmost to save their son and heir, but it was all in vain. The predisposition to tumor formation is given by various constellations: NE = SU/SA; MO = SA/NE; SA = MC; MA = NE. These constellations are found in other tumors and cancers too. The indications of disease of the sexual organs are:

VE = 15° Leo 45', close to 17° Leo, representing the testes
MC = VE/NE: weakness of the genitals
SA = VE/MA: impediments in the sexual life
MA = NE: infectious diseases
NE = MO/VE: abnormal glandular activity; forced continence
PL = MO/SA: bladder trouble, constitutional depression

In June, 1958, when he was 13 years old, he underwent his first operation. However, the cause of the disease must lie in the fifth year of life, when MA and VE crossed the position-line of NE. JU = NE gives the possibility of a false diagnosis attended by serious consequences. Then the paths of SU and ME crossed the position-line of NE. SA was continually creeping nearer to MC and bringing the threat of a serious illness, and the death occurred in 1977 when SU reached the position-line of SA. See figure 91 on page 257.

A study of the declinations will reveal the gravity of the disease, for SA//MC reinforces SA-180-MC. The midpoint SA/MC coincides with MO/VE = NE = JU. This points to a severe disorder of the glands. For good measure we have MA//PL//UR.

MA and PL are very tight together in the Declination Life Diagram, leading us to conjecture that an accident occurred to the native when he was young or that he was forcibly abused by someone, possibly without his parents' knowledge. MA moves to UR and leads to a fresh operation. Also SA_p moves to MC as in the progressed Life Diagram. See figure 92 on page 258.

The early crossing of JU and SU over NE suggests infectious diseases in childhood.

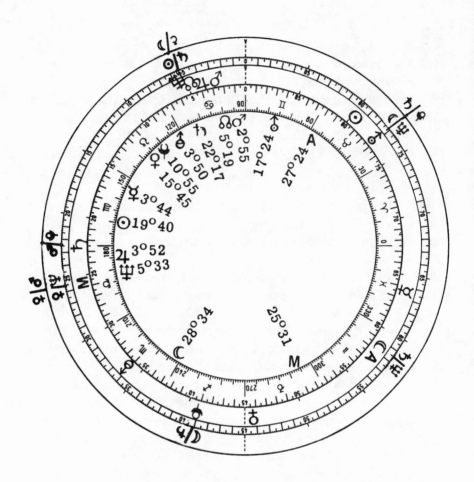

Declinations

$\odot$ = 4°06'N	$\mathbb{C}$ = 16°51'S	$\mathbb{\varphi}$ = 11°22'N	$\mathbb{Q}$ = 16°23'N
σ = 23°29'N	$\mathbb{4}$ = 0°28'S	$\hbar$ = 21°22'N	$\uparrow$ = 22°52'N
Ψ = 0°54'SS	$\mathbb{Q}$ = 23°17'N	M = 21°03'S	A = 19°36'N

Figure 90. Karl, born September 12, 1945. Birth data have been withheld for confidentiality.

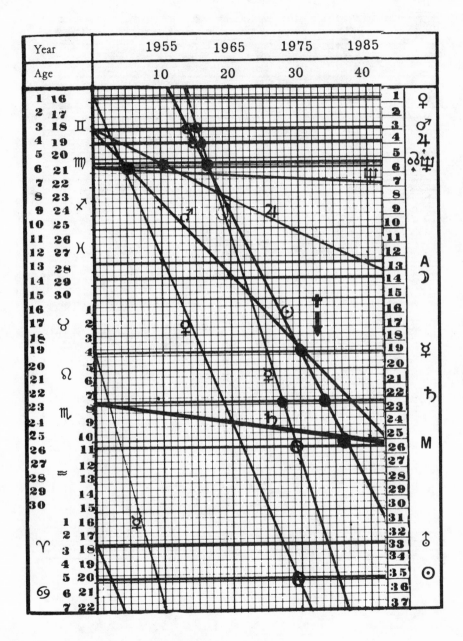

Figure 91. Karl's Life Diagram.

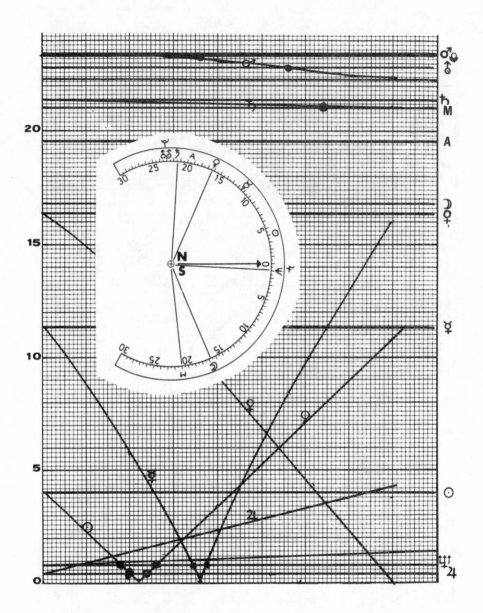

Figure 92. Karl's Declination Midpoint Disc.

In 1975 the doctors had given up hope for the patient, saying that he could not last longer than another two years. Unfortunately, their prognosis was correct. In the autumn of 1976, I warned of a grave crisis, and this occurred in 1977. When SA_T = MA was exact in the July of that year, the patient died.

Cardiac Valve Operation

In cases of heart disease, the first thing to do is to look at the Sun's position and aspects. In M. G.'s cosmogram (figure 93 on page 260, the Sun is in 13° Aries 44' and 135° from Neptune at 28° Leo 55'. This immediately suggests cardiac (Sun) weakness (Neptune). In the *Anatomische Entsprechungen der Tierkreisgrade*, 28° Leo represents the valves of the heart. SU and NE form an axis in the 90° wheel in which we find the midpoints MA/PL and SA/MC. This means that the causes of the disease are agitation and mental suffering. MA/PL often signifies violent treatment of the body (operation). A notable aspect of the cosmogram is MA-90-UR. According to COSI No. 710, this constellation corresponds to functional rhythm, the action of the heart muscle, injury and operation.

On examining the excerpt from the Life Diagram (figure 94 on page 261), UR runs to meet MA; the square is exact at the time of the operation. In addition, NE was retrograde at the time of birth and turned direct after an interval of forty days, so that it was back to normal when the operation was performed. On the other hand, SU cuts the SU-NE axis. And so both constellations relating to disorders of the cardiac valves and to disturbances of the cardiac rhythm were being activated at the time of the operation.

The operation day (see figure 95 on page 261) was well chosen because, in addition to ME = MA, MA = ASC in between Full Moon and New Moon, SU = JU and JU = MO are due; thus the operation was a success and the patient was able to return home four weeks later. Other constellations were due, but have been left out of consideration here so that we can keep to the essentials.

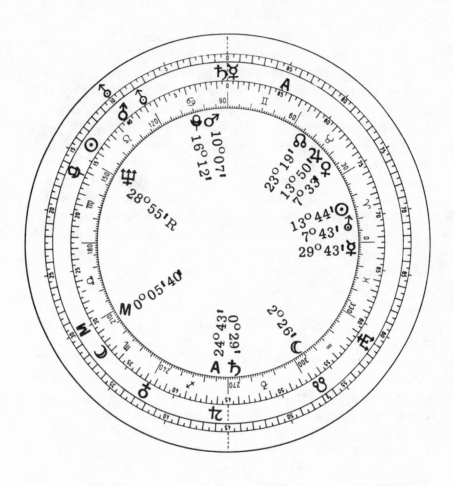

*Figure 93. M.G., born April 4, 1929, 1:45 P.M., in Wolfenbutte.
Cardiac valve operation.*

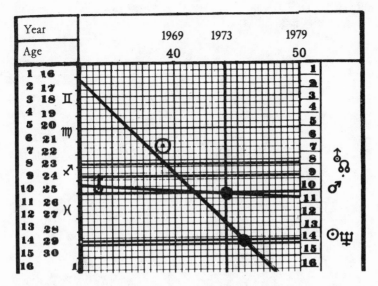

Figure 94. Excerpt from M.G.'s Life Diagram.

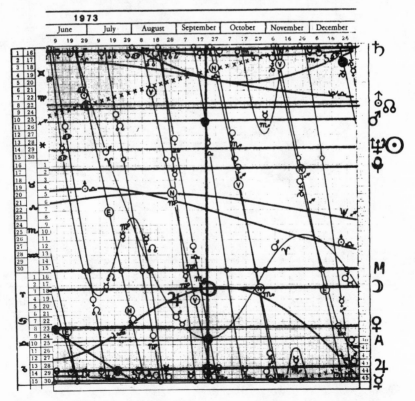

Figure 95. The Annual Diagram.

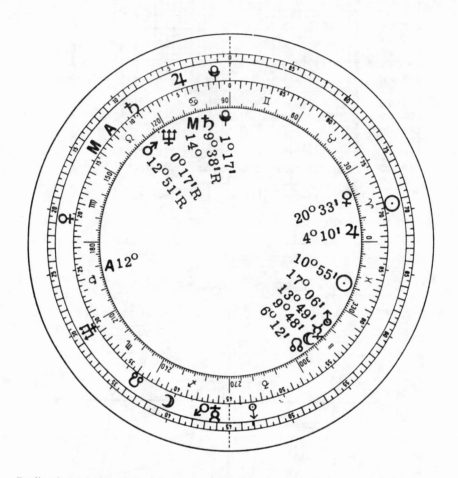

Declinations

⊙ =	07°29'S	☾ =	17°24'S	☿ =	16°57'S	♀ =	8°42'N
♂ =	21°00'N	♃ =	0°43'N	♄ =	22°45'N	⚷ =	16°20'S
♆ =	19°49'N	♇ =	18°20'N	M =	22°43'N	A =	4°48'S

Figure 96. W.G., born March 1, 1916, 8:30 P.M., Leipzig, E. Germany.

A Case of Poliomyelitis

None of the examples of this book have been specially chosen to fit in neatly with the theory of the subject. The reader should understand that there are cases in which it is hard to see relevant correspondences, and that it is not good to jump to conclusions just because some constellation happens to be due. There must be some analogy to the events or illness in question. In the disease now known as poliomyelitis or "polio" for short (formerly called infantile paralyis), PL = SU/ NE has been found repeatedly.

The following case of polio (see figure 96 on page 262) has been supplied by medical assistant Hans Reissmann of Leipzig. A member of his own family was involved, so he was able to state the exact time of the outbreak of the disease. The then schoolchild exhibited the first symptoms of paralyis in Leipzig at 8:00 A.M. on September 6th, 1922. The time is certain because the child's father was just about to leave home for work in the bank, but had to drop everything and run from doctor to doctor in order to fetch help.

On the subject of the disease itself, Reissmann writes: "Spinal infantile paralysis is an infectious disease. It is epidemic and usually appears in summer or autumn. The infective agent is a poliomyelitis virus. There are three varities of the disease. It has an incubation period (the interval between exposure to the disease and its appearance) of between four and twelve days."

On looking for the essential disease constellations, we notice VE = SA/NE; MO = SU/SA. If the positions are adjusted by approximately 6° to match the age, the MC moves into square aspect with VE = SA/NE and a chronic (SA) disease (NE) is activated.

In the day's constellations for the September 6th, 1922, we have NE_T-180-UR (paralyzed rhythm), UR_T = SU (sudden disturbance). If due allowance is made for the above mentioned incubation period, the Sun must have transited NE/PL twelve days previously, so that the disease was caught under SU_T-135-NE.

There is a really striking disease picture in the Declination Diagram (figure 97 on page 264), with a stellium of negative factors compressed within a space of 4°: in particular, SA/MC/MA/NE/PL/ MC/SA echoes MC = SA in the radix. This is underlined by the strong infection constellation NE = MA/PL.

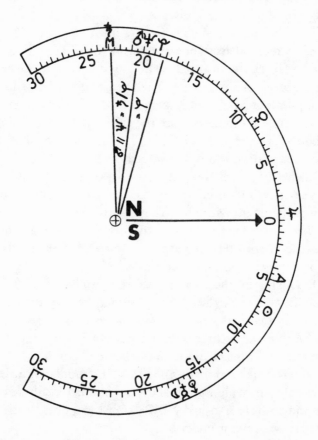

Figure 97. Declination Midpoint Disc for W.G.

The case illustrates that disease constellations will always indicate when trouble is likely to strike, but do not so readily identify the type of disease or the organs affected.

A Second Case of Poliomyelitis

The person concerned was born at 1:45 A.M. on May 12th 1945 in Hirschberg, Silesia. See figure 98 on page 266. Her twin sister came into the world at 2:00 P.M. In the 25th problem set in the magazine *Kosmobiologie* (1959), readers were asked which of the twin sisters developed polio in August of 1948. Twelve contributors sent in the correct answer, and pointed out that the first-born has $MC = MA = UR/NE$. In the fifth year of her life, SA_S activated the midpoint constellation in question. In the Annual Diagram, NE_T-180-UR corresponds to the appearance of the disease. Also, in the cosmogram we have $NE = SU/PL$ within an orb of $2°$. If NE is shifted by a solar arc of $5°$, NE_S-135-SU becomes exact. In the Declination Picture, $SA//UR$ has an orb of only $8'$. UR_P reaches $20° 52'$ at the time of the disease, thus narrowing the orb to $3'$.

He Smoked Himself to Death

Dr. Z., who has been using the Ebertin method for years, writes concerning the following case:

> From time to time, I like to see the light thrown by cosmobiology on what happens to my patients. Here is an example you might find interesting. On looking at the concise ephemerides for 1971/1980, I doubted whether attorney S. would live beyond June 1975. He was smoking himself to death, and did in fact die with Jupiter and Uranus over Pluto shortly before Saturn was over the ASC and Neptune was over Saturn. It was an easy death. I had drawn his life diagram years before.
>
> The patient suffered from dropsy. Enormous quantities of fluid collected in the body tissues and cavaties due to blood

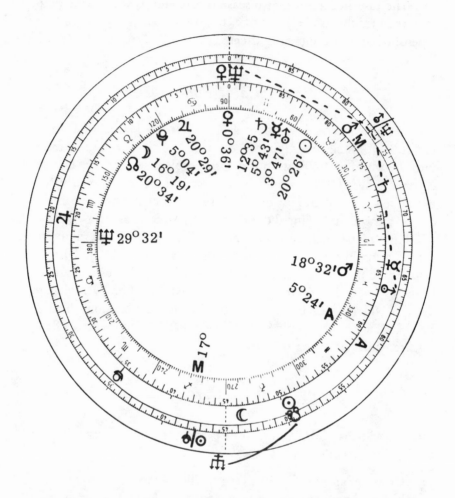

Declinations

☉ = 17°43'N	☾ = 16°45'N	☿ = 22°56'N	♀ = 25°40'N
♂ = 6°11'S	♃ = 22°18'N	♄ = 20°55'N	☊ = 20°47'N
♆ = 1°28'N	♇ = 23°58'N	M = 22°49'S	A = 11°56'S

Figure 98. A second case of polio. Patient born May 12, 1943 at 1:45 A.M., in Hirschberg, Silesia, Poland.

serum being forced out of the capillaries by local and general stasis. However, he would have lived longer than he did if he had not been such a heavy smoker. His body was no longer able to cope with the poisons he had put into it.

The predisposition to a chronic disease is given in the cosmogram by SU = MA = SA/NE: "incurable chronic deterioration."

Diseases caused by overindulgence in such things as alcohol, tobacco and caffeine, are shown usually by SU = NE/PL (COSI No. 999). In the present cosmogram (see figure 99 on page 268), this formula is changed around to become NE = SU/PL = MC. Dropsy is indicated by NE = MA/PL = MC. Furthermore, UR = NE/PL = SA/MC = DR points to an insidious, practically painless disease which may have a psychological origin. The climax of the disease was reached when SU = UR = NE/PL = SA/MC.

The case also illustrates how strongly involved the declinations can be in a disease process. See figure 100 on page 269. In the declination picture, PL = SU/NE = MA/NE signifies the main malady, the dropsy, and points to extensive damage due to the toxication by smoking. UR//NE represents the disturbed rhythm. Now the declination diagram itself is very interesting. See also figure 101 on page 270.

The movements of UR, NE, and SA are minimal, so that it is hard to differentiate them from the position-lines of these planets. $JU_P//MO$ rules the second half of life to give a big increase (JU) in the body's fluid content (MO). Death was precipitated by $MA_P//SA$, $ME_P//SA$ and $SU_P//UR$.

As for the transits, there was a successful stay in hospital in March 1974, represented by SA_T = NE/MC, UR_T = SA and helped by JU_T = MO. In the summer of 1974, the patient was readmitted to hospital under SA_T = MA/SU; death ensued in January 1975, when JU_T and UR_T both transited PL and the transits SA_T = VE/ASC/NE_T = SA and UR_T = PL were nearly due.

Glaucoma and Cerebral Embolism

Eye diseases, especially cataract and glaucoma, are dreaded complaints of old age. But when the corresponding constellations are

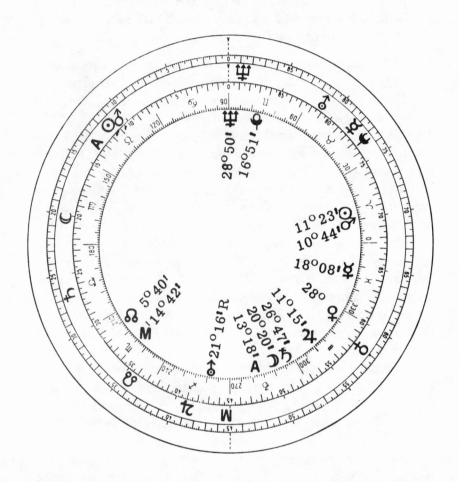

Declinations

$\odot$ = 4°32'N	$\mathbb{C}$ = 16°35'S	$\math233{Q}$ = 6°49'S	$\female$ = 9°28'S
$\mars$ = 3°49'N	$\jupiter$ = 17°50'S	$\saturn$ = 20°44'S	$\node$ = 23°14'S
$\neptune$ = 22°19'N	$\pluto$ = 13°54'N	M = 16°17'S	A = 22°47'S

Figure 99. Attorney born April 2, 1902, at 1:30 A.M., at 40°N, 10°E.

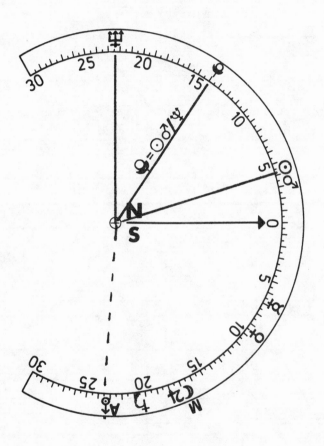

*Figure 100. Declination Midpoint Disc for attorney. PL = SO/NE =
MA/NE: dropsy.*

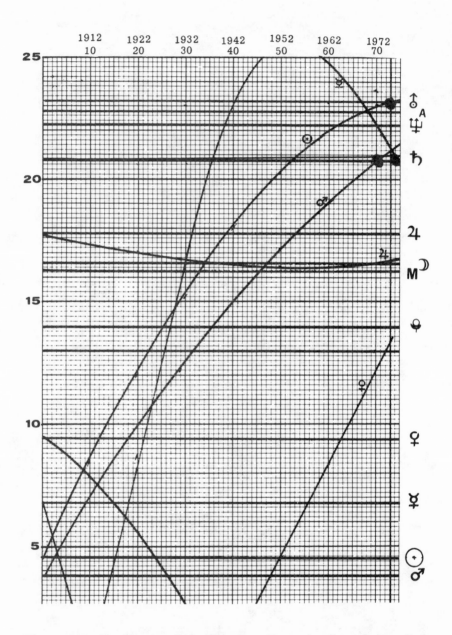

Figure 101. Declination Life Diagram. Born April 2, 1902; died January 25, 1975.

present, it should be possible to take preventive measures in good time. In contrast to cataract, glaucoma affects the whole eye and can easily lead to loss of sight. The leading symptom is increased pressure within the eyeball. The cause is either excessive production of humor in the eye or else the outflow of humor is obstructed or even prevented altogether. The rising pressure in the eye squeezes the retina, the optic nerve and the blood supply. According to the degree and duration of the pressure, there is a more or less quick destruction of the nerve fibers and atrophy of the optic nerve.

The case before us is that of a female born on February 28th, 1900, at 3:00 P.M. in 15° E and 45° 30′ N. See figure 102 on page 271. Without recourse to any special equipment, it should be immediately obvious that ME = NE = SA/PL. In addition, we have SU = JU = MO/NE; SA = PL/MC; UR = MA/NE; PL = MO/SA. The full structural picture is diagrammed below.

SU = MO/NE: Impaired blood supply, accumulation of fluid in the organism, deficient salt utilization (psychological disturbances, eye diseases).

UR = MA/NE: Crippled activities, muscular paralysis, dystrophy, susceptibility to infection, the consequences of infection.

ME/NE: Loss of sensibility, neurasthenia, paralyzed nerves.

SA = PL/MC: Determination to recover, decision to operate, change of therapy. To this I would add: chronic diseases, risk of cancer.

NE = SA/PL: Underdevelopment of the organs, hardening or ossifying of the organs.

NE = VE/MA: Sympathetic and parasympathetic nervous system, vegetative functional disturbances (especially in the intestines and kidneys), menstrual anomalies, varicose veins.

PL = MO/SA: Chronic disturbances of the fluid balance, defects in the mucous membranes, weeping wounds, bladder trouble, constitutional depression, hereditary diseases.

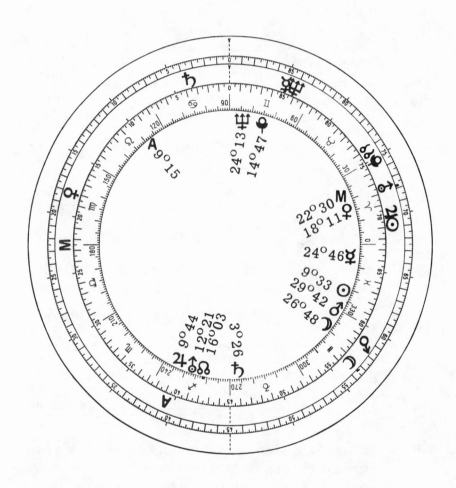

Figure 102. Female, born February 28, 1900, at 45°N30′, 15°E.

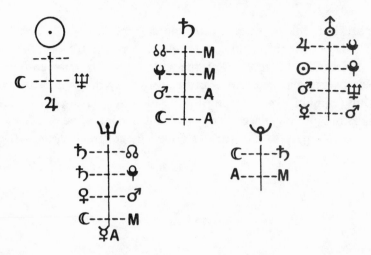

Figure 103. Structural elements of the cosmogram for February 28, 1900.

Obviously, not all the possibilities will materialize. A copy of the case history or a talk with the patient is therefore necessary. A case history provides an opportunity to check the accuracy of the cosmogram. One must never treat the birth chart as a settled fact, but as something that is constantly being modified by directions and transits.

When she was 14, this girl had a congenital glaucoma of the left eye which was surgically removed. According to tradition, the left eye is represented by the Moon and the right by the Sun. If we move the Moon, representing the left eye, through 14° (= 14 years) it approaches Uranus on the 90° dial exactly at the SU/UR midpoint, having already passed SU because the operation was the result of an existing condition. At the same time we should remember that SU = MO/NE indicates eye disease. See figure 104 on page 274.

At age 55, a glaucoma developed in the right eye. If we move MA through 55° (= 55 years), MA is exactly opposite SU, i.e., MA$_s$-45-SU. Once again, SU = MO/NE; the constellation representing eye disease was activated.

When I am making a rough survey, I do not always calculate the exact solar arc, but make do with the simple degree direction corresponding to the year of the patient's life. This is not accurate to the minute but, in any case, a direction seldom takes full effect in a single day but requires time to unfold. See figure 105 on page 275.

On the 23rd August 1960, the patient had a cerebral embolism. An embolism may be defined as the obstruction of a vein or artery by a plug (embolus) borne along by the bloodstream until it becomes lodged in a narrow place. The embolus is dangerous when it cuts off the blood supply to an area not served by collateral vessels. It can

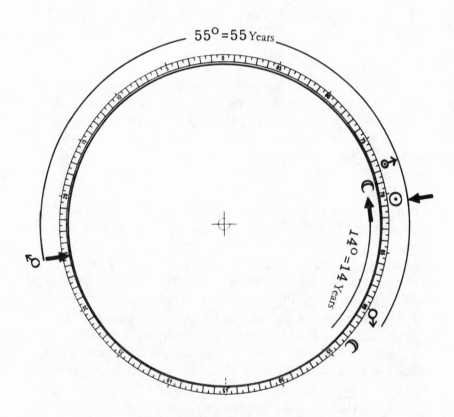

Figure 104. Age 14, glaucoma of the left eye; age 55, glaucoma of the right eye.

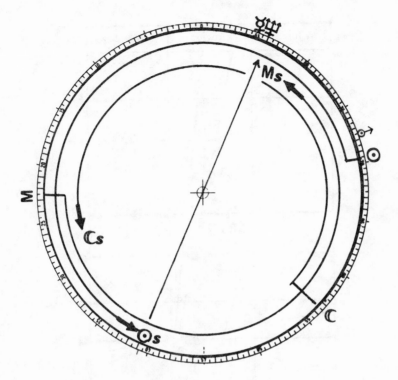

Figure 105. Female born February 28, 1900. Solar arc = 59° 44'. SU^s = NE/ME.

consist of a clot of blood (thromboembolism), of fat (fat embolism), of cellular debris (from cancers or caseous lymph nodes), of foreign bodies or of amniotic fluid. If a plug of this sort does manage to cut off the blood supply, the starved tissues will die.

An embolism in the brain is particularly dangerous; as is shown by the present case, which required a stay in hospital lasting sixteen months. The solar arc for the 60th year is about 60° or, to be exact, 59° 44'. If the individual positions are moved in the 90° wheel, the SU goes to 9° Taurus 16' where it is semisquare ME and NE. A quick glance at the disease constellations shows several relating to disordered nerves and paralysis. In addition, MC$_s$ = NE, MO$_s$-135-UR = MA/NE and MA$_s$-45-PL are all forming. From this we see that disease complexes based on NE, UR and PL are all three being activated simultaneously.

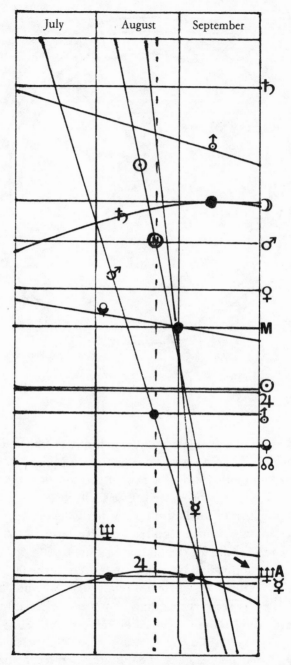

Figure 106. The 45° Graphic Ephemeris for 1960.

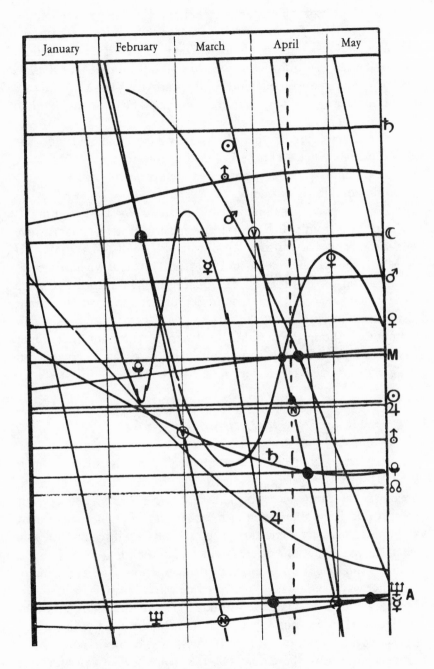

Figure 107. Graphic Ephemeris for 1961.

At the time of the embolism (see figure 106 on page 276) almost every one of these factors is being activated by transits in the annual diagram, and especially by the new Moon. MA crosses the position-line of UR. In addition, SA approaches MO/PL and SU cut the MC line, JU is stationary on NE, and NE is approaching the NE/ASC/ME complex where it is due the following year. So it is not hard to anticipate the outbreak of disease at this time.

We can even predict that the disease will be prolonged, since the slow-moving planet Neptune is creeping toward the NE/ASC/ME complex. NE = ASC signifies an unpleasant or depressing environment—in this instance, the hospital.

Turning now to the graphic 45° ephemeris for 1961 (figure 107 on page 277) from which we are showing the first five months, we notice the danger of a crisis in April, when PL = MC, MA = MC, SU = MC, SA = PL, ME = NE and NE are all due and when there was a new Moon on April 15, 1961. On the night of April 15th, the patient had six attacks of cerebral eclampsia resulting in 50 percent loss of mobility, in loss of the singing voice, and in osteopathy and osteoporosis (bone disease and brittleness of the bones). It might have been possible, with cosmic foresight, to have recognized this danger and to have taken steps to circumvent it.

Death from Drugs

The film actress Renate Ewert was born at 6:28 A.M. on November 9th, 1933, in Konigsberg. See figure 108 on page 280. She began to dream of becoming an actress at a very early age and pestered her parents into letting her attend drama school. After she was content with minor parts for some time, she met the film director Paul May when she was 22, and he offered her a role in the film *08/15*. She was a success, and went on to appear in several films. The opportunity came her way to star with some very fine actors, such as Paul Horbiger, Heinz Erhardt, Dietmar Schonherr, Heinz Ruhmann, and others. However, it was not only in films that she hit the headlines, but also in affairs with married colleagues, which provoked a much stronger reaction in those days than they would evoke now and were well aired in the popular press. Although she longed for a partner for

life, she had no success (VE = SU = UR/NE = NE/PL, MA = VE/
NE = MO/SA, MO = MA/NE, SA/PL = SA/UR).

She suffered from bouts of depression, did everything she could
to gain relief and finally turned to drugs. She took ever increasing
doses until she was no longer fit to appear in front of the camera.
Good friends tried to cure her, but she hid herself away from every-
body, a mere shadow of her former self. On December 10th, 1966,
she was found dead in her flat. The doctor stated that she must have
ended her life some days earlier.

The question as to whether it would have been possible to have
foreseen the tragedy and perhaps to have prevented it can be
answered in the affirmative. For this purpose, it is necessary to take a
closer look at the structure of the cosmogram. See figure 109 on page
281. A strong Neptunian influence is observable, even though the
NE aspects are not exact. Note how informative the midpoints are as
seen in the 90° wheel. UR is joined to PL opposite NE (UR-135-NE-
90-PL). The UR/PL/NE axis crosses the SU/VE axis. The meaning of
SU = NE/PL is given in the COSI as "diseases due to indulgence in
alcohol, tobacco and drugs, etc." Here is a systematic listing of the
various midpoints:

NE = MO/PL: Sentimentality, pessimism, loss of will-power
NE = MO/UR: Loss of energy, muddled endeavors
NE = JU/SA: Pessimism, feeling of abandonment, unbearable
     loneliness
MA = VE/NE: Powerful erotic desires, sexual misconduct
MA = MO/SA: Lack of determination, mental conflicts, disease
VE = UR/NE: One-sided enthusiasm
MO = MA/NE: Nervous debility, addiction
MO = ISA/UR: Mental strain, depression
MO = SA/PL: Sad fate in a woman
SA = PL/MC: Struggle to live, death
MC = SA/NE: Odd character, frequent changes of mood, easily
     discouraged, mental suffering, poor health
MC = MO/MA: Unusual activities, actor
ME = NE/MC: Depressive psychoses, mental disorders
MC = SU/NE: Sensitive, weak, ailing, worn out

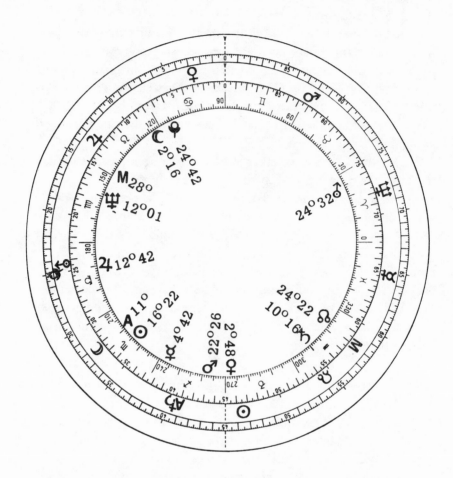

Declinations

☉ = 16°27S	☽ = 26°26N	☿ = 23°15S	♀ = 26°30S
♂ = 24°17S	♃ = 3°58S	♄ = 18°37S	☊ = 8°59N
♆ = 7°51N	♇ = 22°25N	M = 12°10N	A = 15°58S

Figure 108. Renate Ewert, born November 8, 1933, at 6:26 A.M., Konigsberg.

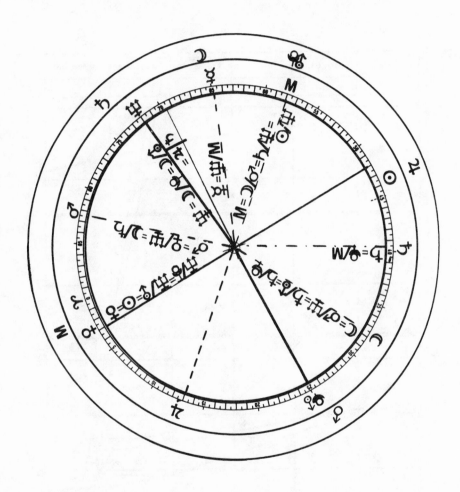

Figure 109. Major configurations for Renate Ewert. The solar arc directions for 1966 are on the outside of the structural picture.

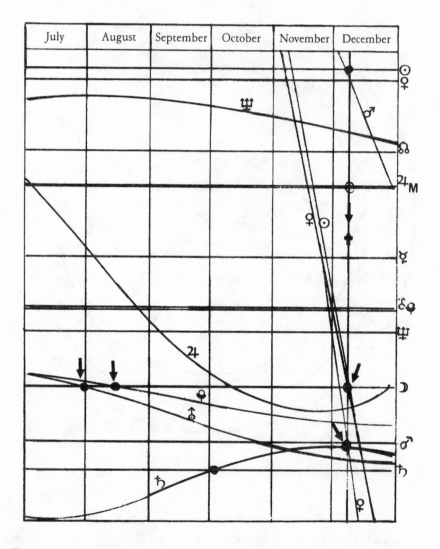

Figure 110. An excerpt from the Annual Diagram for 1961.

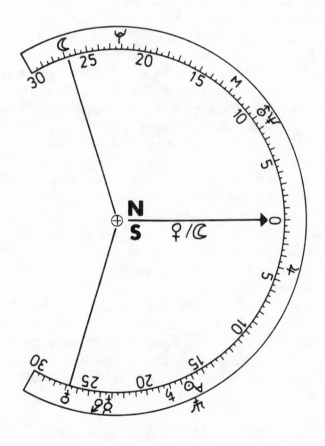

Figure 111. Declination Midpoint Disc for Renate Ewert.

It has to be admitted that these statements are in keeping with the facts of the case, and that everything they predicted happened — because nothing was done to prevent it. The cause of the tragedy lay mainly in the mental state, in the loss of energy, and in the obsession with wishes that seemed to defy fulfillment. The actress was unable to free herself from her depression unaided, and so turned to drugs. She ought to have received psychotherapy at a fairly early stage.

In 1963 transiting Neptune had already reached the place of the Sun, thus activating the basic planetary picture — disease consequent on drug abuse.

The solar arc directions due in 1966 are marked on the outside of the structural picture shown in figure 109. According to these, SA_S had crossed the NE axis two years previously. MA_S had also crossed it. This constellation can be read as $MA/SA_S = NE$ with the meaning: "low vitality, resistance not developed, flagging strength, worn-out condition, life-force sapped by poison, death in mysterious circumstances." $PL = UR_S$ activated $MC = MO/MA = SA/NE = SU/NE$, again pointing to weakness, disease and fatigue.

In the excerpt from the annual diagram, UR and PL had already crossed the position-line of the Moon in August, SA and UR are moving up to the MA and SA position-lines, and death is threatened by $MA_T = SU$, $SA_T = MA$. See figure 110 on page 283.

A look now at the declinations (figure 111 on page 284) reveals an emphasis on affection, love and sexuality. SU-90-SA has an orb of 6° in the cosmogram. $SU//SA$ and $SU//ASC$ reinforce this in a negative way. Equally, UR-90-PL was reinforced by $UR//NE$. If the declinations are calculated for the year of death, $NE_T//SU$ has already formed in October 1966. This constellation represents the weak, sick, enfeebled body, and is fully in keeping with the placement of $SU = NE/PL$ (results of alcoholism, smoking, and drug abuse).

A Life Spent Fighting Anxiety

A long report was sent to me by a lady on whom I shall bestow the pseudonym Pia Wagner. Since it is needful to preserve confidentiality, it is not possible to repeat everything she wrote. Nevertheless, her chart is very instructive in a number of respects; especially with regard to the conjunction of the Moon and Saturn, which is among the causes of her neurosis and subsequent depressive psychosis.

Her father was a revenue officer, and her paternal grandfather and great-grandfather were attorneys. Another ancestor was a Protestant clergyman. Her paternal grandmother was the daughter of a lord of the manor with a long family history, and her greatgrandmother came from France; she had Scottish and Frisian ancestors. One of her forefathers was an astrologer who was raised to the Bohemian nobility by the Emperor Rudolf II.

Her mother was a housewife whose father had been a chief accountant. The other ancestors on this side of the family were independent farmers. One of her great-grandfathers was descended from Portuguese Jews. Her maternal ancestors were mostly marked by the signs Aries, Virgo and Pisces. Table A on page 361 shows the comparative planetary positions of the parents.

Their daughter's birth took place when the following constellations were due in the mother's cosmogram: MA = JU, ASC = UR, MC = VE/MA, MO = MA/UR. On attempting to determine the day of conception, we find the following constellations: in the father, MA_T = VE/MA; VE_T = MO, ME_T = MO; in the mother, MA_T = ME/VE; VE = MO (SA).

Confirmation that the Moon and Saturn were indeed in aspect in the mother's radix is supplied by this description:

> My mother is a very instinctive woman and her activities are colored by repressed aggression [MA-45-UR, MO-135-SA]. Her own parents were very strict with her. She loved my brother more than me. I think I was my father's favorite child. Unfortunately my parents were incapable of being warm and loving. I do not think they loved one another. Both of them take life much as it comes. They seem to have completely drained each other of vital energy while locked in a "cat-and-dog" struggle. The atmosphere in their home has always been like that of a Strindberg play.
>
> In this gray, loveless, puritanical and frugal environment, my brother and I grew up. I was the loneliest child. My brother was always teasing me, and when I got mad at him he would hide behind my mother. Then they would

both have a laugh at me. This is the cause of my later anxiety and aggression neuroses. It is only fair to mention, however, that more recently when I have had to fight against disease and want, my parents have always been very supportive. Today I enjoy a tender relationship with them.

My parents were ambitious to make something of their children. When I was little, I showed musical talent; I was made to learn the piano and it was taken for granted that I was going to become the family virtuoso on that instrument. No one thought of asking me whether I was interested in it. My brother, who has always had a sharp and witty tongue, was set down for a literary career. But he took his fate into his own hands and, when he was 16, he ran away from home to escape the atmosphere of the place. He rented a room and became a cub reporter on the staff of one of the big state newspapers. When he visits his father and mother, he is polite but not affectionate. The family gets together only at Christmas and birthdays. As for me, I left the academy as pianist, composer, and trained music teacher. I couldn't run away from home because I was a girl, and I had to stay there until I was 25. This is what did me so much harm psychologically.

Our parents always wanted children who would excel artistically, but they were in no position to bring up artistic performers because all they did was to fill their offspring with psychological inhibitions and inferiority feelings— properties that are disastrous for a performer. I was constantly nervous of other people. My parents were so frightened of other people, they were positively servile. They invariably sided with others and sacrificed their own children's good to them. Such goings on are enough to drive any child to despair and to give it the idea that nothing but betrayal can be expected from the family. The upshot is a terrible anxiety which ends in neurosis. One simply lacks the self-confidence to overcome fits of depression.

Here we must pause a moment to emphasize that it is entirely possible to overcome the fear and inferiority feelings imparted by

Moon/Saturn. By taking yourself in hand, or through the help of others, you can conquer the negative side of life. The writer of the above report was eventually able to make more of her life and of her capabilities, even though she had wasted a lot of precious time.

The positions in Pia's cosmogram are concentrated almost exclusively in Cancer and Leo, and this in itself points to conflict, seeing that Cancer is negative and Leo is positive. See figure 112 on page 288. The type composition score is as follows: SA = 11, SI = 3, LA = 2 and LI = 8 points. Since the SA score was highest, it was negativism that gained the ascendancy. Nevertheless, SU = PL proved to be a powerful factor which gave Pia enough initiative to achieve some of her goals. SU-45-VE = MA/JU helps the development of creativity, but at the same time, SU-45-SA indicates the hereditary problems and the difficulty in getting on in the world. VE = SA leads to shyness and reserve strongly affecting the love-life.

Confining our attention to those constellations that relate to the body and mind, we observe the following planetary pictures: SU = PL = VE = SA: disappointment, sexual inhibitions, organic disorders, difficult love affairs, desire for freedom from mental pressure, tensions in the love-life. MC = MO/NE: sensitive and easily hurt, but also inspired. ASC = NE = ME/NE = UR/PL: inability to make headway in the face of the environment (the parents), lack of staying power, tendency to be easily led, uncertainty, nervous diseases, difficult circumstances. ME = VE/PL = SA/PL: artistic talent, readiness to solve hard problems. VE = SA = MO/MC: sense of duty, sexual inhibitions, discontent, unhappy love affairs, pessimism. NE = ME/MC = VE/JU = JU/SA: disillusionment, abrasive relationships with others (parents, partner), pessimism, sense of being forsaken, intolerable loneliness.

This case once more demonstrates that the way the life develops cannot be divorced from the state of health. The mother was a very strong influence and exerted unusual pressure on the child:

> I was robbed of the pleasure music had given me, because I did not wish to perform music; I wanted to become an actress. When I entered the music academy, my mother made me practice at the piano so hard that even my professor felt compelled to intervene and protested to her that she

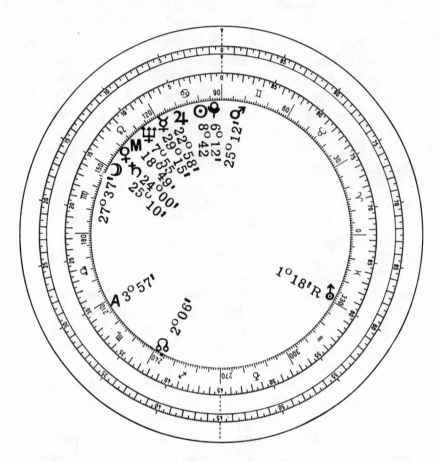

Declinations

☉ = 23°09N	☽ = 7°36'N	☿ = 21°59'N	♀ = 14°45'N
♂ = 23°53'N	♃ = 21°48'N	♄ = 14°26'N	☊ = 11°40'S
♇ = 18°14'N	♇ = 19°25'N	M = 15°11'N	A = 12°46'S

Figure 112. Pia Wagner, born July 1, 1919, 3:00 P.M., 12°N36', 55°E42'.

would soon kill all love of music in me. But she did not want to listen, and his prediction quickly came true. Then, shortly after marrying and leaving home, I became depressive and conceived such a hatred of the keyboard that I sold my inoffensive grand piano and for years I did not practice. Whenever I fancied playing something, I sat down at our old instrument. As a pianist I suffered from stage fright and had lapses of memory. It was years before I was able to enjoy music again.

An examination of the life diagram (figure 113 on page 290) will quickly reveal the complex of SU/VE/SA/MO. The first great turning-point was reached when Pia was twenty. SA = MO was due and, with that, the MO = SA influence was overcome to some extent. Simultaneously, several positive aspects came into play; e.g., MA = SU-45-VE/MC = JU and SU = ME.

In August 1939 (age 20) I became engaged. I was not really in love, but the young man, a fellow-student at the academy, was the first with whom I had really been able to talk seriously and confidentially. We were free to share one another's thoughts. His family (his father wrote for the theater) were very friendly and full of fun, and this wonderful atmosphere was a revelation to me. However, the engagement soon became burdensome, because my fiancé wanted to make love to me physically and I was not ready for it; I was emotionally and erotically inhibited [VE = SA]. I felt the situation was one of mental and physical violence.

These feelings are symbolized by MA-45-SA. In the following years her engagement was broken off.

In 1941, Pia turned Roman Catholic. Even this act fits the future disease picture:

I had always been religious. Love of God, yes, love in general, was the main theme of my life. Well, love and art! These are the areas where I have experienced the greatest suffering, despair and disappointments. The sense of isola-

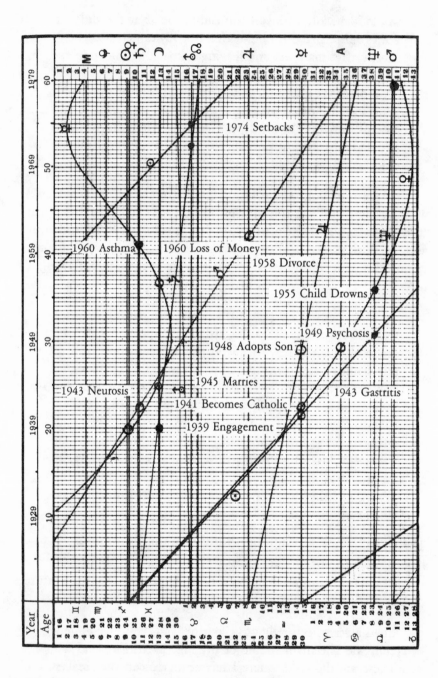

Figure 113. Life Diagram for Pia Wagner.

tion [SA = MO], to which I seem doomed, is accentuated by the fact that I do not look Nordic. I am black-haired and have dark eyes; an inheritance no doubt from my French and Jewish ancestors. I was worthless, that's why I was alone! Men loved and desired me, but only one or two ventured to propose marriage. Of course, I was holier than the Pope and seized the opportunity to tell my fiancé that I could no longer be his mistress. Not till we were married would I sleep with him again. He protested against my chastity [SA = VE] but I was not to be moved.

Inspection of Pia's Life Diagram reveals, in addition to the progression SA_P = MO, a constellation that is less obvious in the cosmogram: MA-45-NE. The two planets face one another on the 90° wheel. In the Life Diagram, NE_P keeps edging closer and closer to MA. This constellation derives its character from ME/MC = JU/SA, which points to the galling relationships (in the parental home), to the unbearable loneliness (lack of marital satisfaction) and to a pessimistic frame of mind.

In the autumn of 1943, the first symptoms of neurosis showed themselves, when I was lying in hospital suffering from gastritis. This was the year in which I fell deeply in love in a purely spiritual way with a young priest who had received me into the Catholic Church. I was aware that he loved me, too; but it scared him and, without warning, he started acting unfriendly toward me. I did not understand his behavior, because everything was so innocent and nothing had happened. His change of attitude came as an emotional shock. Of course, I had been very naïve, I saw that afterwards. I was capable of loving him platonically [due to VE-SA-MO in Leo] but to him I was a physical temptation.

The neurosis and the stomach trouble are associated with SA_P = MO. SA_T-O-MA-45-NE also plays a part. And, in the lower part of the Life Diagram, NE_P-45-MA is gradually forming. These leisurely directions are initially activated by SA_T. In this connection, it should be noted that NE_P-45-MA is not exact until age sixty, but makes itself felt many years in advance. I see here a vindication of my rule that a constellation is effective as long as a planet is within 1° of its exact position. In this instance, NE and MA are within a more generous orb of 2° which works due to the fact that NE_P-45-MA is triggered to some extent by SA_P-0-MO.

The way in which the development of the disease is mirrored by the constellations in the Life Diagram should now be clear to the reader; so the further course of events can be described more briefly. In 1944 there was an opportunity to marry, but Pia discovered that her prospective partner had homosexual tendencies. However, on December 21st, 1944, she wedded a young actor. "I was very impressed; besides, my home life was miserable and I wanted to get away from it." The husband was born at 2:49 P.M. on October 22nd, 1922, in South Jutland. A comparison of the natal charts reveals that the negative constellations play a leading role. VE = SA in the female chart comes in contact with MO in the male chart. MC_F = NE_M leads to disappointment. "I wanted to have children but my husband turned out to be sterile." On October 2nd, 1947, the couple adopted a boy who had been born on September 22nd, 1947. This was one of the few happy moments in Pia's life under JU_P-0-ME. Professionally, too, her prospects looked brighter, and she saw a final hope of doing something creative and artistic by becoming an actress. But the hope was short-lived because, in June 1949, she failed the audition for drama school.

SU_P = NE is found in the Life Diagram under 1949, and this activates NE_P-45-MA. She began to suffer from a severe depressive psychosis. "I felt that there was nothing left to hope for. All my vitality had disappeared; only a thin thread held me back from suicide. It is impossible for me to paint the hell of depressive psychosis. I remained shut up in this hell for almost three quarters of a year. The doctors were unable to help me. All they did was to give me barbiturates, phenobarbitone, etc., which made the so-called stupor phases of the disease even worse." Now, with NE-MA constellations, medication should be avoided as much as possible, because allopathic drugs can aggravate the disease or transpose it. Homeopathic remedies are more helpful because although they act slowly, they have no side effects.

With VE_P-45-NE, Pia suffered a particularly hard blow of fate. While she and her husband were on tour, their child was playing in the harbor and some youths pushed him into the water and he was drowned.

In May 1955, she was engaged to perform in three short films for television. The programs were "hand ballets" in which her fingers were used to perform a dance. In spite of this successful activity, she had to visit a psychoanalyst because her bouts of neurotic depression had become so painful.

After a fresh marital union had ended in failure and divorce, the patient began to suffer from asthma. ME_p = SA had fallen due. The serious disability had its good side in that the performer now received a sickness pension and was no longer forced to work.

The Life Diagram shows SA_p-180-UR and SU_p-180-UR looming up next. This corresponds to a series of setbacks which helped to worsen the disease.

Thanks to an advance from the inheritance her parents will one day leave to her, this trained musician plans to buy a small house where she can play the piano and practice chamber music without disturbing the neighbors.

A Case of Mental Aberration

The following item is taken from a newspaper report: "An angel of death mounting heavenward was the favorite figure of the 34 year old graphic designer. This sinister theme ran like a red thread through many of his water colors and other works. On Monday night (22nd–23rd September 1974), the mentally sick artist himself played the part of death's ghastly messenger."

Erich Postenrieder, a baker's son, was born at 8:55 P.M. on May 26th, 1940, in Baden bei Wien. See figure 114 on page 294. After trying his hand for a short time as a baker's apprentice, he immersed himself in literature; especially in the writings of Dante, Klopstock, Goethe, Hölderlin, and James Joyce. He also amused himself by composing morbid poems. Because of his brilliance at drawing, he was sent to the Academy for Applied Art in Vienna and, when still very young, he matured his painting technique by visits abroad to France and Italy. His main occupation was that of artist, but for brief

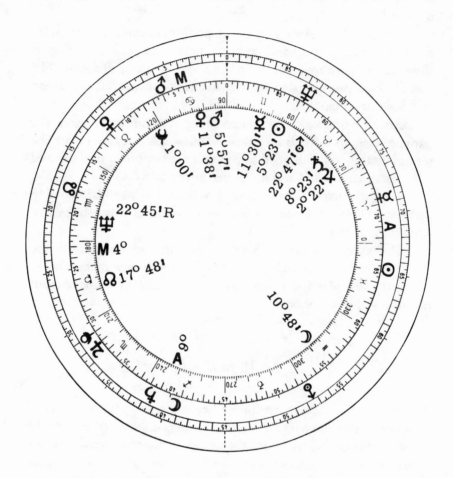

Declinations

☉ = 21°13'N	☾ = 12°52'S	☿ = 23°16'N	♀ = 25°58'N
♂ = 24°26'N	♃ = 11°16'N	♄ = 12°11'N	☊ = 18°12'N
♆ = 4°01'N	♇ = 23°41'N	M = 1°36'S	A = 21°49'S

Figure 114. Erich Posternrieder, born May 26, 1940, at 8:55 P.M., Baden bei Wien, W. Germany.

periods he had been a croupier, then a medical student and, in fact, had tried all sorts of jobs.

On looking at his cosmogram, we note the following constellations: MO-90-SA, the significance of which we have already seen in previous examples, SA-135-NE and SA-135-MO, or NE = MO/SA. These all suggest the possibility of mental disturbance, with a tendency to bouts of depression and a lack of self-confidence. On the other hand, artistic talent and opportunities for success are shown by SU = VE/PL = MA/JU, VE = MO/ME, JU = VE/UR, PL = VE/UR. The radical square MO-90-SA is reinforced by the parallel MO//SA.

A quick glance at the positions for the 30th and 60th days after birth reveals that SA_P-90-MO, JU_P = SA-135-NE and NE_P-135-SA are due.

These directions show up very clearly in the Life Diagram. See figure 115 on page 296. The already narrow distance between NE and JU continually decreases. When the native is about eighteen years old, SU crosses the position-lines of NE and SA; SA_P reaches the MO line some six years later.

The biographical details state that the artist suffered his first attack of mental aberration when he was 24, after which he had to be confined to an institution for a long time. In his unstable and depressed state, he executed original drawings and water colors which art critics interpret as a "warning to the sick world."

The Life Diagram shows the virtual impossibility of conquering the disease, for NE is approaching 23° Virgo and therefore the sesquisquare of SA. Between 1967 and 1970, JU crosses the position-lines of SA and NE. In 1973 the native had to be readmitted to the mental hospital, but was soon discharged being apparently more cheerful and full of vitality. He married and a daughter was born of the union. This is represented in the Life Diagram by VE over MC and ME over JU. But SU over MA = SU/SA is also forming.

In view of the constellations in the Annual Diagram for 1973 (figure 116 on page 297), the patient should not have been discharged on any account. True enough, a few Jupiter transits gave him a certain amount of uplift, but Uranus and Neptune move to the position-line of the Sun. This signifies, on the one hand, great agitation (UR) and, on the other hand, weakness and stupefaction (NE).

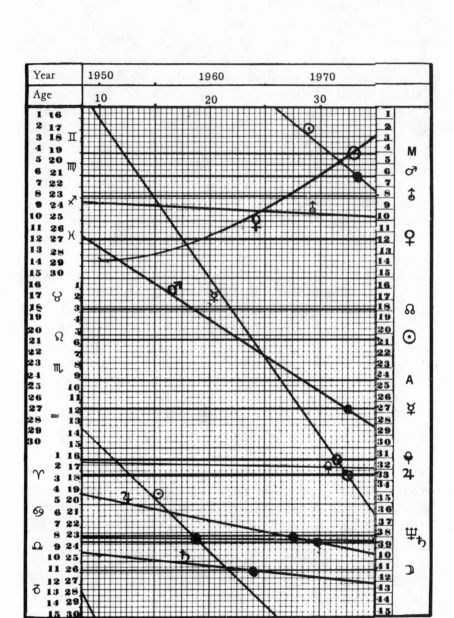

Figure 115. Life Diagram for Erich Posternrieder.

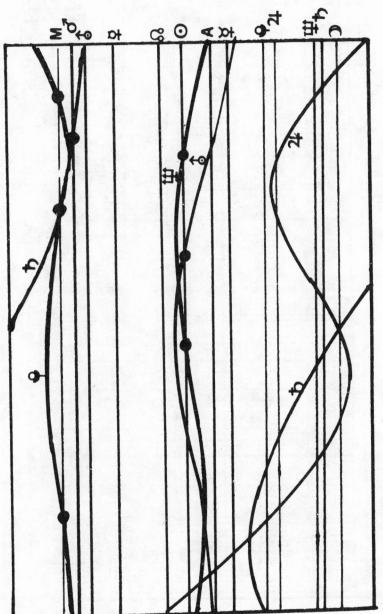

Figure 116. Annual Diagram for 1973.

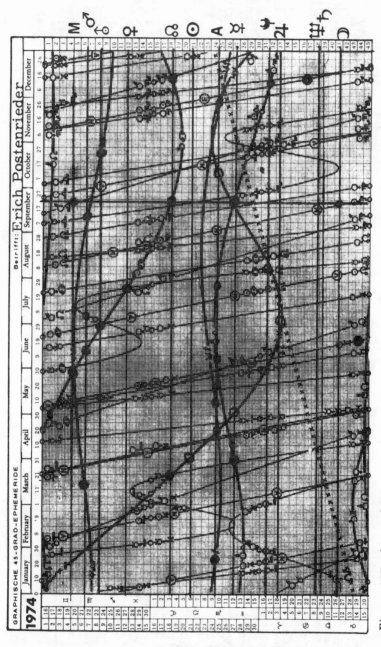

Figure 117. Annual Diagram for 1974.

UR and NE are capable of switching off the conscious mind and of handling the individual over to the uncontrolled impulses of the unconscious. At the top right of the diagram we have some fairly ominous constellations, as SA and PL simultaneously cross MC and MA. These constellations can lead without warning to brutality and violence. A physician trained in cosmobiology would never have risked releasing a patient into the community when such directions were active. Only by checking their astrological charts as a backup to the medical diagnosis is it possible to make a wise decision regarding the discharge of mental patients. The same applies to the release of convicts, if one wishes to ensure that they will not commit fresh crimes on being paroled or let out of prison at the wrong time.

In the Annual Diagram for 1974 (figure 117 on page 298), PL is threading its way through the MC/MA/UR complex; SA also crosses this constellation in the summer. When MA also crossed the complex on the night of the 22nd/23rd September, "the Angel of Death struck." A contemporary newspaper article reported as follows:

> Erich Postenrieder, who has recently held successful exhibitions in the Basilisk and Kaiser Galleries in Vienna, and whose paintings and drawings have been purchased by the Albertina and the Lower Austrian government, was a patient for more than a year in the Gugging state hospital. [He must have been discharged when JU was stationary for a considerable period over its own position-line.] After his condition had apparently improved, the doctors released him. The oversight, or as Gugging medical superintendent Friedrich Lorenz calls it, "the lack of provision for aftercare," had disastrous consequences and relapse. When his condition worsened a few days ago [PL_T = MA = SU/SA and SA_T = DR = MO/NE = MA/PL], Erich Postenrieder avoided the doctors. The big, corpulent man, who seemed to have every hope of becoming an established artist after his discharge, was suffering from fits of depression again. His young, attractive wife, who had finished an insured leave of one year after childbirth, wanted to leave their child with grandparents in Baden. She discussed her husband's condition with her in-laws. It was decided at a fam-

ily council, and with apparent agreement of Postenrieder, that he should be taken to see the doctor early Monday morning.

That night the artist's sleep was troubled. When he rose at 1:15 A.M., ostensibly to take some medicine, his wife followed him into the kitchen. Suddenly she no longer saw her husband facing her, but the Angel of Death who had been haunting Postenrieder's brain in a terrifying way ever since his first committal. The artist was standing naked in the kitchen with something held behind his back. Silvia scarcely had time to speak before he stabbed her with a kitchen knife; then, with a punctured lung, she fled down the stairs leading from their attic flat in 18 Mozart Street.

A Hofrat's widow living in the same block heard the screams, looked up the stairs, and horrified by the sight of the naked man, slammed her door shut. Silvia hid in a lavatory and was later taken to hospital. Postenrieder went back into the flat and completed his grisly work: he killed his darling daughter as she lay in her cot, and knifed his parents in a desperate struggle in the kitchen. Then he cut his throat and threw himself from a window, hitting the ground thirty-six feet below.

A number of obvious constellations warn of the event of September 23rd, e.g., $SU_T = MA/NE = SA/PL$, $MO_T = UR_S = MO/SA/NE_T = MA/SA$, $SA_T = DR = MA/PL$, $MA_T = MA = SU/SA$, $PL_T = MA$, $MC_T = MA/PL$. I feel it is important to realize that such tragedies can be foreseen and averted. It would have made a vital difference here if only the doctor had arranged for proper aftercare when the patient was under critical constellations.

Elma Must Stay Fat!

On examining our next cosmogram (see figure 118 on page 302) we notice a clear indication of disease in the 90° wheel, namely SA-90-VE. Other inauspicious signs are UR-90-PL and the relationship of these planets to NE. The first thing likely to happen in this case is a disturbance of the glandular system (SA = VE), in which the kidneys play a big part. If the kidneys are malfunctioning, water collects in the body and induces obesity. Whenever the fluid balance of the body is upset, we should take a look at the Moon. Here we have MO = MC = SA/NE. Thus the Moon is in the disease axis.

Next, we ought to inquire if the individual planets are forming aspects with one another. This is best seen in the Life Diagram. SA_p = VE takes effect in the years between thirty and forty; allowance being made for the fact that (as experience shows) such constellations always start to operate years ahead of time. In the center of the Life Diagram, UR_p = PL and NE_p = PL are slowly forming. The critical point came at the age of thirty, when SU and VE crossed the position-line of NE.

Elma Karlowa was a very popular actress. She had starred in more than thirty films and had played opposite many well-known actors. But a gradual change came over her formerly immaculate body. In 1958 a film producer told her: "Elma, you are putting on weight; take care or no more parts will come your way!" At this, she began to live in dread of growing stout and of quickly reaching the end of her career. "I received a psychological shock," she told a reporter, "because I wasn't fat and wasn't going to get fat either." But in 1963, Peter Alexander refused to appear with her. Her weight had increased from 110 to 150 pounds. She fasted, and tried various treatments, but nothing seemed to help. Colleagues began shunning her. What had gone wrong? The answer lies in SA-90°-VE and SA_p = VE, a glandular disorder.

She said at that time: "I tried to take my life with an overdose of sleeping tablets. But I was saved. . . . My unconscious would not allow me to die. . . . I hardly know how to explain it. I guess I just didn't want to die looking homely. I was 21 [MA_p = JU] when a German film producer discovered me, and I became a star almost overnight. The plunge back from sudden riches to sudden poverty was not too strange, but it was mighty grim."

She still had a little money left, but she needed an occupation, also the feeling that she was still useful to somebody; and so she became a charwoman, a washerwoman, a canvasser and a cravat-maker. (See figure 119 on page 303).

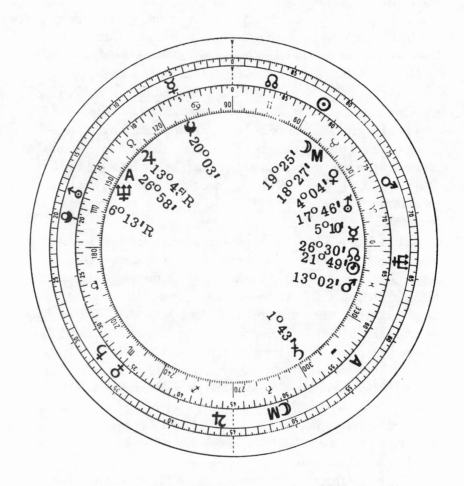

Declinations

⊙ = 3°14'S	☾ = 21°33'N	☿ = 1°29'N	♀ = 13°52'N
♂ = 8°00'S	♃ = 17°40'N	♄ = 19°58'S	☊ = 6°25'N
♅ = 9°58'N	♇ = 22°22'N	M = 17°20'N	A = 12°31'N

Figure 118. Cosmogram for Elma Karlowa, born March 12, 1932, 3:40 P.M., Zagreb, Yugoslavia.

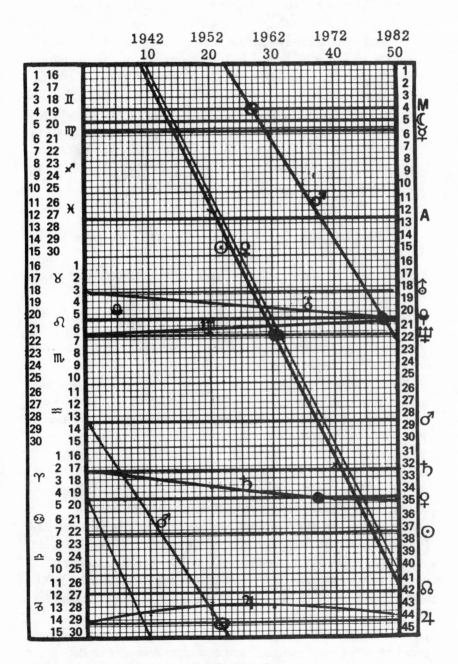

Figure 119. Life Diagram for Elma Karlowa.

But Karlowa was tough. She managed to endure eighty days in hospital on a null diet. She became slimmer, although not so slim as before, and soon secured a role. Ironically, she was cast in a comedy in which she had to stuff herself with chocolate creams, so she rapidly became fatter. But now they wanted her that way: she had to stay fat. In her prime she used to be paid fifty thousand to two thousand marks per film; now she has to be content with a comparative pittance. But she has not given in. From time to time she appears on television as well. At all events, she has succeeded in mastering her fate, and is living proof that there is no need for us to be worsted by critical constellations.

In Double-Quick Time to the Operation

A young married couple who went on a world tour every year always had an annual diagram prepared so that they could adapt their travel plans to the constellations. The result was that everything went well, even when their journeys took them through the trouble spots of Southeast Asia. On the other hand, ignorance of the cosmic situation can prove very prejudicial, as is shown by the following case.

In the natal chart for my client (see figure 120 on page 305) you'll see two complexes, UR/VE/MA and NE/DR/SU, are immediately obvious in the 90° wheel. These two complexes are separated by 35° to 40° so it is likely that a crisis affecting health could occur between the ages of thirty-five to forty. In this connection, SU/NE points to weakness and disease, and UR/VE/MA points to sexual matters and the female organs. Now look at SA, midway between the complexes. This suggests growths, a tumor, or cell death.

Inspection of the excerpt from the Annual Diagram for 1966 (figure 121 on page 306), in which all the essential factors are given, instantly reveals that nearly all the slow-moving planets are forming ominous constellations. NE_T is weaving its way through the UR/VE/MA complex where it dwells on the position line of VE. PL and UR_T are moving over the lines of JU and SA; SA_T is stationary on the position-line of ME. Anyone acquainted with cosmic laws would avoid travel at such a time. Here is a circumstantial report of the course of events.

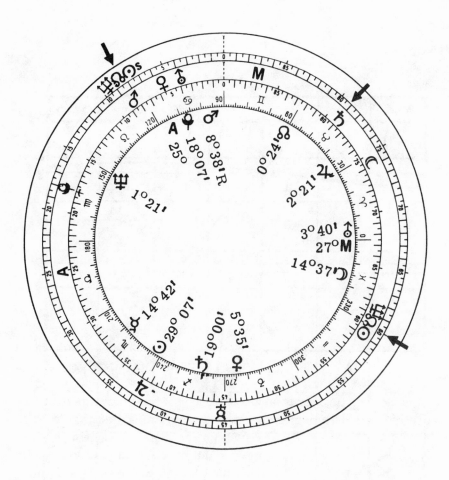

Figure 120. Female born November 22, 1928. Birth data withheld for confidentiality.

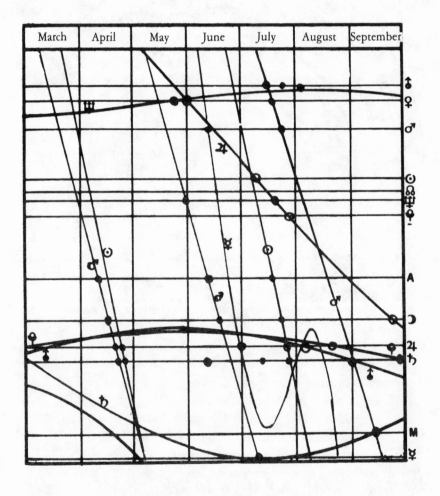

Figure 121. Annual Diagram for 1966.

On April 13th, 1966 my client experienced abdominal pains while at work. MA$_t$ was crossing the lines of ASC and MO. It seemed as if the case was one of inflammation (MA). The patient put off going to the doctor until April 23rd, 1966 and, when she did, he diagnosed a uterine myoma. Myomas are benign tumors of connective tissue that do not develop before the 20th (or more usually) the 35th year of life. If they grow very rapidly and there is a deterioration in the general health, this is cause for concern and they ought to be surgically removed. The doctor gave her injections every five days, but the course did her no good. She remained tired and listless. An appointment was made for her to see him again in three month's time.

In spite of her condition, she went on vacation with her husband on June 30th. It was glorious weather at the seaside, and they stayed at a good hotel where the food was excellent and the other guests were good company. The sun and the salt water toned up their skin and started to give them a tan. But appearances were deceptive. Jupiter and Neptune together mean "fictitious good luck," and JU$_T$ and NE$_T$ met on the position-line of Venus at the time. MA$_T$ over NE was not a good sign either.

On July 13th, the patient's abdomen was struck by a heavy wave while she was bathing. She recalls, "It felt as if something had burst inside me. My husband had to help me out of the water. I felt ill, and had sharp tummy pains which made me vomit." MA$_T$ was crossing the lines of UR and VE, and NE$_T$ was approaching the position line of UR.

Although she was in such bad shape, the couple visited a large town on July 14th. "I felt obliged to pull myself together," she said, "so as not to spoil my husband's holiday. On the 15th of July we went against my will to a small island; I was longing to go home. I fainted in the street but was able to rest for a while in a house. I slept there for two hours while my husband saw to our luggage. From the 19th through the 20th July, I lay in bed unable to eat anything and, apart from brief periods of relief, was in agony day and night."

The local doctor advised that the patient should return home as soon as possible. The journey was undertaken on July 22nd, with the pain increasing until it was almost unbearable. They arrived on the 23rd at 7:30 A.M. and their own doctor started to examine her ten minutes later. She was immediately admitted to the hospital and, at 12 noon, was wheeled into the operating theater for surgery that lasted two-and-a-half hours. The doctor had acted like lightning. MA_T conjunct MA_T expedited the operation besides representing the surgery itself. It was a good thing that $JU_T = PL$, $UR_T = JU$ and $PL_T = JU$ were due on the following days. As early as the 6th of August the patient was fit to be discharged.

Nevertheless, difficult constellations followed. SA moved over MC, and UR and PL moved over SA, while NE dipped back towards VE. As the case notes show, the emotional shock after the operation was extraordinarily great when the patient realized that she was no longer able to bear children. She could console herself, however, that she had survived the crisis well and that her husband still loved her. Early warning of what was in her cosmogram and annual diagram would, if heeded, have stopped her going away on holiday. Certainly, the first attack of severe pain should have sent her rushing home to consult the surgeon.

The Childless Queen

The problem of children often plays a very big part in marriage, especially in ruling houses where the call for an heir to the throne is so imperative. A well-known example is the fate of Queen Soraya, the former consort of the late Shah of Persia.

A superficial glance at the natal chart (see figure 122 on page 310) leaves one wondering why ever this lady should be infertile seeing her Moon is in opposition to Jupiter and her Mercury is conjunct Venus. However, consideration of SU = MA/SA = NE/PL reveals that she may be inadequate in certain areas, for she suffers from diseases brought on by indulgence in poisons such as nicotine. She was a notoriously heavy smoker, and this and her other addictions caused her infertility. Now, MO = SA/NE points not simply to disease in general but, more specifically, to female (MO) disorders (SA/NE).

MC = SU/SA = MA/NE indicates infectious diseases, and obstructions to her personal development in spite of her impetuous spirit (MC = VE/PL). The former constellation is reinforced by ASC

= MA = SU/SA. ME = VE = MA/JU = MO/MA gives a strong desire to be procreative, which is unfortunately frustrated by other constellations. MA = VE/PL = SU/SA reveals passion but denies the birth of a child. JU = SU/VE shows the possibility of happiness in love but JU = SA/NE speaks of illnesses. The constellations SA = SU/NE, UR = VE/SA, NE = VE/SA, PL = VE/SA have the same purport.

Soraya was betrothed to the Shah in October 1950, and the royal wedding took place on February 12th 1951. She was then eighteen years, seven months and twenty days old. The solar arc for the event was 17°, 35′. According to this, SA_S = MO was due, which is not a very favorable constellation — especially for a woman. MO = SA/NE was also activated. SU_P had crossed PL and was now at the UR/PL midpoint, showing the exceptional demands being made on this young woman.

In the life diagram (figure 123 on page 311), we see that the semisquare between NE and PL is exact. Also the activation of this constellation by SU_P is imminent. Perhaps the young woman was so upset at this time that she kept on smoking cigarettes in order to calm herself. In the Life Diagram, VE and ME reach SU, which is at MA/SA = NE/PL however.

Already in 1954, when SU = NE/PL was exact in the Life Diagram, rumors were going round of an intended divorce on account of childlessness. The divorce was granted in 1958. In the Life Diagram we see how, at this time, MA is approaching SA, after SU_P has crossed the position-line of UR. During this period the young queen must have experienced a great upheaval.

The annual curve that I have devised gives a very clear idea of Soraya's situation. See figure 124 on page 312. One key is to look for triangles standing on (positive) or hanging from (negative) a base line. The difference in height depends on how long it takes a planet to traverse 1°. In the case of Jupiter, for example, the difference can be anything from 4–26 days. With Neptune, the differences can run to several weeks. These variations arise because of the times when the planets are stationary (as seen from earth). In Soraya's and in the Shah's curve, the rise indicates the marriage; but then, in Soraya's case, the curve descends steeply under the influence of NE_T-90-MC. Nevertheless, striking as this is, the reader is cautioned not to study

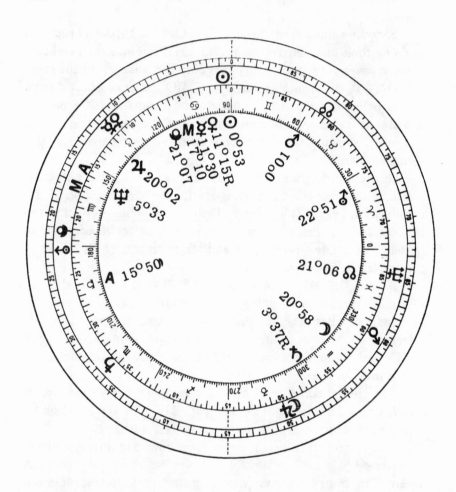

Figure 122. Cosmogram for Queen Soraya, born June 22, 1932, 1:13 P.M., Esfahan, Iran.

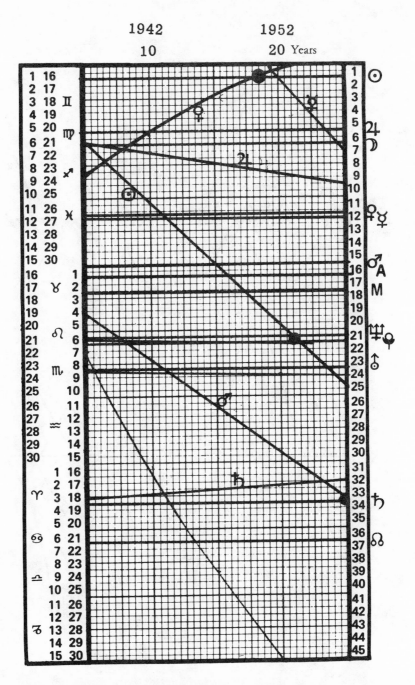

Figure 123. Life Diagram for Queen Soraya.

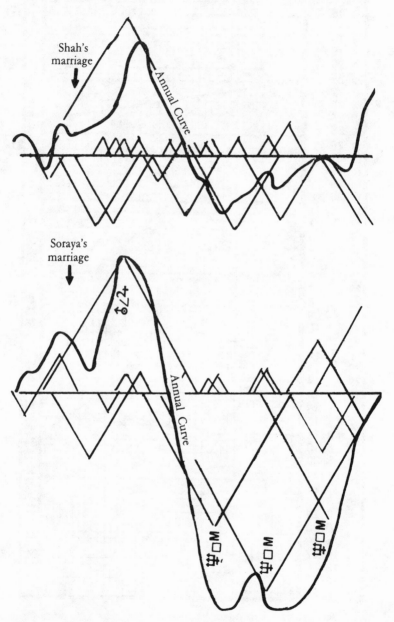

Figure 124. Annual Curve.

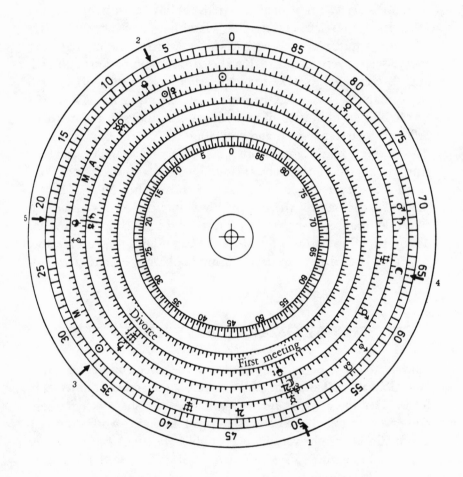

Figure 125. Contact Cosmogram for Shah Reza of Iran and Queen Soraya.

the annual curve in isolation but always to look at the directions when assessing a situation.

The possibility of childlessness and subsequent divorce figures in *Das Kontaktkosmogramm* (The Contact Cosmogram).[73] Both partners have an extraordinarily good constellation, shown by arrows 1 and 2 (see figure 125 on page 313), which was activated when they met. ME and PL_M (m = male, f = female) link up with MO, JU and DR_F opposite SU/VE. This signifies a fateful love alliance (PL = SU/VE) with a fortunate (JU) woman (MO). At first, the marriage was indeed seen as very fortunate. But the critical combination of NE, UR and PL_F is exposed to MO_M, suggesting disappointment (NE) through the woman (MO). Also, in the same constellation, we have PL = VE/SA = NE; an indication of exceptional difficulties in the marriage followed by estrangement and separation.

One very significant feature is the contact between SU_M and SA_F, which is marked on the Contact Cosmogram by arrow 3 (figure 124). It warns of the separation that actually occurred when NE_T passed this place. That it was not the man who was infertile in this instance is shown by the fact that the Shah himself did have children later on. The relationship between the Shah and Farah Diba was considerably better, as is explained in detail in my book on the contact cosmogram.

A Queen With No Heir

Queen Fabiola of Belgium is the sixth of the seven children of Count Don Gonzalo de Mora, one of the richest large landed proprietors in Spain. Her three sisters married young, while she led a retiring, domestic life (VE-180-SA) and engaged in social work. She is a devout Catholic, not very keen on public functions but a lover of music and literature (SU = MO/SA = SU/VE). See figure 126 on page 316 for her cosmogram.

On September 16th, 1960, the world was taken by surprise when the betrothal of Fabiola and the Belgian King Baudouin was announced. The couple had met two years previously (SU_P-90-MA) = JU/UR) but had kept their association a close secret. The wedding took place on December 15th, 1960 (VE_S = PL, JU_S = MA/PL). The well-matched and discrete royal couple waited in vain for an heir to the throne. Their hopes were blighted by the miscarriages suffered by the very delicate Queen in 1961, 1963 and 1966. In 1971 the eldest son of Albert, Baudouin's brother, began training for future kingship since there was no prospect of any other crown prince coming along.

The retiring life-style of the queen-to-be gave early warning that she might be subject to various obstructions and organic disorders. VE-180-SA indicates a disturbance of the internal secretions, with special reference to the ovaries. Since VE = SA = UR/NE, we gather that the native is hypersensitive and liable to defective body rhythms. This constellation is also influential in stillbirths (COSI No. 938). MO = MA/NE can represent poisons in the body which would not accumulate except for faulty elimination. JU = SU/SA can signify hereditary afflictions. SA = SU/VE is a further portent of disorders of the glandular tissues (COSI No. 206).

An examination of the dates of the stillbirths reveals how the above mentioned constellations are confirmed. At the time of the first stillbirth on June 26th 1961, we have NE_T-135-MO = MA/NE and SU_T = SA/NE = VE/NE, and at the third stillbirth on June 11th, 1966, UR_T = SA = VE = UR/NE was due. Nevertheless, this royal marriage, although childless, was due. Nevertheless, this royal marriage, although childless, was not dissolved; nor would we expect it to be, given the religious beliefs of the partners. The contact cosmogram bears this out too. In the fuller discussion to be found in *Das Kontaktkosmogramm*,[74] I have already stated that there is no likelihood of further births.

The mutual constellations are numbered in the Contact Cosmogram (figure 127 on page 317). 1) ME = MA_M = UR_F can produce unpleasant commotions and surprises, as exemplified by the stillbirths; 2) JU = UR_M = PL_F heralds shared happy events; 3/4) PL_M = NE_M = MA represents insuperable opposition. On the other hand, VE_M = JU_F = SU_M = VE_F can be recognized as the constellation that guarantees a harmonious marriage in spite of all adversities (SA).

It was pointed out that where childlessness is concerned, each case is unique. There is a difference in Iran and Belgium between similar cases owing to the different outlooks and religious attitudes in the two countries. Say, for example, the Sun and Moon in contact represent the marriage, and Mars and Jupiter in contact represents

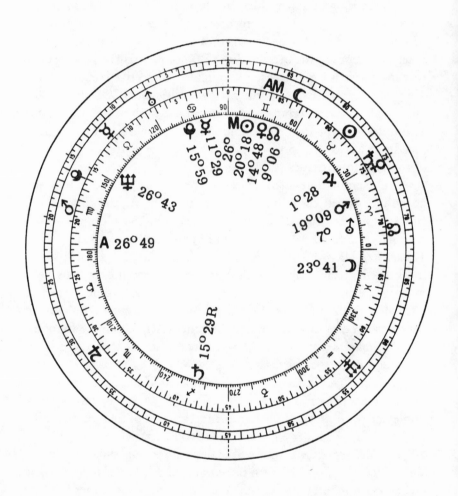

Figure 126. Queen Fabiola of Belgium, born June 11, 1928, 1:13 P.M., in Madrid, Spain.

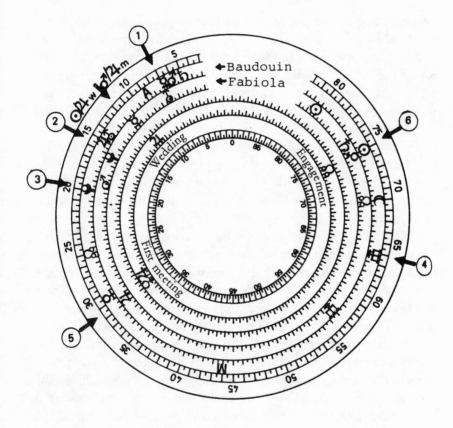

Figure 127. The Contact Cosmogram for Fabiola and Baudouin.

births, it is not a foregone conclusion that the interference of Saturn with these contacts will deny progeny.

We must constantly remind ourselves that the planets on their own can tell us nothing certain, and that other factors such as the heredity, character and current circumstances of the native must be taken into account.

Born with Brain Damage

Our next case is a boy found to be suffering from brain damage. See figure 128 on page 319. The mother had already borne five children and had been torn each time. This time the birth was easier, but the top of the baby's head bulged above his forehead and he showed no signs of life. The doctor immediately gave him an injection and said they would know by 4 P.M. whether the child would ever open its eyes. The little fellow lived but, after a few days, began to suffer from epileptic fits. He was taken to a university hospital, where the conclusion was reached that there was strong pressure on the left side of the brain. Water was constantly filling a cerebral cavity and pressing on the brain to produce fits. When the boy was older, he had to sit on the sofa all day. If he got up he would fall over.

The doctors thought he might be suffering from a split personality or schizophrenia. Just before an attack he used to call out, "Momma, bad boys are coming!" and, when the attack was over, he would say, "Momma, we are going to be good friends again." These words seem to indicate that the disturbances originated in the unconscious. They actually sound like some form of possession.

In the second cosmogram for this case, the geocentric and heliocentric positions of the planets have been combined in a way that is not done in ordinary horoscopes. See figure 129 on page 320. In the center is the Sun. As far as possible, the planets have been placed in their orbits accurately, according to scale. Straight lines have been drawn from the Earth (represented by a cross in a circle) through the various planets to show where we would see them in the zodiac. The position of Mercury is very significant. It is rather hard to make out in the diagram, but lies between the Earth and the Sun. Here is it liable to disturb the solar radiation travelling earthward. A similar effect

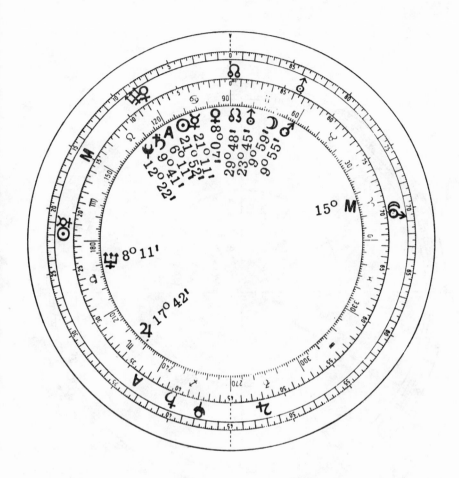

Declinations

☉ = 21°40'N	☾ = 22°36'N	☿ = 16°58'N	♀ = 23°15'N
♂ = 21°46'N	♃ = 16°11'S	♄ = 18°31'N	☊ = 23°25'N
♆ = 1°51'S	♇ = 23°35'N	M = 5°55'N	A = 18°47'N

Figure 128. Brain damaged boy, born July 15, 1947, 5:50 A.M. Birth data withheld for confidentiality.

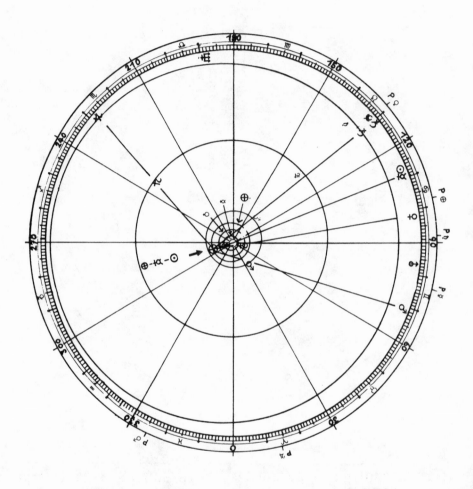

Figure 129. Heliocentric zodiac diagram for brain damaged boy.
Includes orbits of the planets from Mercury through Saturn. (This
idea was conceived by Reinhold Ebertin, designed by Simon Wolff,
and drawn by Hqas Hausemann.

happens at new Moon, when it is the Moon that interposes itself between the Sun and the Earth and occasions disturbances. The case is quite different at the superior conjunction of Mercury, when the planet lies beyond the Sun, and the Sun comes between Mercury and the Earth.

Now, because Mercury has to do with the speech center, the cranial nerves and the intellect, its position may certainly be taken as one explanation of the disturbances in the patient's brain. As the diagram makes clear, Mercury is in its closest position to the Earth, whereas Venus is approaching its furthest position from us. This would not have been known unless the heliocentric situation had been displayed.

The trans-Saturnian planets (Uranus, Neptune and Pluto) can not be entered at their true distances from the Sun in a drawing of the present size. Even so, we continue our investigation by means of the separate geocentric and heliocentric charts.

In the heliocentric chart (figure 130 on page 322), Mars is square Saturn and Pluto, as is visible at once in the 90° wheel. The SA/PL midpoint is 12° 13′; MA is 12° 07′—a difference of no more than 6′. This constellation, which represents "suffering violence and having to fight for one's life" is not present in its geocentric form, but even the geocentric cosmogram gives several indications of the severity of the disease. The reference to suffering violence may be interpreted as injury to the head at birth.

The MC at 15° Aries has some surprising correspondences to offer. In Fritz Brandau's table of anatomical correspondences,[75] 13° Aries represents the ventricles of the brain, 14° represents the frontal lobe, and 15° the parietal lobe of the brain. Now MC = SU/NE points to brain injury or disease. The epilepsy that commenced shortly after birth is depicted by UR = MO/VE. In COSI No. 344 we read, "Epilepsy and other convulsive conditions." UR = MO/NE indicates disturbed states of consciousness. SA = MO/NE indicates hopelessness, pessimism, inhibitions, handicaps.

The declinations have a similar story to tell. See figure 131 on page 323. I have noted SU//MA, VE//UR//PL, and SA//ASC. Further confirmation is provided by my specially developed Declination Diagram. Never before have I seen such a stellium within so few degrees. In addition, SU and MA, the representatives of the vital

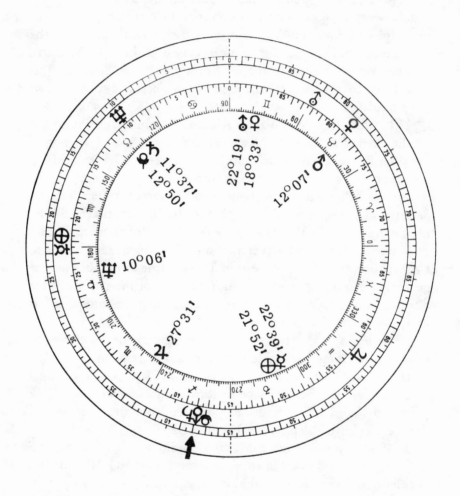

Figure 130. The heliocentric chart for the brain damaged boy born July 15, 1947, at 5:50 A.M.

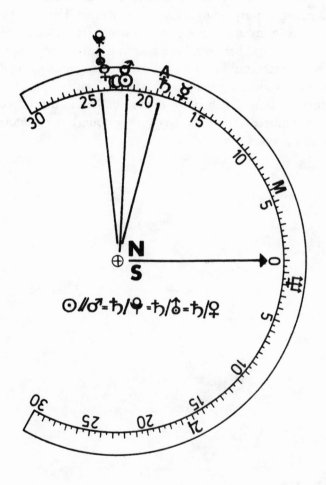

Figure 131. Declination Midpoint Disc for July 15, 1947.

force, are at the midpoints SA/PL = SA/UR = SA/VE, corresponding to the heliocentric MA = SA/PL, but do not emerge from the longitude cosmogram.

Reliance should not be placed in one of the above methods on its own; the situation needs to be examined from various angles for a well-informed opinion. There is not much one can do after the event but, if the constellations for a birth are calculated in advance, it should then be possible to help. In the present state of midwifery, it is not hard to induce or postpone a birth. Here, Mercury interposes itself between the Earth and the Sun as a disturbing factor, and the position of Mars could do with improvement too. Incidentally, I used always to include the superior and inferior conjunctions in our pocket ephemerides but, as nobody seemed interested in this improvement, it is now omitted. The data may still be found in astronomical and nautical almanacs.

CHAPTER NINE

CALCULATING A SUITABLE DAY FOR SURGERY

NOWADAYS, THERE ARE MANY SURGEONS who pay attention to such factors as the new Moon and full Moon, biorhythms, and the effect (in mainland Europe) of the hot, dry föhn wind; unless an operation is so urgent (in the case of an accident, say) that cosmic influences and weather conditions have to be ignored. Many surgeons are also prepared to oblige patients who state a strong preference for surgery on a certain day. Heavy hemorrhaging after full Moon surgery and attacks of weakness after new Moon surgery are already very well documented.

There is an old astrological rule that surgery should not be performed when the Moon is in the sign representing the body part concerned. Thus abdominal operations ought to be avoided when the Moon is in Scorpio, kidney operations are inadvisable when the Moon is in Libra, and the head should be left alone when the Moon is in Aries.

If a patient asks for a favorable operation day to be calculated, my first question is whether surgery has to take place fairly soon or not. For urgent operations I usually decline to advise, because if it turns out that there is a narrow choice between negative constellations and one is reduced to "making the best of a bad job," the patient would probably become apprehensive, and this would have an adverse effect on the progress and success of the operation. But if one has several months or even a year in which to decide, the most favorable time can certainly be worked out, and will then help to relieve the patient of anxiety and to strengthen his or her faith in eventual recovery.

Here is a case in point, verified by an exchange of correspondence. The daughter of Mrs. Bauer (not her real name) wrote to me on September 15, 1975, as follows:

> I wish to thank you at long last for your trouble. And now I have another request. My mother feels she ought to have an operation in the autumn, but will not visit the surgeon before hearing from you what her chances are. Mother is short of breath, apparently because of a swollen thyroid gland. She has already had two operations for goiter. After the second, she suffered a circulatory collapse, was clinically dead and needed fifty injections to revive her. This operation took place fifteen years ago last spring. As you will appreciate, she is frightened of further surgery. You would do me a great favor by letting us have your opinion soon, for, as I say, Mother refuses to put herself in the hands of the surgeon before hearing what you advise.

The above lines demonstrate the tremendous trust placed in a cosmobiologist after he has successfully advised a family on a number of occasions.

The operation fifteen years earlier was performed on April 11, 1960, when, according to the ephemeris, the Moon was full. In the morning the Moon was 9° Libra 51' and, at midnight, it was 24° Libra 03'. The Sun was 21° Aries 06' in the morning. Therefore the Moon must have been full in the evening shortly after the operation. In addition, other critical constellations were due: SU_T-180-ASC = MA/PL, MA, NE-90-MA and SA_T = NE/PL = MO/MA. When there have been previous operations, it is always necessary to find out how the patient reacted to the cosmic constellations at the time.

From Anna's cosmogram (figure 132 on page 328), we can list the following disease constellations. However, before doing so, it is worth mentioning that in the *Anatomischen Entsprechungen der Tierkreisgrade* 17° to 18° Taurus represent the thyroid gland. These degrees are not occupied, but Uranus at 18° Aquarius 37' does form a square to them. The following constellations in the cosmic structural picture (figure 133 on page 329) give warning of disease:

PL   = MO/VE concerns the glandular system (thyroid).

UR   = MO/VE concerns glandular malfunction.

SA   = MC = UR/PL concerns pulse and respiration or shortness of breath.

SU   = SA/NE concerns disease tendencies in general. The fact that Aquarius and Leo are involved indicates faulty circulation and heart trouble.

NE   = SU/MA concerns debility and disease.

MA   = SU/UR concerns injuries and surgery.

On looking at the declinations (figure 134 on page 330), we see the northern SA//MC and NE//PL and the southern SU//MA. Since the same degrees north and south are involved, these positions are all parallel. Therefore, SU//MA has been placed between brackets in the Declination Midpoint Disc (figure 134). The main aspects in the cosmogram (SA = MC, SU-180-SA, SU-180-NE) are considerably strengthened by the declinations.

Turning now to the progressions for the fifty-ninth day after birth, March 21, 1917, we note that NE$_P$ is slowly approaching the Sun—an intimation of future weakness not boding well for surgery later in life. Yet JU$_P$ is nearing MA, which offers hope that an operation would be successful. The solar arc positions are:

SU	= 29° Pisces 46'		PL	= 2° Virgo 17'
VE	= 6° Pisces 19'		ASC	= 19° Sagittarius 28'
SA	= 26° Virgo 17'		MO	= 26° Aquarius 57'

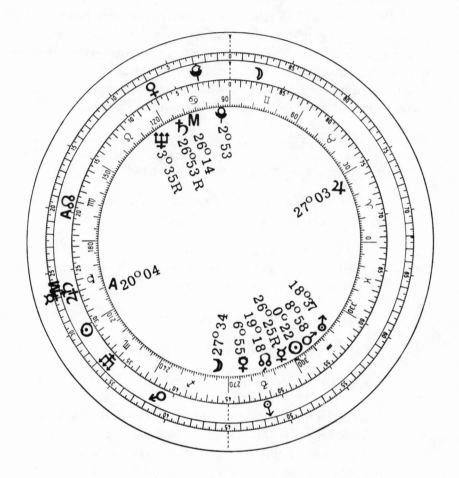

Declinations

⊙ = 20°05S	☾ = 25°09S	☿ = 17°47S	♀ = 22°56S
♂ = 19°03S	♃ = 9°23N	♄ = 20°59N	☊ = 15°53S
♅ = 19°08N	♇ = 18°33N	M = 20°54N	A = 7°50S

Figure 132. Anna Bauer, born January 21, 1917, at 12:30 A.M., in Aachen, W. Germany.

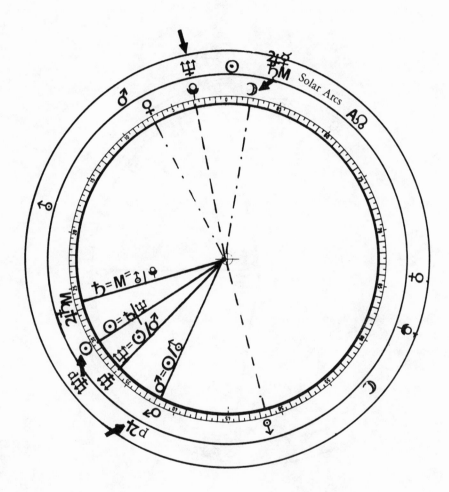

Figure 133. The major constellations from Anna's cosmogram.

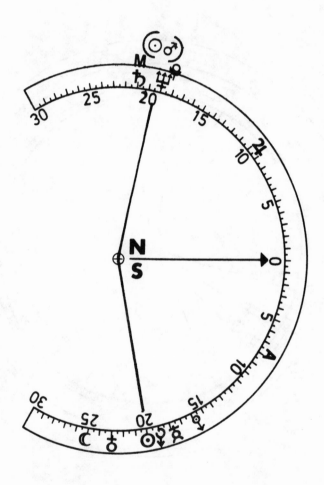

Figure 134. Declination Midpoint Disc for Anna Bauer.

MA	=	8° Aries 22'
UR	=	18° Aries 21'
DR	=	18° Pisces 42'
ME	=	25° Pisces 49'

JU	=	26° Gemini 27'
NE	=	2° Libra 57'
MC	=	25° Virgo 38'

These directions have been calculated for the date of birth, January 21, 1976. The positions are set out in the outer circle of the structural picture. NE_S has moved a few minutes beyond PL = MO/VE = UR. The complex associated with SA_S is approaching MO, making it preferable to get the operation out of the way quickly before this direction is exact.

Now we want to discover the day on which the operation ought to be performed. The annual diagram is not very encouraging (figure 135 on page 332), since NE_T is twisting around the MC/SA/JU/ME complex. What is more, SA_T joins it for part of the way; so that, in spite of a Jupiter transit, the prospects are not very bright early in the year. In May SA_T has left the complex and NE is not making any exact aspect.

The midpoint MA/UR is specially indicative of operations and the ideal situation is when JU is situated at this midpoint. Then we are likely to have a successful or safe (JU) operation (MA/UR). The midpoint MA/UR lies in 13° Aquarius 47'. Its course is drawn as a broken line in the annual diagram and, in May, this line is cut by the path of Jupiter.

The transit table on page 333 shows the exact transits for May. It reveals that JU_T-90-MA would have made the beginning of the month favorable if SA_T-90-JU had not been due as well. The full Moon and new Moon are signified by "F" and "N"; the days of the 13th and 29th on which they occur are out of the question. On the 18th, JU-135-MO = MA/UR is due. This is a Tuesday. The Moon is moving from Capricorn to Aquarius, and is therefore not in Taurus — the sign associated with the site of the proposed operation. On the 19th, MO transits MA = SU/UR. This is another operation constellation. The 18th and 19th of May were accordingly recommended as suitable days for surgery. The operation was performed on the 19th and was free from complications — as the patient reported to me with delight and gratitude.

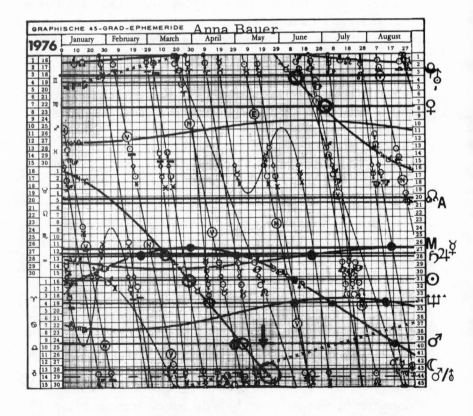

Figure 135. Annual Diagram for 1976.

Table 18. Transit table for May 1976.

Day	Transits
1	
2	♃ □ ♂, ♄ □ ♃
3	
4	
5	
6	
7	
8	☉ □ ☊
9	♂ ☌ M ♂ ☿
10	♂ □ ♃
11	
12	
13	Ⓕ
14	
15	
16	♂ □ ☉
17	
18	♃ ⚷ ☽ = ♂/☊
19	☽ ☌ ♂ = ☉/☊
20	≈
21	
22	♂ ☌ ♆
23	
24	
25	
26	☽ ♉
27	☽ ♉
28	
29	Ⓝ
30	
31	♂ □ ♂

This instance should not be brushed aside as a "happy accident" since, in nearly sixty years of practice, I have successfully calculated many favorable days for operations, both with and without the cooperation of medical men. However, astrological work of this type ought never to be undertaken unless the practitioner is very experienced and is prepared to devote to it time and patience. The responsibility for getting the right answer is a heavy one.

On the 22nd of May MA-0-NE is due. The fact of this constellation coming so quickly on the heels of the operation caused me some concern. The patient was advised to be careful what she ate and to avoid pain-killers and sleeping pills as far as possible. Fortunately, beneficial transits of Jupiter were due in June and July. The fact is worth noting, because good transits after an operation contribute to recuperation. If the transits relate to the Sun, so much the better.

The following two examples show how the success of an operation (or otherwise) can be reflected in the annual curve. In the first case, the curve rises immediately after the operation, but, in the case where the patient died, the curve is held down by powerful negative constellations. Both cases are included in the book, *Die Jahreskurve* (The Annual Curve), but are re-interpreted here.

Successful Gallbladder Operation

The first case was originally presented by Erich Modersohn in an article entitled, "Possibilities and Limits in Making a Prognosis."[76] The patient's attention was drawn to a critical period in the autumn. To begin with, everything went well. Then from October 1956, there were increasing disappointments, promises were not kept and relationships at work were strained. At the beginning of November the region of the gallbladder felt tender, and the pain grew worse and worse until it was unbearable. No gallstones showed up in the clinical investigation but, when an operation was performed on the 16th of November, pebble-sized calculi were removed from the gallbladder.

The general diseased condition is represented in the cosmogram by SU-90-NE (figure 136 on page 335). Now if the ruler in the 90° wheel is placed on SU and NE, we have SU = NE = MO/JU. The

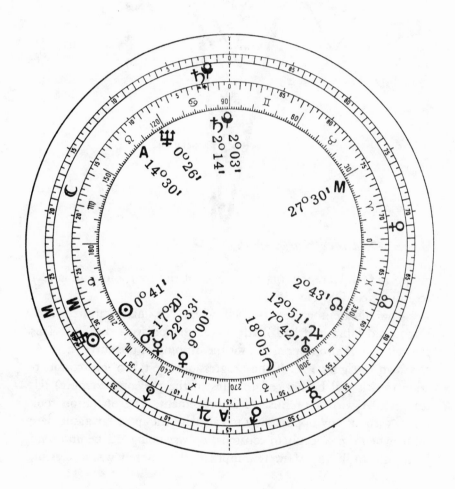

Figure 136. Male birth, October 24, 1914.

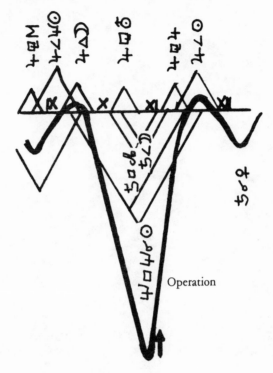

Operation

Figure 137. Annual Curve for 1956.

midpoint MO/JU represents the region of the liver and gallbladder according to COSI No. 362.

The disease manifested itself when NE_T had transited Leo, Virgo, and Libra and had made a conjunction with the Sun. This constellation is also responsible for the dipping of the curve in 1956, as shown in figure 137. If the progressions are taken into consideration too, it will be noticed that (as in the previous example) JU_P reaches MA with a promise of improvement. The operation took place, without any opportunity to calculate the most favorable date for it, when the Neptunian constellation was being left behind, and JU transits to JU and SU were imminent. The surgery was successful.

Unsuccessful Prostate Operation

Now let us look, by way of contrast, at the cosmogram for September 14, 1889. See figure 138 on page 337. After the patient had suffered

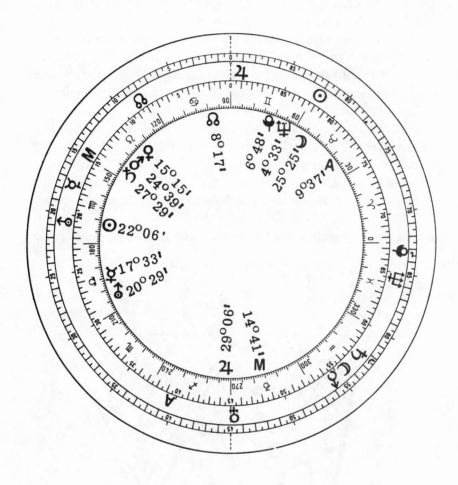

Figure 138. Male born September 14, 1889, 7:28 P.M.

from prostatic hypertrophy (a swollen prostate gland) for a number of years, the matter became urgent and an operation was performed at 9:20 A.M. on June 25th, 1956. Further postponement was out of the question. The operation lasted two-and-a-half hours and was followed by great physical weakness. Water collected in the tissues and the patient suffered from shortness of breath; thrombosis occurred in an otherwise healthy leg. The limbs slowly stiffened and, in the night of 6th–7th October, 1956, the patient died.

At the time of the operation SU-90-SA had just come into effect and indicated a grave crisis. The transits due were SA_T-90-SA and JU_T = SA. PL transits play a big part in depressing the curve and the one or two good transits are too weak to bring about an improvement. See figure 139.

The enlarged prostate is indicated in the natal chart by MO, MA and SA at the VE/UR midpoint in 11° Cancer 01′ and 26° Taurus 01′ respectively. They coincide with MA/SA in 26° Leo 04′. These constellations were activated within a very narrow orb by SA_T in 27° Scorpio 06′—illustrating yet again how accurately the cosmos works.

The moral of these examples is that, if surgery is required, it should not be put off to the last moment, when it may be impossible

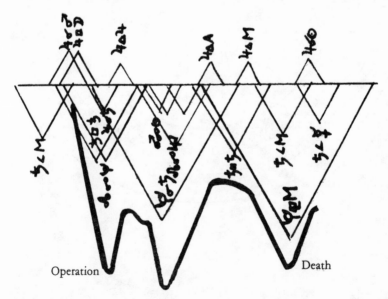

Figure 139. Annual Curve for 1956 showing operation and death.

to avoid the sort of critical constellations found in the second case. On the contrary, an attempt should be made to ensure favorable transits after any operation.

An Operation Happily Avoided

A middle-aged woman going through the change of life complained that she had suffered from persistent hemorrhages for several years. Nothing seemed to stop them and they were very weakening. Her physician advised removal of the ovaries, and so she inquired when would be the best time for an operation. Glancing at Asta's cosmogram (figure 140 on page 340), we note four planets bunched together between 78° and 80° on the 90° dial, all fronting the Sun and nearby Mars and Saturn.

The annual diagram will show these connections even more clearly; with Neptune threading its way for a number of years through the Saturn/Mars/Sun/Venus/Moon/Jupiter/Uranus complex, and presumably evoking the pathological hemorrhages. See figure 141 on page 341.

As early as 1976, Uranus and Saturn entered the complex while Neptune began to skim over the Mars/Saturn line. In 1977 Neptune was still hugging the Mars/Saturn line, and Saturn traversed the complex beneath it. In 1978 Neptune reached the core of the complex (bounded by the Sun and Uranus), and was still there in 1979. See figure 142 on page 342.

By 1980, however, Saturn and Neptune have lost contact with all but the lower edge of this complex; the whole of which is crossed by Jupiter in August (see figure 143, page 343). On this basis, the following advice was offered: "Unless there are urgent medical reasons against it, put off having the operation at least until August. Only then, if there is no improvement, should surgery be considered."

On the 9th of March, the lady reported to me that the hemorrhage had stopped. A doctor had prescribed a remedy which stanched the bleeding within a few days and made the operation unnecessary. What so amazed her was that the sudden relief occurred when the

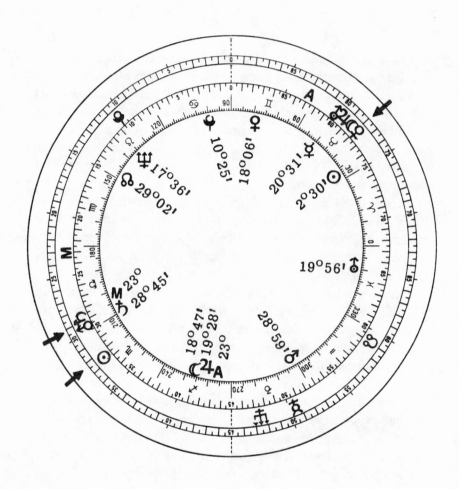

Figure 140. Asta Fehling, born April 22, 1924. Birth data withheld for confidentiality.

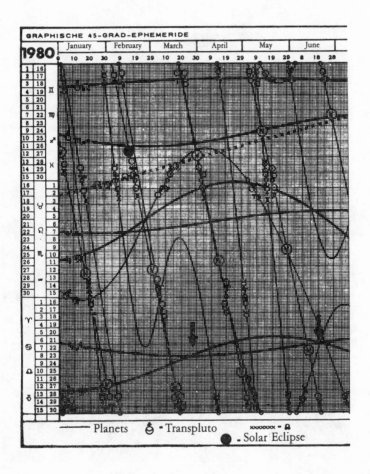

Figure 141. Annual Diagram for 1980.

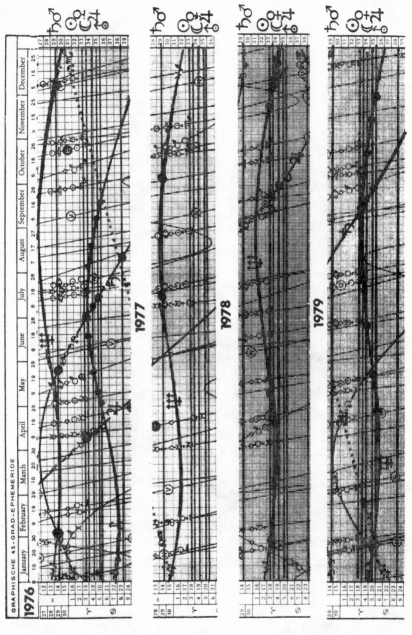

Figure 142. Details of the Annual Diagrams for 1976–1979.

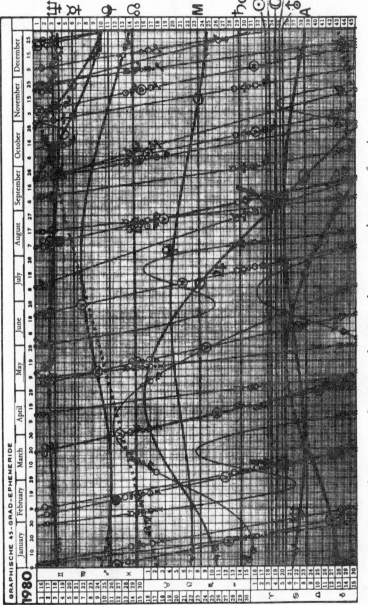

Figure 143. Annual Diagram for 1980 showing the energy changes after August.

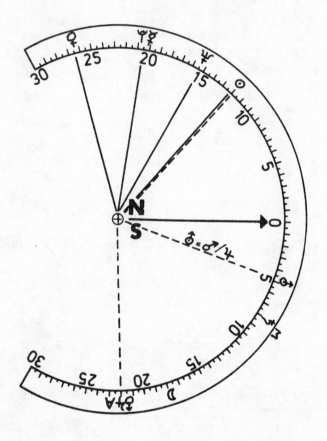

Figure 144. Declination Midpoint Disc.

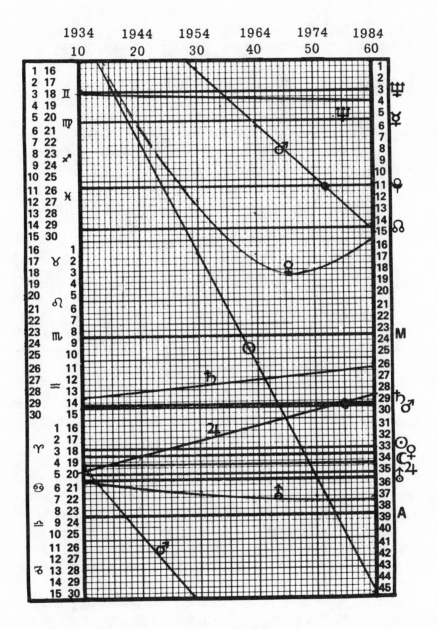

Figure 145. Life Diagram for Asta Fehling.

Sun conjunct Uranus square Venus and the Sun with Mercury were apparently parallel to Uranus.

On studying the declination program (figure 144, page 344), we find UR in SU/JU, giving prospects of a fortunate (JU) sudden change (UR) in the physical state (SU). The pathological condition is identified by ME = PL = VE/NE as serious disease (PL) of the female organs (SU/VE).

Although the trouble had been cleared up, I wanted to discover what else the Life Diagram had to say, and found that in 1976, MA$_P$ crossed the PL line. See figure 145 on page 345. One of the ovaries had been removed at that time. The proposed second operation was for the removal of the other ovary, which could now be left intact.

The movement of JU$_P$ over SA and MA in 1980 is rather striking. Could it have some connection with the hemorrhages? Biological correspondences for Jupiter given in COSI No. 78 include the mention: "the organism, the blood, the menopause." Since the hemorrhages were associated with the menopause (change of life), this is our answer. The periods did not dry up at the right time, but went out of control. An operation under this constellation might easily have endangered the patient's life.

The recommendation to delay Asta's operation if at all possible encouraged her to consult other doctors; and one of them suggested the remedy that stopped the hemorrhages.

Epidemics

Every now and then there are periods when epidemics occur, in which people, often for some obscure reason, fall victim in large numbers to a particular virus. They spread the infection from one to another, and soon fill hospitals to overflowing. Although such scourges as cholera and the dreaded Black Death of the Middle Ages are seldom encountered today, certain diseases do sometimes assume epidemic proportions, mainly due to the weather or to big catastrophes.

In many instances, these epidemics coincide with long-term constellations. For example, there is a well-established statistical correlation between waves of influenza and Jupiter/Saturn aspects. Advance warning of these and other epidemics can often be obtained from the graphic 45° ephemeris and also from the declination ephemeris.

In the early part of 1980, Saturn and Neptune were square for several weeks, the square being exact around the end of March and middle of June. As early as February, the press was reporting that millions of people had fallen ill due to the inclement weather. In March, two hundred thousand cases of sleeping sickness were being treated in Uganda.

Mass diseases can be recognized in the declinations too. Thus, in July 1975, I heard that twenty-five members of the American Legion had suddenly died of a mysterious illness, the causes of which were then unknown. Another hundred and thirty people were being nursed in intensive care units. This so-called Legionnaire's disease was accompanied by high fever, severe chills, pains in the head and chest, a dry cough and shortness of breath.

The disease broke out between the 21st and 24th of July 1976. Usually, infectious diseases make their appearance under Neptunian constellations. There are none of these as far as the planetary longitudes are concerned, but in the declination ephemeris for the days in question, the Sun, Venus and Mercury cross the position-line of Neptune as shown in figure 146 on page 348.

After a very dry hot season, these constellations brought not only the longed-for rain (Neptune), but floods of rain—especially in Mexico, where one hundred and twenty people were killed and a hundred thousand were rendered homeless: conditions which form a good breeding-ground for epidemics. In addition, food was being poisoned by pesticides. A poisonous cloud (Neptune) was also reported drifting over Milan.

In *Der kosmische Beobachter* (The Cosmic Observer) for October 1976,[77] I pointed out the number of similar constellations due between the 16th and 26th of November of last year, namely: ME//NE on the 16th, MA//NE on the 24th, and SU//NE on the 26th.

During this period, mass suffering arose mainly through natural disasters. In my diary, I noted: "16th November 1976, the industrial city of Tanshan in China destroyed by earthquake. 20th November 1976, cold weather, non-stop rain in Italy, some snow. 24th November 1976, earthquake in Turkey, three towns in ruins, five thousand dead. 25th November 1976, two hundred Turkish villages destroyed

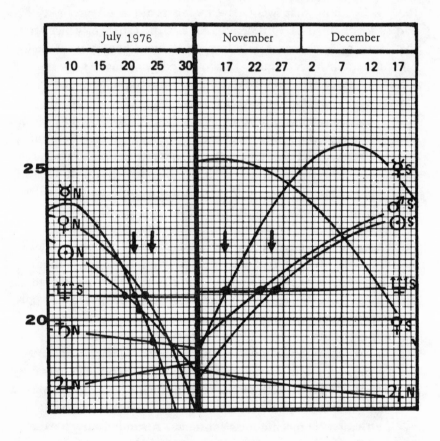

Figure 146. Mysterious disease.

by quake, blizzards in Turkey, hundreds of the homeless killed by
–20° frost." At the same time, an increase in the number of people
suffering from occupational diseases in West Germany was
announced in the media.

What we now need to know is whether we are dealing with
parallels having only a short-term effect, or with parallels exerting an
influence over weeks or even months. Well, SU//NE or MA//NE is
effective for no more than a few days, but SA//UR or SA//NE makes
its presence felt over a longer period.

In 1979 it almost escaped notice that SA//PL was due in February and in July. Many people suffered in the persistent cold of February, and also in the "summer we never had." That spring, a hundred
thousand cases of influenza were treated in West Germany alone.
Many children died in Naples. In March, ten million South Ameri-
cans were said to be suffering from thyroid trouble. The Russians
went down with jaundice. Contagious diseases were being carried by
refugees in Southeast Asia.

As these examples show, there is a connection between cosmic
constellations (both in longitudinal aspect and in parallel aspect) and
the weather and disease. The different factors should therefore be
studied together. In scientific literature, attention is generally confined to the weather and disease, while the cosmic influence is
ignored. Nevertheless, many diseases are known to be connected with
sunspots and to run through the same eleven-year cycle. Michel
Gauquelin wrote as follows:

> At a closed session of the French Medical Academy held in
> Paris on the March 3, 1958, Dr. J. Poumailloux, a physician
> at the Saint-Antoine hospital, and his collaborator, the
> meteorologist R. Viart, presented their learned colleagues
> with a sensational report, according to which cardiac infarct
> was not a random occurrence but one with a frequency
> governed by specific solar constants. A sudden increase in
> solar activity affects the blood vessels in the human body
> and causes the formation of blood clots in susceptible peo-
> ple. In some circumstances, these clots can block the coro-
> nary artery and so deprive the heart tissues of their necessary
> blood supply. The researchers gave as one example the year

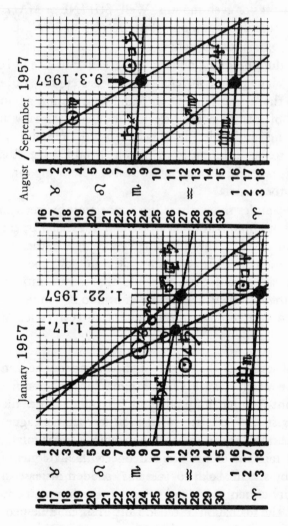

Figure 147. High incidence of cardiac infarcts in January and September, 1957.

1957: in which they observed a large number of cardiac infarcts between the 17th and 22nd of January, then an absence of cases from April through July, followed by another surge between the 1st and 3rd of September. Now, most of that year the Sun was fairly quiet, but it flared into activity from the 17th through the 25th of January and from the 28th of August through the 3rd of September.[78]

I have investigated the days concerned and have discovered that there were similar constellations during both periods.

On January 17, 1957, SU-45-SA was due shortly after the full Moon, and SU-90-NE and MA-135-SA were due on January 22nd; then, on September 3rd, 1957, SU-90-SA and MA-45-NE were due. As you will see from figure 147 (on page 350), very nearly the same degrees in the 45° wheel were involved each time.

It remains to be seen to what extent the heliocentric constellations (which, like the declinations, are usually ignored) are connected with the weather, natural catastrophes and disease. This matter has been broached in my book *Das Doppelgesicht des Kosmos* (The Two Faces of the Cosmos),[79] where the special significance of aspects between Mars and Neptune is shown.

Rapid Astromedical Diagnosis

It is not often that patients will bring their cosmograms with them when they pay a visit to the doctor or naturopath. And, of course, the practitioner can hardly be expected to cast a chart straight away for each patient. However, with the help of an ordinary ephemeris and a graphic 45° ephemeris, it is possible to determine the prevailing cosmic situation in a few minutes during the consultation. One day, such work will be placed in the hands of a trained assistant.

When the King and Queen of Sweden were about to pay a state visit to West Germany in March 1979, it was known that Queen Silvia was seven to eight months pregnant, and I was commissioned to examine the Queen's current constellations. I shall now explain how this can be done quickly.

Queen Silvia was born Silvia Sommerlath on 23rd December, 1943, in Heidelberg. The hour of birth is disputed: at one time it has been given as 6:00 A.M., at another as 2:58 A.M. When the hour of birth is unknown, it is customary to take the noon positions. The 1943 ephemeris gives the midnight positions as:

SU	=	0° Capricorn 16'	DR	=	8° Leo 40'
VE	=	16° Scorpio 49'	JU	=	26° Leo 55'
UR	=	5° Gemini 52'	MO	=	6° Scorpio 37'
PL	=	8° Leo 22'	ME	=	20° Capricorn 15'
MA	=	7° Gemini 06'	SA	=	22° Gemini 34'
NE	=	4° Libra 11'			

From these midnight positions it is possible to make an approximate estimate of the noon positions for the Sun and the inferior planets (which are the only ones to move significantly in half a day). The Moon cannot be accurately located, since it traverses more than 13° per day. The Sun can be given another 30'; Mercury can be advanced to barely 21° Capricorn and Venus to fully 17° Scorpio. See figure 148 on page 353.

It will be observed that, on the left side of the graphic 45° ephemeris, there are three columns each containing thirty degree numbers and four different zodiac signs. See figure 149 on page 354. The Sun has been entered at ca. 0° 45' in the first column, because it is in Capricorn. Neptune, at 4° Libra 11', also comes in the first column. Uranus at 5° Gemini 52' comes in column three. It should be mentioned that for each degree, the horizontal lines above and below the degree-number mark the beginning and end of that degree. Therefore the planetary positions can be made accurate to almost a quarter of a degree. Saturn at 22° Gemini 34' is entered at the bottom of column three. Jupiter at 26° Leo 55' is entered in the central column. Mars at 7° Gemini 06' is set down just below Uranus. Venus at 16° Scorpio 49' comes at the top of column two. Mercury in ca. 21° Capricorn is in the middle of column one. The Dragon's Head and Pluto stand together in ca. 8° 40' of the central column.

Horizontal lines are drawn across the graph from the above positions, and these lines intersect the preprinted planetary paths. Chief importance has to be attached to the slow-moving planets. At the end of April, Uranus reaches the position-line of Neptune, and from the end of April through the middle of May, Saturn is stationary

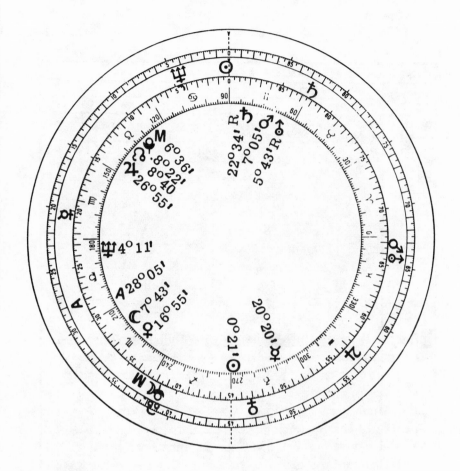

Declinations

☉ = 23°27'S	☽ = 9°09'S	☿ = 23°06'S	♀ = 14°46'S
♂ = 24°01'N	♃ = 13°25'N	♄ = 21°51'N	☊ = 21°12'N
♆ = 0°23'S	♇ = 23°30'N	M = 18°39'N	A = 10°47'S

Figure 148. Her Majesty Queen Silvia of Sweden, born December 23, 1943, 2:58 A.M., Heidelberg, W. Germany.

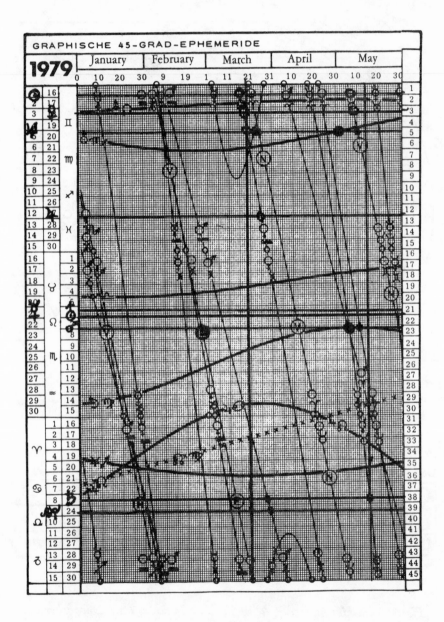

Figure 149. Annual Diagram for 1979.

on the position-line of Mars. Both these are critical transits and should warn an expectant mother to take extraspecial care.

In such cases, the weaker transits also require study. On the day their majesties were due to arrive in Germany, VE_T crosses VE and NE. Then, shortly before New Moon, SU crosses NE, indicating debility. VE over JU represents great rejoicing and acclamation, but MA_T crosses SA and PL before the month is out.

I made the following prognosis in my manuscript (the published version was edited): "In the days around the 25th of March, Queen Silvia will not feel very well, as the Sun transit in opposition Neptune is due. Possibly the exertion of the visit will tell on her in her pregnant state. There are some very critical constellations for her in May, so she will have to take every precaution to ensure a safe delivery. . . . Unfortunately, the 27th of March, the final day in Lübeck, is not under the best constellations and mishap cannot be ruled out."

According to press reports, "Queen Silvia was already depleted of energy by the 23rd March, for she collapsed into a chair." This was the advance working of SU_T-180r NE. On the 25th of March, the Queen was indisposed, and the King had to pay the visit without his consort, who turned back to Sweden completely exhausted.

As was established later, the Queen was not in the seventh but in the eighth month of her pregnancy. The child was born on May 13, 1979. According to the official bulletin, the birth was normal. That was not quite true. The public learned afterward that the Queen had not had an easy time and, in view of $SA_T = MA$ and $MA_T = MA$, this is very understandable. On account of the difficult presentation of the baby, she had to be narcotized. When she regained consciousness, she was not allowed to take the baby in her arms; every effort had to be made—so Professor Borell declared—to avoid infection. Finally, for the same reason, the controversial "triple inoculation" was rejected as an unacceptable health hazard to the child.

From the above example, it will be clear how many useful facts can be gleaned from a rapid diagnosis. Nevertheless, it is always important to cast an accurate cosmogram when the time of birth is known; it is important, too, to consider the declinations when judging the situation. Sometimes a rapid diagnosis fails to yield any relevant data at all; and then, of course, a more thorough investigation is essential.

DISEASE CORRESPONDENCES

Table A. Disease Correspondences of Significant Midpoints

Number	Midpoint	Disease Correspondence
1	SA = SU/VE	Diseases arising from sexual activity
2	NE = SU/MA	Delicacy, disease
3	SA = SU/JU	Disease
4	NE = SU/JU	Influences undermining the health
5	ME = SU/SA	Tendency to hearing problems, nervous disorders
6	VE = SU/SA	Diseases to do with sexual activity and marriage
7	NE = SU/SA	Lack of vitality, debility
8	PL = SU/SA	Diseases due to mental stress or adverse circumstances
9	DR = SU/SA	Hospitalization
10	MC = SU/SA	Diseases due to lack of development opportunities
11	SO = UR	Cardiothymia
12	MA = SU/UR	Accident, injury
13	NE = SU/UR	Sudden weakness, possibly due to approaching death
14	PL = SU/UR	Severe physical suffering, physical impediment
15	SO = NE	Weakness, disease
16	MO = SU/NE	Disease due to mental suffering
17	VE = SU/NE	Debilitation of the female organs
18	MA = SU/NE	Weak sexual impulse

Table A. Continued

Number	Midpoint	Disease Correspondence
19	SA = SU/NE	Impure blood, circulatory disorders, mental suffering
20	UR = SU/NE	Sudden weakness, spasms, nervousness
21	DR = SU/NE	Hospitalization
22	NE = SU/PL	Hypersensitivity, disease, martyrdom
23	SA = SU/MC	Tendency to depression
24	SA = MO/VE	Unsatisfied desire, female diseases
25	UR = MO/VE	Glandular disorders, spasms, epilepsy
26	NE = MO/VE	Disturbed glandular function
27	NE = MO/MA	Low potency, infection, diseases of the genitals
28	PL = MO/MA	Periodic disorders in the female organism
29	SA = MO/JU	Disease of liver or gallbladder, gallstones
30	MO = SA	Disturbances of the fluid balance, retention of urine, bladder disease, weeping wounds, defects in the mucous membrane, melancholy, depression
31	MA = MO/SA	Inflammatory diseases
32	NE = MO/SA	Melancholy
33	PL = MO/SA	Depressions due to organic complaints

Table A. Continued

Number	Midpoint	Disease Correspondence
34	ASC = MO/SA	Close confinement in institutions, hospitalization
35	MC = MO/SA	Indisposition, feeling unwell
36	MA = MO/UR	Injuries and accidents
37	SA = MO/UR	Sudden illness
38	MA = MO/NE	Sexual debility, nervous disorders due to unnatural sexual practices
39	SA = MO/NE	Manic depression, a feeling of being paralyzed or constrained
40	PL = MO/NE	Hypersensitivity
41	SA = MO/PL	Mental suffering, depression
42	UR = MO/PL	Nervous disorders
43	NE = MO/PL	Sentimentality, hypersensitivity, prostration
44	UR = MO/MC	Irritability, nerviness, unusual mental states
45	UR = ME/MA	Agitation, frenzy, delirium
46	UR = ME/SA	Diseases of the nerves
47	NE = ME/SA	Depression
48	NE = ME/UR	Nervous disorders
49	PL = ME/UR	Superexcitement of the nerves
50	SA = ME/NE	Gloomy thoughts, pessimism, touchiness
51	UR = ME/NE	Spasmodic disorders originating in the nervous system

Table A. Continued

Number	Midpoint	Disease Correspondence
52	UR = ME/PL	Superexcitement of the nerves, nervous breakdown
53	NE = ME/PL	Nervous sensitivity, anxiety states
54	SA = ME/MC	Pessimism, depression
55	UR = ME/NE	Unusual exciteableness
56	SA = VE/MA	Morbid sexuality
57	UR = VE/MA	Rape, criminal assault, abdominal operations
58	NE = VE/MA	Tendency to perversions, sexual diseases, appendicitis
59	VE = SA	Suppression of inner secretions, glandular disorders (kidneys)
60	SU = VE/SA	Sexual inhibitions, glandular disorders
61	MO = VE/SA	Depression
62	NE = VE/SA	Diseases caused by mental distress
63	MC = VE/SA	Sexual inhibitions
64	SA = VE/UR	Late or difficult birth
65	NE = VE/UR	Glandular disorders, abdominal disease
66	MA = VE/NE	Perversions, infections, diseases of the genitals
67	SA = VE/NE	Morbid eroticism, diseases due to sad love life
68	UR = VE/NE	Perversions
69	MA = VE/PL	Risk of sexual assault or interference

Table A. Continued

Number	Midpoint	Disease Correspondence
70	SA = VE/MC	Unsatisfied desire, depression
71	NE = VE/MC	Psychosomatic complaints
72	SA = MA/JU	Difficult birth, illness through setbacks
73	SU = MA/SA	Low vitality, danger to life
74	MO = MA/SA	Depression, mental suffering, grief
75	UR = MA/SA	Sudden illness, danger to life
76	NE = MA/SA	Sapping of the vitality by poison, gas, medicines
77	PL = MA/SA	Physical injury, amputation, danger to life
78	MC = MA/SA	Disease, grief, preoccupation with death
79	MA = UR	Injury, accident, operation
80	SU = MA/UR	Physical injury, accident, operation
81	MO = MA/UR	Injury, operation (in a female)
82	ME = MA/UR	Nervous strain, superexcitement of the nerves, injury, operation
83	VE = MA/UR	Abdominal operation
84	JU = MA/UR	Successful operation
85	SA = MA/UR	Severe injury, surgery, amputation
86	PL = MA/UR	Forced injury, serious operation
87	NE = MA/UR	Bouts of weakness, infections following operation or injury, danger from poisons, narcotics

Table A. Continued

Number	Midpoint	Disease Correspondence
88	MC = MA/UR	Injury, accident, operation
89	SU = MA/NE	Lack of vitality, infections, bouts of weakness
90	MO = MA/NE	Sensitivity, nervous debility, infections, ill effects of indulgence in alcohol, tobacco, etc.
91	ME = MA/NE	Nervous debility due to indulgence in alcohol, tobacco, etc., to wrong medication (sleeping pills) or to self-abuse
92	VE = MA/NE	Low fertility, perversions, infection
93	SA = MA/NE	Body toxins, weakness, disease
94	UR = MA/NE	Sudden paralysis, states of weakness, life-threatening crises
95	PL = MA/NE	Disease through injury, poison, wrong medication
96	MC = MA/NE	Debility or illness, addiction
97	SU = MA/PL	Forcible injury, accident, operation
98	MO = MA/PL	Injury, results of strain
99	ME = MA/PL	Superexcitement of the nerves
100	VE = MA/PL	Rape, indecent assault, abdominal operation
101	UR = MA/PL	Suffering violence or cruelty, disasters

Table A. Continued

Number	Midpoint	Disease Correspondence
102	NE = MA/PL	Concealed injury, disease due to surgical error, catastrophes involving water
103	ASC = MA/PL	Accident, danger to life
104	MC = MA/PL	Danger from Act of God, operation, amputation
105	SU = JU/SA	Disruptions of life, pulmonary disease
106	UR = JU/SA	Sudden illness, loss of consciousness, accident
107	NE = JU/SA	Depression, impure blood, circulatory disorders
108	JU = NE	Flaccidity of the organs, false diagnosis
109	SU = JU/NE	Loss of energy, disease
110	SU = SA/UR	Disease due to strain, dysrhythmia
111	MO = SA/UR	Manic depression, mental illness leading to organic disorders
112	ME = SA/UR	Nervous disorders
113	MA = SA/UR	Injury, accidents, disasters, operations
114	NE = SA/UR	Loss of vitality, no love of life
115	SA = NE	An axis (or pivot) of disease
116	SU = SA/NE	Poor health, physical suffering
117	MO = SA/NE	Depression, female diseases
118	ME = SA/NE	Nervous diseases, nervous debility, disorders of the sense organs

Table A. Continued

Number	Midpoint	Disease Correspondence
119	VE = SA/NE	Deficient glandular activity, glandular troubles (kidneys), sexual problems
120	MA = SA/NE	Lack of energy, little love of life, chronic diseases
121	JU = SA/NE	Emaciation, liver or lung disease
122	UR = SA/NE	Sudden weakness or illness, disease due to upsets
123	PL = SA/NE	Serious illness, chronic suffering (cancer)
124	DR = SA/NE	Hospitalization
125	MC = SA/NE	Disease due to mental suffering
126	MA = SA/PL	Suffering ill-treatment, having to fight for one's life, disaster, operation
127	JU = SA/PL	Problems caused by illness, underdevelopment of organs, swellings, indurations
128	UR = SA/PL	Sudden assaults, violent attacks, outrages
129	NE = SA/PL	Diseases due to water, poison, gas, drugs
130	MO = SA/DR	Mental suffering caused by others or by isolation
131	NE = SA/DR	Diseases of the underprivileged, bad effects of hospitalization
132	SA = MC	Ego disorders, loss of self-awareness, disorders due to inhibited development, no perseverance

Table A. Continued

Number	Midpoint	Disease Correspondence
133	SU = SA/MC	Mental illness or affliction, low powers of resistance
134	MO = SA/MC	Mental suffering, depression, psychosis
135	ME = SA/MC	Dejection
136	MA = SA/MC	Lack of vitality, low spirits
137	SU = UR/NE	Sensitivity, little will to live, disease
138	MO = UR/NE	Bouts of weakness, lack of mental balance, disorders of consciousness
139	MA = UR/NE	Low powers of resistance, sense of paralysis
140	SA = UR/NE	Pessimism, unusual conditions
141	MC = UR/NE	Nervous breakdown, disorders of consciousness
142	SU = UR/PL	Superexcitement of the nerves, nervous breakdown
143	MA = UR/PL	Injury, accident, sudden illness, operation
144	NE = UR/PL	Exhaustion, nervous disorders, drug symptoms
145	SU = NE/PL	Sensitive body, diseases due to addictions or medical poisons (sleeping pills)
146	MO = NE/PL	Strange mental states, melancholy
147	ME = NE/PL	Nervous debility, nervous disorders, confusion

Table A. Continued

Number	Midpoint	Disease Correspondence
148	MA = NE/PL	Lack of energy, control by alien forces (possession)
149	SA = NE/PL	Pessimism, declining energy
150	UR = NE/PL	Hypersensitive nerves, sudden attacks of disease hard to identify, disturbed consciousness
151	MO = NE/MC	Delusions and self-deception
152	SA = NE/MC	Disease due to wrong treatment and mental suffering, mental illness
153	UR = NE/MC	Mental illness and confusion, diseases the origin of which lies in the unconscious
154	NE = PL/MC	Serious illness, chronic disease (cancer), consequences of mental suffering, perhaps through disparagement or lack of scope for personal growth

Table B. Correspondences between Signs, Organs and Diseases

Sign	Primary Influence	Secondary Influence	Diseases
Aries	Head, face, ears, eyes, nerves	Kidneys, liver	Headache, brain disease, apoplexy, epilepsy, neuralgia, rashes on face (with impaired kidney function)
Taurus	Neck, throat, tonsils, respiratory organs	Sexual and excretory organs, glandular system	Goiter, pharyngitis, tonsilitis, laryngitis, diphtheria, choking fits, mumps, disorders of the thyroid gland, heart disease, abdominal disorders
Gemini	Shoulders, arms, hands, lungs, 1st through 4th dorsal vertebrae	Thigh, digestive organs	Pulmonary diseases, asthma, bronchial catarrh, fractures of arms or legs, nerve troubles
Cancer	Chest, stomach, lungs, breasts (mammary glands)	Knee, bones, tibia (kidneys)	Stomach disorders, eructation, hiccups, heartburn, dropsy, failure of peristalsis, under-active lymph glands, inebriety, depression, nodularity (breast)
Leo	Heart, circulation, back, 5th through 9th dorsal vertebrae	Cardia (upper end of stomach), all blood vessels, disorders of veins and abdomen	Heart disease, circulatory disorders, anemia, arteriosclerosis, venous diseases, abdominal disorders, impotence, spinal trouble, neurosis, throat trouble

Table B. Continued

Sign	Primary Influence	Secondary Influence	Diseases
Virgo	Digestive organs, spleen, liver, gallbladder	Pancreas, feet, toes	Intestinal disorders, peritonitis, diarrhea, constipation, disorders of liver and gallbladder, intestinal ulcers
Libra	Kidneys, bladder, lumbar region	Uterus, region around navel, head	Nephritis, gravel, retention of urine, impure blood, poor skin condition (due to deficient kidney function), nervous disorders, erysipelas
Scorpio	Sexual and excretory organs, uterus, testicles, rectum	Nose, throat, tonsils, bladder	Bladder complaints, gravel, retention of urine, impure blood, poor skin condition, rheumatism, nasal polyps, nasal catarrh, furuncle, hemorrhoids, neurasthenia, sexual diseases, operations to do with the sexual organs
Sagittarius	Muscular system, thighs, lumbar region	Shoulders, arms, digestive apparatus	Hip disease, rheumatism, sciatica, gout, locomotor disturbances, arteriosclerosis, nervous disorders, impure blood
Capricorn	Skin and bone system, knee	Chest, stomach, lungs	Rashes, scald (scab on head), polyarthritis, tuberculosis of the bones and joints, furunculosis, scrofula, predisposition to indurations, keratosis (horny growths on skin)

Table B. Continued

Sign	Primary Influence	Secondary Influence	Diseases
Aquarius	Shin, calf, ankle, circulation	Heart, back, circulation	Fractured ankle, dislocations, sprains, cramp in calf muscle, phlebitis, swollen legs, varicose veins, blood diseases, spinal disorders, locomotor disturbances, heart trouble
Pisces	Feet, toes, calcaneus (heel bone)	Digestive organs, spleen, nerves, lungs, liver	Weak feet, flat feet, diseases due to chills, rheumatism, gout, alcoholism, scrofulosis, poisoning

Table C. Correspondences between Planets, Organs and Diseases

Planets	Biological Correspondences	Disease Tendencies
Sun/yang	Heredity, health, vitality, heart, circulation, right eye, cerebrum, hyperemia	Disorders of the heart and circulation, asthenia, impotence, blood disorders, eye complaints, scrofulosis, rickets
Moon/yin	Fertility, fluid balance, blood serum, lymph, stomach, mucous membranes, cerebellum, psyche	Gynecological disorders (a badly placed Moon is more critical in the female cosmogram than it is in the male), gastric disorders, dropsy, glandular troubles, ulcers, swellings, depression
Mercury/yin	Motor nerves, organs of speech and hearing, hands, fingers	Nervous disorders, speech disorders, defective hearing, mental overexcitement, rapid breathing, tremors
Venus/yin	Glands, especially the kidneys, veins, cheeks, mouth, skin, female breasts	Glandular disorders, kidney disease, ulcerated tonsils, bladder troubles, cellulitis (inflammation of connective tissue), growths, women's diseases
Mars/yang	Muscles, ligaments, red blood corpuscles, bile, nose, sexual functions	Inflammation, fever, bilious attacks, severe hemorrhages, sexual diseases, proneness to injuries and accidents

Table C. Continued

Planets	Biological correspondences	Disease tendencies
Jupiter/yang	Fluid enrichment, nutrition, putting on weight, liver, gallbladder, lungs, swellings, glycogen balance	Plethora, liver and gallbladder troubles, obesity, autointoxication through faulty diet, diabetes, tendency to apoplectic fits, hemorrhoids
Saturn/yin	Skeleton, joints, spleen, skin, teeth, white blood corpuscles	Metabolic disorders, accumulation of toxins, indurations, stone and gravel, rheumatism, gout, chronic diseases
Uranus/yang	Vital rhythms, meninges, spine, pituitary	Disordered rhythms, nervous complains, spasms, spinal trouble, accidents, operations
Neptune/yin	Pineal gland, solar plexus, subconscious mind	Prostration of organs, paralysis, poisoning, abuse of alcohol, tobacco and other drugs, psychological disturbance, sleep disorders, coma
Pluto/yang	Not yet fully investigated, but experience to date links it with physical changes due to action taken by the authorities or by Act of God	Growths, amputations, injurious operations, diseases due to large-scale events (disasters, epidemics, war, terrorism)
Lunar nodes/yin	Disorders connected with other people	Infections picked up in crowds, hospitalization

SOME COSMIC
CORRESPONDENCES OF DISEASE

Anal pain occurs mainly in hemorrhoids, constipation and enteritis, when there are placements of Mars, Saturn, Sun, Moon in Taurus, Virgo, Scorpio.

Anxiety states often have their cause in angular relationships between the Moon and Saturn or Neptune in Cancer, Leo, Virgo, Capricorn, Pisces, also in aspects of Uranus to the Sun.

Backache can be caused by inflammation around the vertebrae, disc injury, irritation of the spinal cord. Pain extending the whole length of the spinal column is a sign of polyarthritis. Fever, anemia and lung disease often produce pain in the region of the shoulder blades. Pain in the right shoulder is characteristic of liver and gallbladder trouble. Backache is especially associated with Leo and Aquarius; the Sun can be aspecting Uranus, Saturn or Neptune. Saturn and Neptune are often involved in rheumatic diseases.

Bladder pain can be due to diseases of the urinary bladder, to the suppression of urine (Moon/Saturn) and to certain female complaints. Particular attention should be paid in such cases to Libra and Scorpio and to their opposite signs Aries and Taurus. Often there are relationships between the Moon, Venus and Mars.

Buzzing in the ear can be due to dirt or to an accumulation of wax, but it can also be due to inflammation of the middle ear, to anatomical changes in the ear, to nervous irritation or to medical poisons. A clue may be found in the relationship between Mercury and Saturn. Aries and Taurus could also be involved, especially the degrees around 7° Aries and 10° Taurus.

Chest pain probably has a psychic cause when the discomfort is concentrated in the solar plexus. Pain made worse by breathing can point to pleurisy or pneumonia; often it is indicated by Jupiter aspecting Saturn or Neptune in Gemini or Cancer. Pain in the lower thorax is frequently associated with rheumatism. Girdle pain points to shingles or spinal trouble, and is quite likely to involve Cancer, Leo, Virgo and the planets Mars and Uranus.

Cough can be produced by diseases of the respiratory organs: swollen mucous membranes in the air passages, an accumulation of mucus, laryngitis, bronchial and pulmonary catarrh. The aspects for which to look are those between the Moon, Mercury and Venus in Taurus, Gemini and Scorpio. Cough can also occur when food is regurgitated due to deficient digestion; in which case there may be aspects to the Moon and Mercury involving Cancer and Capricorn. Coughs such as the above, which have some organic cause, must not be confused with a self-conscious nervous cough.

Headaches can spring from numerous causes. They can originate in the stomach and intestines when the gases find no outlet and rise to the head. The faulty digestion will probably show up in the cosmogram in connection with the Moon and Saturn and with the signs Cancer, Virgo, Scorpio or their opposites. Weakness of the stomach and intestines may also be revealed by Neptunian aspects. In anemic people, who generally have Sun/Neptune or Sun/Saturn aspects in their charts, the headache can sometimes be relieved by placing the head between the knees. Yoga asanas like the shoulder stand and the head stand can help too. Other causes of headache are colds, sinusitis and nose blockages that make it difficult to breathe. In this case it is worth looking at Aries, Taurus and Scorpio, and the planets Venus, Saturn, Neptune and the Moon. Headache is often an accompaniment of cerebritis (inflammation of the brain), colotyphoid, infectious diseases and wrong medication. Neptune is nearly always involved in such cases.

Hiccup (hiccough) is a reflex movement of the diaphragm. The disorder arises from faulty feeding, so that gas is trapped by a muscular spasm as it tries to escape. Babies tend to suffer from it unless they are properly "burped" after meals. Cosmic correspondences can be found in Taurus, Cancer, Virgo, Scorpio and in the Moon, Sun, Saturn and Uranus. Hiccups may also have a more serious cause in peritonitis or intestinal obstruction.

Itching skin (pruritis) is usually due to an accumulation of autotoxins which can be eliminated only through the skin. A child who is being fed at the mother's breast may suffer from irritation of the skin if she smokes heavily or poisons herself with some other indulgence. Hyperacidity can result from a faulty diet. One child used to suffer from an irritating rash immediately after enjoying a plate of sausage and bacon. Diseases of the liver, gallbladder, intestines and kidneys can all play a part. Sugar diabetes is another possible cause. External applications like ointments do little good; the cure must take place from within. An alkaline diet should be adopted. Packs of healing earth or skimmed quark may ease the violent itching. The disturbed fluid balance is generally attributable to aspects between the Moon and Saturn or Neptune posited in Cancer, Virgo, Libra, Scorpio or Capricorn.

Liver disorders are hard to diagnose at times, because they are often painless. In hepatitis, the liver swells slightly and the skin turns yellow. The factors mainly involved in the cosmogram are Virgo, Pisces and Jupiter. Mars plays a part in inflammations. Liver damage caused by wrong feeding and wrong medication is represented by Neptune. When difficult directions of Jupiter, Saturn, and Neptune are on their way in the life diagram, prophylactic measures against chronic diseases (including cancer) should be taken in good time. Liver complaints ought never to be treated without medical advice.

Lung disease is usually indicated by a badly placed Jupiter in the cosmogram. Jupiter can also stand at an unpropitious midpoint such as Saturn/Neptune. Gemini and Sagittarius are the signs generally associated with pulmonary disease. But the rule is not invariable. Dr. F. Schwab in his book *Sternemächte und Mensch* (The Stellar Powers and Humanity) produced statistics in which Libra is the most heavily occupied sign in lung disease. Thus the zodiac signs are not so reliable as the position of Jupiter.

Palpitations of the heart frequently originate in the frame of mind, in general unrest, in agitation over important interviews or examinations, and in quarrels. Transits of Mars and Uranus are often involved. Palpitations accompanied by shortness of breath occur in anemic persons when climbing the stairs, walking in the mountains or exerting themselves more than normal. The Sun, Mars and Uranus in Leo, Aquarius, Taurus and Scorpio can be prominent in the cosmogram. Palpitations may also be found in obesity and rheumatism, and feature Jupiter, Saturn, Uranus and Neptune.

Perspiration (excessive) occurs not only during strenuous physical activity and in very hot weather, but when sweat is secreted in response to nervous stimulation, as in the cold sweat of fear. In debilitated individuals suffering from such complaints as anemia, chlorosis and cardiac insufficiency, even the slightest exertion can produce perspiration. In fevers, the sweating is necessary to cleanse the body of its toxins. Here sweat production is part of the healing process.* Even night sweats serve to eliminate toxins. Suppressed perspiration is a sign of dermal malfunction. In this case the elimination of toxins via the kidneys should be promoted with the help of the appropriate herbal infusions. Sweaty hands are often found in kidney disease and diabetes. The cosmic factors usually involved are Aries, Libra, Scorpio and the Moon (fluid balance), Saturn (suppressed secretions), Venus (kidney and bladder function), Mars (inflammation), Neptune (autointoxication).

Stomachache can be due to indigestion or to a gastric ulcer. The factors to examine first are the Moon, Cancer and Capricorn. Connections between the Moon and Saturn or the Moon and Neptune are often involved. Stomach pains caused by some form of nervous strain or upset usually implicate Uranus. Virgo and Scorpio come into play when digestive disorders are chronic.

Vertigo (dizziness) results from a disturbance in the sense of balance, the center for which is the labyrinth in the inner ear. The

---

*In fevers, the body is usually fighting not only its own toxins but the bacterial or viral infections they encourage. The toxins can sometimes be eliminated in good time by a Turkish bath or sauna or, if these would strain the system, by resorting to a rubber sweatsuit. *Tr.*

usual cause is impaired circulation and a temporary shortage of blood in the brain. Yoga asanas, especially the shoulder stand and head stand, and breathing exercises, can prove helpful. The planets most likely to be involved are the Moon, Mercury and Saturn. When accompanied by vomiting, vertigo can be due to gastric and intestinal disorders. Vertigo may also be a symptom of epilepsy, myelopathy, brain disease, and brain tumor. Therefore it if recurs fairly often, it should not be treated lightly.

The above notes on correspondences between diseases and cosmic factors make no pretension to being complete. They are intended merely as an introduction to the subject. In no circumstances can they take the place of clinical diagnosis.

With these remarks I conclude my book in the hope that it will prove thought-provoking to doctors, lay healers, and ordinary citizens; even to the extent of persuading them of the great practical use of cosmobiology both when we are ill and when we are well.

CHRONOLOGY OF
COSMOBIOLOGICAL MEDICINE

2000–1700 B.C.	Enoch and Abraham.
ca. 1250 B.C.	Moses.
668–628 B.C.	King Assurbanipal founded a library of cuneiform tablets, among them some showing the relationship of the position of the Moon to disease.
628–538 B.C.	The Neobabylonian Empire became a center for the astrology of Chaldea, so that the word Chaldean was later used as a general term for astrologer.
540–480 B.C.	Heraclitus of Ephesus, a Greek philosopher, taught that all things, including the other elements earth, air and water, arose out of primeval fire.
490–430 B.C.	Empedocles, a Greek philosopher who lived on the south coast of Sicily, believed that the "roots of all things" were to be found in the four elements, fire, earth, air and water.

460–377 B.C.   The lifetime of the physician and astrologer Hippocrates, the "father of medicine" and an exponent of the doctrine of the elements.

458–388 B.C.   The period of the Biblical prophet Ezra, to whom a lunar medical almanac has been ascribed.

427–347 B.C.   Plato, Greek philosopher, a pupil of Socrates, had contact with the Chaldeans.

ca. 400 B.C.   Ktesias, physician at the court of the Persian king, wrote a work called *Persica*.

356–323 B.C.   Alexander the Great. Under him there began a new astrological era. Different lines of development in various parts of the Ancient World (Mesopotamia, Egypt, Greece) were brought together. The start of scientific systematization of the subject.

ca. 330 B.C.   Diocles of Karystos practiced as a physician in Athens, and took the age of the Moon into account when giving treatments.

ca. 300 B.C.   Original form of the Hermes Trismegistus corpus. In which, among other things, diseases and remedies were discussed, including ophthalmic and gynecological disorders. Doctrine of the correspondence between the body and the zodiac.

ca. 300 B.C.   Transition from universal astrology to individual astrology, and so to iatromathematics or the science of astrological medicine. Doctrine of the correspondence between medical plants and zodiac signs.

384–322 B.C.   Aristotle, son of the court physician Nicomachus, was the ablest of Plato's students and became in 343 B.C. the tutor of the young prince who was to become Alexander the Great. In his teachings he created an astrological picture of the world. He discussed the four fundamental qualities and developed ancient humoral pathology (which ascribes disease to a faulty mixture of the body's humors).

372–320 B.C. Theophastus, a pupil of Aristotles.

3rd cent. B.C. Alexandria in Egypt grew into a center of Hellenistic science.

161–127 B.C. Hipparchus of Nicaea, astronomer, mathematician, and astrologer. Said to have invented the 360° circle. Compiled the first scientific star catalog. Reformed astronomy and astrology, especially where melothesia is concerned — the rule of parts of the body by the planets and zodiac signs.

Mid-2nd cent. B.C. Astrology becomes widely popular in Rome, where it is then forbidden.

106–43 B.C. Cicero, statesman and philosopher, sought to introduce Greek philosophy into Roman thought. Also occupied himself with astrology.

100–50 B.C. Timaios employed the four cardinal points in astrology and counted them correctly in a clockwise direction.

End of the 1st cent. B.C. The poet Manilius wrote the first self-contained exposition of astrology, *Astronomica*, in which he has something to say about melothesia (the astrological correspondences).

99–45 B.C. Nigidius Figulus, Roman senator, recognized as the first learned Roman politician, also studied how human health is fated.

70–19 B.C. Virgil, the greatest poet of the Augustinian age, embodied astrological ideas in his works.

65–8 B.C. Horace, the renowned poet, interested himself in astrology.

33 B.C. Second proscription of astrology in Rome. Expulsion of astrologers and sorcerers. Attack on debased astrology.

20 B.C.–50 A.D.	Philo of Alexandria, the chief representative of Hellenistic-Jewish astrology, divided the exterior and interior of the head, the soul, and the whole body into seven parts corresponding to the seven planets. Development of the seven-year rhythm.
15 B.C.–19 A.D.	Germanicus, son of Trusus, victor over the Germans, was interested in astrology.
20–36 A.D.	Thrassilos of Alexandria was chief astrologer and friend of the Emperor Tiberius. His son, Tiberius Claudius Balbillus, is said to have made a special study of the term of life in the horoscope.
23–79 A.D.	C. Plinius Secundus wrote an encyclopedia under the title *Naturalis historia* (Natural History) containing information on astrological medicine.
Mid-1st cent. A.D.	Thessalos, physician and astrologer, wrote an iatromathematical herbal. He was the first to lay down rules on when and where herbs should be gathered.
55–120 A.D.	Tacitus, the Roman historian, immersed himself in astrology.
ca. 60 A.D.	Krinas of Messalia, astrologer and fashionable physician, practiced in Rome in the time of Nero. He treated his patients according to the current positions of the planets.
ca. 100–178 A.D.	Claudius Ptolemy, mathematician, astronomer, astrologer and physician, the last great scientist of antiquity, incorporated in his works the results of earlier investigations. His book, *Tetrabiblos*, is still extant. In it he refers to heredity and free-will and writes extensively on planetary diseases. He is the acknowledged "king of astrologers," and his books form the basis of all later expositions.
129–200 A.D.	Galen of Pergamum was the most celebrated medical man of imperial Rome and was per-

sonal physician to the Emperor Marcus Aurelius. He is thought to have elaborated the theory of temperaments, and wrote the *Prognostikon* on the diseases of bedridden patients.

Second half of the 2nd cent. A.D.	Antigones of Nicaea wrote about the horoscopes of historical notabilities.
ca. 160 A.D.	Vettius Valens wrote an astrological work.
232–304 A.D.	Porphyry wrote an extensive commentary on Ptolemy.
ca. 335 A.D.	Firmicus Maternus penned the most exhaustive textbook on astrology that had yet appeared. His eight volumes appeared under the title *Mathesios libri*. Until his conversion to Christianity in 337 A.D., he regarded astrology as a "divine science," but then renounced it.
ca. 370 A.D.	Paulus Alexandrinus wrote an introduction to astrology and enjoyed a big reputation. In his discussion of disease, he paid special attention to the effects of the menopause.
Up to 394 A.D.	Hephaestion, an astrological author living at the Thebes of Egypt, recapitulated various texts and traditions.
5th–6th cent. A.D.	Assimilation of astrology by Christendom.
754–775 A.D.	Caliph Al-Mansur indited the book, *Propositiones*.
ca. 805 A.D.	The greatest Arab astrologer, Abumassar, was born at Balkh in Khorasan; he was a pupil of the Persian court physician Alkindi.
860–901 A.D.	The astrologer Thedit. No known astromedical texts.
877–928 A.D.	Albategnis. No known astromedical texts.
919–998 A.D.	Abu Nassr al Faradi. No known astromedical texts.
ca. 1093 A.D.	Ebn Ezra. No known astromedical texts.
ca. 1100 A.D.	Adelandus. No known astromedical texts.

ca. 1150 A.D.	Albetragius, Morocco. No known astromedical texts.
1093–1180 A.D.	Albertus Magnus.
1098–1179 A.D.	Hildegard of Bingen.
1200 A.D.	The Archduke Leopold of Austria, Bishop of Freising, published his *Tractatus decem de astrorum*.
1214–1291 A.D.	Michael Scot, personal physician to Frederick II.
1216–1294 A.D.	Roger Bacon referred to the heavens as the cause of the organization of all things.
1219 A.D.	Gilbertus Anglicus wrote a treatise on "The Diagnosis of Disease by Astrological Rules Without Resort to Urinoscopy."
1224–1274 A.D.	Thomas Aquinas, pupil of Albertus Magnus, discounted astrology.
1230–1300 A.D.	Guido Bonati, court astrologer to Frederick II, founded the doctrine of half-sums.
1250–1316 A.D.	Peter of Albano, physician, astrologer and magician is to some extent the parent of graphic ephemerides.
1250–1327 A.D.	Cichus Asculus (Francesco della Stabili) was a mathematician, physician and astrologer.
1256 A.D.	Death of John of Sacrobosco, who copied out an extract from Ptolemy's *Almagest*.
14th cent. A.D.	In the first half, Johann de Luna practiced as a physician and astrologer in Bologna.
1350–1425 A.D.	Peter of Ailly, astronomer, astrologer and theologian.
19th Sept. 1398	Jean Charlier, in his capacity as chancellor of the Sorbonne in Paris, launched a sharp attack on astrology, and issued an edict in which a number of magical and astrological doctrines were condemned as heretical errors.
1401–1464 A.D.	Nicholas Cusanus emphasized human individuality.
1423–1483 A.D.	The lifetime of Louis XI of France, who was devoted to astrology.

1425 A.D.	Jacques Ganivet, professor of theology, wrote a work entitled *Amicus medicorum*.
1433–1499 A.D.	Marsilius Ficinus issued the *De vita coelitus comparanda*.
1436–1461 A.D.	Johann Müller (Regiomontanus) freed King Matthias Corvinus of Hungary from a morbid fear. He is known as the "father of German astronomy."
1437–1508 A.D.	Rabbi Isaac Arbabanel made a special study of the conjunctions of Jupiter and Saturn.
1440–1493 A.D.	Reign of the Emperor Frederick III, who encouraged astrology.
1452–1531 A.D.	Johannes Stöffler.
1463–1494 A.D.	Count Giovanni Pico della Mirandola denounced the abuses of astrology.
1473–1543 A.D.	Nicolaus Copernicus, founder of the heliocentric system, was also an astrologer, as is stated on his gravestone.
1476–1558 A.D.	Lucas Gauricus, papal favorite, published numerous astrological books.
1477–1547 A.D.	Johann Schoner proved that astrology is fully compatible with the Copernican system.
1484–1485 A.D.	Johann von Lichtenberg wrote on the grand conjunction of Jupiter and Saturn in the year 1484.
1486–1535 A.D.	Cornelius Agrippa, personal physician to the mother of Kin Francis I.
End of 15th cent. A.D.	Hieronymus de Manfredi, professor of medicine at Bologna, publisher of almanacs giving medical elections.
1493–1541 A.D.	Theophrastus Bombastus von Hohenheim (Paracelsus), physician, philosopher and astrologer, expressed the opinion that a doctor with no astrological knowledge is a "pseudomedicus" (a sham doctor).
1st half of 16th cent. A.D.	Georg von Tanstetter, physician and astrologer, worked at the University of Vienna.

	Andreas Perlacher was active at the University of Vienna at the same time as Tanstetter.
1501–1559 A.D.	Jacob Milich, mathematician, physician and astrologer, chiefly taught the medicine of Hippocrates.
1501–1575 A.D.	Hieronymus Cardanus, physician and astrologer.
1503–1566 A.D.	Michael Nostradamus.
1513–1588 A.D.	Jean Ferrer (Ferrius) physician-in-ordinary to Catherine de' Medici.
1513–1521 A.D.	Pontificate of Pope Leo X.
1514–1534 A.D.	Albrecht Dürer engraved "Melencolia" for Maximilian I. Pontificate of Pope Clement VII (1523–1534).
(?)–1576 A.D.	Georg Joachim (Rhaeticus) calculated the first heliocentric ephemerides according to the Copernican system.
1525–1590 A.D.	Franz Junctinus, mathematician, astrologer, philosopher and theologian wrote the most comprehensive astrological textbook of his time.
1534–1549 A.D.	Pontificate of Pope Paul III.
1527–1579 A.D.	Johann Stadius, mathematician, calculated ephemerides for 1544–1606.
1529–1574 A.D.	Leovitius.
1530–1575 A.D.	Johann Garvaeus, professor of theology at Wittenberg and famous astrologer.
1526–1580 A.D.	Count Heinrich von Rantzau was an important man of learning of his era and the author of several books on astrology.
1546–1601 A.D.	Tycho Brahe, Danish astronomer, attacked the excesses of astrology and tried to bring about a reform.
1555–1617 A.D.	Johann Antonius Maginus, doctor of medicine and mathematics, was a member of the Commission for Calendar Reform. He wrote a book on the use of astrology in medicine.

1557–1636 A.D.	David Herlich (Herlicus) lectured on mathematics, astrology, rhetoric and logic at the University of Greifswald.
1561–1656 A.D.	Francis Bacon rose from advocate to lord chancellor. He considered that astrology was useful for weather forecasting and for agriculture and that it was invaluable in questions of health.
1561–1656 A.D.	Thomas Fink, M.D., professor of mathematics, published astronomical and medical treatises.
1571–1630 A.D.	Johann Kepler, imperial mathematician and astrologer, tried hard to reform astrology and to rid it of superstition.
(?)–1592 A.D.	Martin Pegius wrote the first astrological textbook in the German language to refer to astromedicine.
1572–1621 A.D.	Rudolf Goclenius, professor of medicine at Marburg, published several astrological textbooks.
1574–1637 A.D.	Robert Fludd, English* physician, astrologer and Rosicrucian, described the interplay of macrocosmic and microcosmic forces.
(?)–1593 A.D.	Johann Antonius Roffinus, author of *De laudibus astrologiae*.
ca. 1581 A.D.	Johann Antonius Roffinus, author of *De laudibus astrologiae*.
1587–1656 A.D.	Jean Baptist Morin, M.D., personal physician to the Duke of Luxembourg and later to Louis XIII. He wrote the celebrated work *Astrologia gallica*.
1597–1669 A.D.	Abdias Trews, clergyman, professor of mathematics and physics, wrote among other things *Astrologia medica*.
	Antonio Tattoni, public health officer, a follower of Placidus, published a compendious astronomical work in Italian.

---

*The German text calls Fludd Scottish, but his immediate ancestry was English and he was born in the English county of Kent. *Tr.*

1602–1681 A.D.	William Lilly achieved fame as an astrologer and was noted for the astounding accuracy of his predictions.
1603–1668 A.D.	Placidus de Titis, "father of modern horoscopy." In addition to commentaries on Ptolemy, wrote a comprehensive medical work entitled *De diebus decretoriis et agrorum decubio.*
1603–1664 A.D.	Andreas Goldmayer was a physician and astrologer who did much to improve chart technique.
1617–1681 A.D.	George Wharton practiced as a physician in London. He was raised to the peerage. His astronomical writings were published by Gadbury.
1619 A.D.	Founding of the Rosicrucian Brotherhood by Johann Vanentin Andreae (1586–1654).* Astromedicine was one of the things practiced by this secret society.
1632–1682 A.D.	Aegidius Strauch, professor of history and mathematics, produced an astromedical textbook.
1669 A.D.	Tobias Beutel, amateur astrologer, and art curator to the Elector of Saxony, Johann Georg II, published a widely read textbook of astrology.
(?)–1740 A.D.	Eberhard Welper wrote *Speculum atrologicum,* the second part of which deals with bloodletting and medication.
1767–1854 A.D.	August Wilhelm Schegel said in his lectures, "Astronomy will have to become astrology again."
1772–1801 A.D.	Friedrich Leopold von Hardenberg (Novalis) devised a magical cosmogony in which astronomy is the "true metaphysics."

---

*This would probably be challenged by some students of the Rosicrucian movement, even though they might accept that Andreae was heavily involved in it at some stage. *Tr.*

1774–1835 A.D.   Johann Wilhelm Pfaff was the last university professor in Germany to promulgate astrology. In his dissertation *Über das Wesen der Astrologie* (The Rationale of Astrology), he called for the subject to be recognized once more as a legitimate science.

1775–1854 A.D.   Friedrich Wilhelm Schelling, the well-known philosopher, described the cosmos as a harmonious work of art.

1788–1860 A.D.   Arthur Schopenhauer, philosopher, called astrology "a science with no object," but in his *Vom Unterschied der Lebensalter* (On Age Difference) he became more sympathetic towards it.

1800 A.D.   Raphael (R.C. Smith) commenced publication of his yearly almanacs in London. He also published *Medical Astrology*, which referred to medicinal plants.

1800–1878 A.D.   Dr. Carl Friedrich Zimpel.

1830–1860 A.D.   Astrometeorology aroused great interest under C. Murphy.

1831 A.D.   Naval lieutenant (ensign) Morrison started to publish ephemerides under the pen name Zadkiel.

1840 A.D.   Birth of Alfred John Pearce, who styled himself Zadkiel II. He published several works in English which are recognized as scientifically reliable.

1845 A.D.   Medical man and astrologer, Dr. William Simmonite, wrote an astrological textbook (partly) in the form of a catechism.

1860 A.D.   Morrison-Zadkiel founded the Astrometeorological Society with a membership that quickly swelled to two hundred.

1860–1916 A.D.   George Wilde, a well-known English astrologer, wrote a number of books.

1888–1897 A.D.	Paul Flambart (Choisnard), in his *Astrologie scientifique*, instituted statistical research into the subject.
1888–1921 A.D.	Dr. Feerhow (Wehofer), medical astrologer in Vienna.
1898–1899 A.D.	The Hamburg astrologer, Albert Kniepf, wrote books on *Die physischen Wirkungen der Gestirne* (The Physical Effects of the Heavenly Bodies) and *Die Physik der Astrologie* (The Physics of Astrology) in which he ascribed the influence of the stars to electromotoric stimulation.
1904 A.D.	In England, Alan Leo founded the monthly, *Modern Astrology*, and published a series of textbooks which were later translated into German.
1909 A.D.	Alexander Bethor (nom de plume of Aquilin Backmund) started the periodical *Zodiakus*.
1910 A.D.	Dr. M. Duz published his book, *Astro-Medizin*, in Geneva; German edition 1950.
1910 A.D.	Karl Brandler-Pracht launched the *Astrologische Rundschau* (The Astrological Review), later amalgamated with the *Monatsschrift für Astrologische Forschung* (The Monthly Magazine for Astrological Research).
1913 A.D.	The Second International Congress for Experimental Psychology. Dr. Allendy declared that it was impossible to do without astrology in medicine.
1914 A.D.	The first impression of Dr. Feerhow's *Medizinische Astrologie*.
1917 A.D.	First appearance of Elsbeth Ebertin's almanacs, *Ein Blick in die Zukunft* (Glimpse of the Future).
1921 A.D.	The first edition of *Astrologie und Medizin* (Astrology and Medicine) by G.W. Surya and Sindbad.

1925 A.D.   Baron von Klöckler founded the monthly, *Sterne und Mensch* (The Stars and Humanity).

1926 A.D.   The issue of *Astrologie als Erfahrungswissenschaft* (Astrology as an Empirical Science) by Baron von Klöckler, with a preface by Professor Hans Driesch.

1926 A.D.   First Astrological Congress, convened by A.M. Grimm.

1927 A.D.   Publication of *Die Grundprobleme der Astrologie* (The Fundamental Problems of Astrology) by Dr. Karl Th. Bayer.

1928 A.D.   Reinhold Ebertin commenced publication of the periodical *Astrologischer Ratgeber* (The Astrological Adviser), renamed after a year *Neue Sternblätter* (New Stellar Papers), later again called *Mensch im All* and, since 1948 *Kosmobiologie* (Cosmobiology).

1928–1929 A.D.   The first *Jahrbücher für Kosmobiologische Forschung* (Yearbooks for Cosmobiological Research) were published by Dr. Arthur Strauss.

1932 A.D.   Congress of "Astrological Pioneers" held in Erfurt under R. Ebertin and Chr. Meier-Parm.

1935 A.D.   The Fourth German Astrological Congress in Vienna.

1938 A.D.   Reinhold Ebertin took over the annual *Ein Blick in die Zukunft* (A Glimpse of the Future) and changed it into the *Kosmobiologischen Jahrbücher* (The Cosmobiological Yearbooks), which until 1978 reported the international conferences.

1949 A.D.   Reinhold Ebertin organized the first Conference for Cosmobiological Research at Aalen. This became an annual event with an international character.

1955 A.D.   Baldur R. Ebertin and his father Reinhold Ebertin obtained permission to conduct an investigation at the University Hospital in Innsbruck, and were able to establish that there was a close relationship between the Moon and Pluto in various cases of schizophrenia.

3rd Aug. 1956 A.D. Professor Köberle, professor in ordinary of evangelical theology at Tübingen, expressed the view that a fruitful encounter might be possible between cosmobiology and pastoral care.

4.8.1956 A.D. At the Eighth Aalen Conference, Dr. Hagenbuchner, of the University Hospital in Innsbruck, declared that every genuinely concerned physician is grateful for any indication from a cosmobiologist that might be helpful in pushing back the frontiers of medicine.

Nov. 1956 A.D. Founding of the Cosmobiological Academy at Aalen, with a preponderance of medical men as founding members, including Professor Urban, Dr. Heinrich Reich, Dr. Walter Gollner.

1956 A.D. Dr. Hagenbuchner called for a "systematically designed technical terminology," and this was produced the following year mainly through the efforts of Reinhold Ebertin.

9th Aug. 1957 A.D. Dr. Vereno, of the Theological Institute at Salzburg, stated that any Catholic was at liberty to take an interest in astrology and cosmobiology, provided they did not fall into the error of fatalism. This countered attacks by other theologians on sensible astrology and cosmobiology.

1958 A.D. Professor Rudolf Tomaschek, a geophysicist of international repute, declared at the Tenth Conference that the various celestial influences were open to accurate scientific study.

1958 A.D. Dr. Siegfried Rilling published an article on the relationship among the stomach, the mother and the Moon, and said, "When something goes wrong with the stomach, then we know there has been a lack of maternal love."

1959 A.D. Dr. Baldur R. Ebertin drew attention to the tests of Prof. Eugster, "which have succeeded in demonstrating the effects of cosmic radiation and human tissues."

1966 A.D.   Dr. Wilhelm Folkert explained, for the first time, how remedies can be selected from the cosmogram on the basis of the cosmic circle of the elements.

1968 A.D.   Reinhold Ebertin developed the life diagram, which gives an opportunity for the early diagnosis of chronic diseases, so that prophylactic measures can be taken in time.

1969 A.D.   Dr. Heinz Fidelsberger of Vienna, said at the Twenty-first Conference: "Modern physics and, in particular, cybernetics, are extending a hand, so to speak, to us cosmobiologists. They give us the opportunity to place cosmobiology on an exact scientific basis."

1969 A.D.   The Jesuit priest, Dr. Agoston Terres, of Oslo, spoke on syndromes in the cosmogram as follows: "One of the most significant results of modern physics is the general theory of relativity, which clearly has a cosmopsychological tendency."

1971 A.D.   Professor Robert Bünsow of Göttingen said, "Plants build their materials out of the forces of the cosmos and of the earth. That is why they are able to form the basis of animal and human life. Special possibilities for healing arise from an intimate knowledge of human beings and they way they related to nature."

1971 A.D.   Professor M.A. Charneco of Puerto Rico declared at the Twenty-third Conference: "We have been able to establish that certain planetary reference points proposed by the Cosmobiological School play an important part in detecting mental and spiritual diseases."

1974 A.D.   Dr. Agoston Terres S.J. referred to the findings of solar physics in these words, "The positions of the planets cause variations in the earth's magnetism. These are reflected statistically in growth processes, in certain disease symptoms, in crimes and in other phenomena."

1974 A.D.   Erich Modersohn developed his Down's syndrome program in order to prevent, by cosmobiological counselling, the procreation of mongoloid children.

1976 A.D.   Reinhold Ebertin recognized the role played by planetary declinations in the life-pattern and in disease.

1977 A.D.   Reinhold Ebertin delivered the lecture which forms the basis of the present book.

1978 A.D.   Date of the last issue of the *Kosmobiologische Jahrbuch*, containing the most significant contributions to the conference. After sixty years, publication had to be discontinued due to insufficient outlets and rising production costs.

1978 A.D.   The Ebertin Verlag (publishing house) was amalgamated with the Hermann Bauer Verlag. The periodicals *Kosmobiologie* and *Kosmischer Beobachter* were combined in the new production *Meridian*.

28th Aug. 1980 A.D. Reinhold Ebertin addressed the Cosmopathy Congress under the auspices of the scientific association Imago Mundi on "Cosmobiological Aspects in Chronic Diseases." This enabled another bridge to be built in the direction of official science.

19th Sept. 1981 A.D. Lay medical practitioner Ulrich Jürgen Heinz pointed out, presumably for the first time, certain processes of alchemical change in plants and in their healing power in the human organism.

Endnotes

1. Boll, Fr., *Sternglaube und Sterndeutung*. Berlin, 1928.
2. Gundel, W. and G., *Astrologumena*. Wiesbaden, 1969.
3. Pollak, Kurt, *Wissen und Weisheit der alten Ärzte — die Heilkunde der frühen Hochkulturen*. Dusseldorf/Wein, 1968.
4. Gundel, W. *Neue astrologische Texte des Hermes Trismegistos — Funde und Forschungen auf dem Gebiet der antiken Astrologie*. Munich, 1936.
5. Winkel, E., *Claudius Ptolemaus*. Berlin, 1923. English translations have been made by J.M. Ashmand (published by Foulsham, London) and F.E. Robbins (published in the Loeb Classical Library Series). The Robbins translation is accurate and complete and reproduces the original Greek text along with the English.
6. Hildegard von Bingen, *Heilkunde: Das Buch von dem Grund, dem Wesen und der Heilung von Krankheiten*. Salzburg, 1957.
7. Hildegard von Bingen, *Heilkunde*.
8. Hildegard von Bingen, *Gott ist am Werk*. Olten, 1958.
9. Hildegard von Bingen, *Gott ist am Werk, Wisse die Wege, Scivias* (Salzburg, 1955). *Scivias* is available in English from Bear & Company, Sante Fe, NM, 1985.
10. Pegius, Martin, *Geburtsstundenbuch*. First printed in Basel in 1570 and reprinted in Freiburg, 1977, with a detailed exposition by Bonati.
11. Strauss, H.A., *Der astrologische Gedanke in der deutschen Vergangenheit*. Berlin, 1926.
12. Pegius. *Geburtsstundenbuch*.
13. Sindbad-Weiss, *Bausteine der Astrologie*. Munich, 1935. A useful abridgement by Jean Hieroz of Morin's *Astrologia gallica* was published by Les Cahiers Astrologiques in Nice, France, in 1941. In his introduction to Morin's work, the editor expressed regret that the unsettled conditions of the war years made it impossible to reissue it entire. *Tr.*
14. Trews, M.A., *Grundriss der verbesserten Astrologie*, 1661, and translated into German by Josef Fuchs, 1927.

15. Feerhow, Friedrich, *Die medizinische Astrolgie unter Berucksichtigung der Pfanzenheilverfahren, der Homoopathie, Hygiene und Biochemie*. Leipzig, 1914.

16. Feerhow, *Die medizinische Astrologie*, page 1.

17. Feerhow, *Die medizinische Astrologie*, page 8.

18. Feerhow, *Die medizinische Astrologie*, page 9.

19. Von Klöckler, Baron Herbert, *Astrologie als Erfahrungsweissenschaft*. Leipzig, 1927.

20. Von Klöcker, *Astrologie als Erfahrungsweissenschaft*.

21. Bayer, T.H., *Die Grundprobleme der Astrologie*, page 119.

22. Anschütz, G., *Psychologie*. Hamburg, 1953, page 475.

23. Anschütz, *Psychologie*, page 430.

24. Anschütz, *Psychologie*, page 475.

25. Hellpach, W., *Geopsyche—die Menschenseele unter dem Einfluss von Wetter und Klima, Boden und Landschaft*. Leipzig, 1935, page 152 ff.

26. Kritzinger, H.H., *Todesstrahlen und Wünschelrute*, page 26.

27. Schwab, Fritz, *Sternenmachte und Mensch*. Zeulenroda, 1933.

28. Ruts, *Neue Relationen im Sonnensystem und Universum*. Darmstadt, W. Germany, 1915.

29. Von Ungern-Sternberg, Olga, *Die innerseelische Erfahrungswelt am Bilde der Astrologie*. Stuttgart, 1975, page 85.

30. Guthman, H., "Ergebnisse bioklimatscher Untersuchungen aus dem Gebiet der Frauenheilkunde" in *Die medizinische Welt*, Vol. 10, 1963, page 953.

31. Heckert, Hilmar, *Lunationsrhythmen des menschlichen Organismus*. Leipzig, 1961, page 38.

32. Andrews, E.L., "Moon Talk: The Cyclic Periodicity of Postoperative Hemorrhage," in *The Journal of the Florida Medical Association*, Vol. 46, May 1960, pages 1362–1366.

33. Ebertin, Reinhold, *Kosmobiologische Jahrbucher 1938 bis 1978*. Erfurt und Aalen.

34. Surya, G.W., *Pflanzenheilkunde auf okkulter Grundlage und ihre Beziehungen zur Volksmedizin*, 4th edition. Pfullingen.

35. Duz, M., *Astro-Medizin und Therapeutik*. Hamburg, 1950.

36. Surya, G.W., *Astrologie und Medizin*. Lorch, 1933.

37. Ebertin, Reinhold, *Lebensdiagramme*. Aalen, 1968.

38. Herlbauer-Virusgo, Richard, *Praktische Astro-Medizin*. Erfurt, 1935.

39. Müller-Freywardt, H.G., Teirkreis-Tees. Reformhaus Alpina, Stuttgart 31.

40. Müller-Freywardt, H.G., "Kosmisches Denken: Eine praktische Realitat arztlichen Tun und Lassens," *Kosmobiologisches Jahrbuch, 1963*. Aalen, 1962.

41. Müller-Freywardt, H.G., "Sinn und Unsinn astromedizinischer Diagnosen," *Kosmobiologisches Jahrbuch, 1970*. Aalen, 1969.

42. Folkert, Wilhelm, *Sphäron: Eine west-ostliche Synthese der Heilkunst*. Frankfurt, 1958.

43. Ebertin, *Lebensdiagramme*.

44. Ebertin, Elsbeth and Reinhold, *Anatomische Entsprechungen der Tierkreisgrade*. Frankfurt, 1958.

45. Brandau, Fritz, *Organuhr der anatomischen Entsprechungen*. Aalen, 1978.

46. Wachsmuth, Günther, *Erde und Mensch: Ihre Bildekrafte, Rhythmen und Lebensprozesse*. Contance, W. Germany, 1952. An earlier book by Wachsmuth, *Die atherischen Bildekrafte in Kosmos, Erde und Mensch*, and covering some of the same ground, was translated into English by Olin D. Wannamaker and published in 1932 by the Anthroposophic Press, New York, as *The Etheric Formative Forces in Cosmos, Earth and Man*. It has gained a high reputation among those who have read it.

47. Stiefvater, E.W., *Die Organuhr*. Heidelberg.

48. Von Bernus, Alexander, *Alchemy und Heilkunst*. Nurnberg, 1948.

49. Müller, Alexander, *Kosmos und Mensch*. Kreuznach, 1926.

50. Wachsmuth, *The Etheric Formative Forces in Cosmos, Earth and Man*.

51. Zimpel, Carl Friedrich, *Zimpel's spagyrisches Heilverfahren*. Gottingen, 1952.

52. Steiner, Rudolf, *Kranheitsfälle und andere medizinische Fragen*. Stuttgart, 1920. Available in English as KSP

53. Hauschka, Rudolf, *Substanzlehre* (Frankfurt, 1950), *Ernährungslehre* (Frankfurt, 1951), *Heilmittellehre* (Frankfurt,

1965). Available in English as *The Nature of Substance*, Anthroposophic, Hudson, NY, 1983.

54. Hauschka, *Heilmittellehre*, page 100.

55. Von Korvin-Krasinski, Cyrill, *Tibetanische Medizinalphilosophie*. Zurich, 1953.

56. Huibers, Jaap, *Gesund sein mit Metallen*, 2nd edition. Freiburg, 1981.

57. Ebertin, Reinhold und Baldur, *Die kosmischen Grundlagen unseres Lebens*. Aalen, 1955/1956.

58. Ebertin, Reinhold, *Grundlagen der kosmobiologischen Heilkunde*. Aalen, 1976.

59. Rilling, S., *Vagus und Sympathicus in Diagnostik und Therapie*. Ulm, 1957.

60. Winkel, *Claudius Ptolemaus*.

61. Boll, *Sternglaube und Sterndeutung*.

62. See also von Korvin-Krasinski, *Tibetanishe Medizinalphilosophie*.

63. See Anschütz, *Psychologie*, page 475.

64. Retschlag, M., *Die Heilkunst der Geheimwissenschaft*. Leipzig, 1924.

65. See Ebertin, *Grundlagen der kosmobiologischen Heilkunde*.

66. Christiansen-Carnap, *Lehrbuch der Handschriftendeutung*. Stuttgart, 1947.

67. Von Klöckler, *Astrologie als Erfahrungswissenschaft*, page 54.

68. Ebertin, Reinhold, *Mensch im All*. Aalen, 1974. Also available in English under the title *Man in the Universe*. AFA, Tempe, AZ, 1973.

69. Ebertin, Reinhold, *Deklinationsparallelen im Geburtsbild*, 2nd edition, Freiburg, 1980.

70. Ebertin, Reinhold, *Kombination der Gestirneinflüsse*. 11th edition, 1981, Freiburg. Available in English as *Combination of Stellar Influences*. AFA, Tempe, AZ, 1973.

71. Ebertin, Reinhold, *Kosmobiologische Diagnostik*. Freiburg, 1980/1981.

72. See Ebertin, Reinhold, *Das Jahresdiagramm*. Aalen, 1976. Available in English under the title *The Annual Diagram as An Aid in Life*, AFA, Tempe, AZ, 1973.

73. Ebertin, Reinhold, *Das Kontaktkosmogramm*. Aalen, 1973.

74. See also Ebertin, Reinhold, *Transite: Welcher Tag ist gunstig fur Mich?* Freiburg, 1981.

75. See Brandau, *Organuhr der anatomischen Entsprechungen*.

76. Modersohn, E., "Moglichkeiten und Grenzen einer Prognose," *Kosmobiologie*, Vol. 5, Aalen, 1957.

77. Ebertin, Reinhold, "Geheimnisvolle Krankheit," *Der kosmische Beobachter*, Vol. 10, Aalen, 1976.

78. Gauquelin, Michael, *Wetterfruhling: Einfluss des Klimas auf die Gesunheit*. Ruschlikon, 1973. Available in English as *How Cosmic and Atmospheric Energies Influence Your Health*. Santa Fe, New Mexico, 1971.

79. Ebertin, Reinhold, *Das Doppelgesicht des Kosmos*. Aalen, 1962.

Index